Consequences of Reference Failure

C000257396

This book defends the Direct Reference (DR) thesis in philosophy of language regarding proper names and indexical pronouns. It uniquely draws out the significant consequences of DR when it is conjoined with the fact that these singular terms sometimes fail to refer.

Even though DR is widely endorsed by philosophers of language, many philosophically important and radically controversial consequences of the thesis have gone largely unexplored. This book makes an important contribution to the DR literature by explicitly addressing the consequences that follow from DR regarding failure of reference. Michael McKinsey argues that only a form of neutral free logic can capture a revised concept of logical truth that is consistent with the fact that *any* sentence of *any* form that contains a directly referring genuine term can fail to be either true or false on interpretations where that term fails to refer. He also explains how it is possible for there to be true (or false) sentences that contain non-referring names, even though this possibility seems inconsistent with DR.

Consequences of Reference Failure will be of interest to philosophers of language and logic and linguists working on Direct Reference.

Michael McKinsey is Professor Emeritus of Philosophy at Wayne State University, Detroit, Michigan.

Routledge Studies in Contemporary Philosophy

For more information about this series, please visit: www.routledge.com/
Routledge-Studies-in-Contemporary-Philosophy/book-series/SE0720

Consequences of Reference Failure

Michael McKinsey

Routledge
Taylor & Francis Group

LONDON AND NEW YORK

First published 2020 by Routledge

2 Park Square, Milton Park, Abingdon, Oxon OX14 4RN
605 Third Avenue, New York, NY 10017

Routledge is an imprint of the Taylor & Francis Group, an informa business

First issued in paperback 2022

Copyright © 2020 Taylor & Francis

The right of Michael McKinsey to be identified as author of
this work has been asserted by him in accordance with sections
77 and 78 of the Copyright, Designs and Patents Act 1988.

All rights reserved. No part of this book may be reprinted or reproduced
or utilized in any form or by any electronic, mechanical, or other means,
now known or hereafter invented, including photocopying and recording,
or in any information storage or retrieval system, without permission in
writing from the publishers.

Notice:
Product or corporate names may be trademarks or registered trademarks, and
are used only for identification and explanation without intent to infringe.

Publisher's Note

The publisher has gone to great lengths to ensure the quality of this reprint but
points out that some imperfections in the original copies may be apparent.

Library of Congress Cataloging-in-Publication Data
Names: McKinsey, Michael, author.
Title: Consequences of reference failure / Michael McKinsey.
Description: New York : Routledge, 2019. | Series: Routledge
    studies in contemporary philosophy ; 130 | Includes
    bibliographical references and index.
Identifiers: LCCN 2019040072 (print) | LCCN 2019040073 (ebook) |
    ISBN 9780367363109 (hardback) | ISBN 9780429345579 (ebook)
Subjects: LCSH: Reference (Linguistics) | Reference (Philosophy) |
    Language and logic. | Semantics.
Classification: LCC P325.5.R44 M385 2019 (print) |
    LCC P325.5.R44 (ebook) | DDC 121/.68—dc23
LC record available at https://lccn.loc.gov/2019040072
LC ebook record available at https://lccn.loc.gov/2019040073

ISBN: 978-0-367-36310-9 (hbk)
ISBN: 978-1-03-233776-0 (pbk)
DOI: 10.4324/9780429345579

Typeset in Sabon
by Apex CoVantage, LLC

In loving memory of
Pamela Sears McKinsey

Contents

Acknowledgements

I am especially indebted to Scott Lehmann, whose seminal work and kind correspondence on neutral free logic made it possible for me to write this book. I am grateful to Ben Caplan, Robert Henderson, Eric Hiddleston, and Dan Yeakel for useful discussions, comments, and suggestions about these matters. I am also grateful to two anonymous referees for their incisive points and useful suggestions. I would like to thank the graduate students in several incarnations of my seminar in philosophy of language at Wayne State for their useful points and questions concerning this material, especially Mohammed Abouzahr, David Baxter, Travis Figg, Joe Hinkins, Jonathan Jones, Mark Reynolds, Jim Schwartz, Khristy Wilkinson, and Tom Wood. I am also grateful to Peter Lang GmbH, Internationaler Verlag de Wissenschaften, for giving me permission to reprint here parts of my article "Truths Containing Empty Names", which was originally published in *Philosophical Approaches to Proper Names*, edited by Piotr Stalmaszczyk and Luis Fernández Moreno, 175–202. (Bern: Peter Lang GmbH, 2016); permission conveyed through Copyright Clearance Center, Inc. Finally I would like to give special thanks to my late wife, Pamela Sears McKinsey, who was a brilliant and hardworking professional historian (as well as loving mother and grandmother), but who also was able to give me a lifetime of love, support, and encouragement. She was especially happy when I had (finally!) written a book (this one).

1 Direct Reference and Descriptivism
History and Problems

According to the Direct Reference thesis, or DR for short, the proper names and indexical pronouns of natural language are what Bertrand Russell called "names in the logical sense" (Russell 1918, 201). Any term of this sort, which I will call a *genuine term*, is a term whose sole semantic contribution to the propositions expressed by sentences containing the term is simply the term's *semantic referent*.[1] This idea, I take it, is equivalent to the idea that the proposition expressed by a sentence containing a genuine term is a strict *function* of the term's semantic referent.[2] Following standard practice, I will call the propositions expressed by sentences containing genuine terms 'singular propositions'.

Like many others, I endorse DR. There in fact seems to have been a consensus among philosophers of language for the past four decades or so that DR is true. In my own case – and I suspect in the case of many others – the main motivation for endorsing DR lies in the modal considerations first raised by John Searle (1958) and later clarified and forcefully applied by Saul Kripke (1972a), which show that proper names do not have the meanings of contingent definite descriptions. (A definite description in English is a term of the form 'The F', where F is a simple or complex predicate. A *contingent* definite description is one like 'the inventor of bifocals', which an object can satisfy in one possible world and yet fail to satisfy in another possible world.) Similar related points were raised by David Kaplan (1977), which persuasively support the conclusion that like names, indexical and demonstrative pronouns are also genuine terms.[3]

Historically, the main competitor of DR is the view that proper names and indexical pronouns have the meanings of or are abbreviations for definite descriptions. I'll call this view 'Descriptivism'. As we shall see, Kripke's modal arguments don't by themselves refute Descriptivism regarding proper names. Additional arguments are required. Moreover, even if in the end we think, as I believe we should, that Descriptivism is false, we should not assume that it follows that DR is true. Many philosophers, including Kripke, who believe that Descriptivism is false, are agnostic regarding the truth of DR. (This in some cases may be because they are agnostic about the existence of abstract singular propositions, to which DR is committed.)

I have two primary goals in this monograph. First, I wish to show in some detail that DR has important but rarely discussed consequences regarding the notions of logical truth and valid inference. These consequences follow from the fact that genuine terms (proper names and indexical pronouns) sometimes fail to refer, are 'empty'. Second, I wish to suggest and defend an important qualification to DR, on which a small subclass of proper names that (following Gareth Evans's (1979) terminology) I will call 'descriptive names', are allowed (by an idiomatic convention of natural languages) to be used as short for descriptions in a small range of sentential context-types. This suggestion will allow me to solve both the substitution problem for DR that Frege (1892a) discovered (see this chapter, Section 3) as well as the problem for DR emphasized by Russell (1918) that in some contexts, sentences containing empty names can nevertheless be true or false. (See this chapter, Section 5.)

In Chapter 2, I will argue that the DR-thesis implies that no sentence of natural language that contains a non-referring genuine term (*used as* a genuine term) can have a truth value, that is, can be either true or false. It follows that the only type of first-order logic that can be correctly applied to (the first-order fragments of) natural languages is a neutral free logic on which *no* sentence that contains *any* individual constant (proper name) is a logical truth.

In Chapter 3, I will describe and defend a formal semantics for neutral-free logic that is largely derived from the neutral free semantics proposed by Scott Lehmann (1994, 2001, 2002), but that differs from his semantics in its treatment of the quantifiers. Also in Chapter 3, I will propose a formal semantics for quantified modal logic that is based on my neutral free logic. It will turn out that many classical logical truths that contain individual constants (such as truth functional tautologies), while they cease to be logical truths on the modal semantics, re-emerge as *a posteriori* necessary truths under interpretations where the contained constants all refer.

In Chapter 4, I will defend my approach to reference failure by considering and criticizing a range of alternative approaches, some of which are proposed by other defenders of DR, while others are proposed by defenders of Meinongian semantics and defenders of substitutional quantification.

Finally in Chapter 5, I will propose and defend an account, consistent with a slightly qualified version of DR, of how there can be sentences of specific types that are either true or false, even though they contain non-referring names. The account will also provide part of a solution to the second major classical problem facing DR, the problem raised by the apparent fact that substitution of co-referring names in cognitive contexts fails to preserve truth value. The existing literature on these two problems for DR is truly huge, but in my view, none of the proposed solutions so far (including one of my own) succeed.

In the remainder of this chapter, I will discuss the history of the major literature concerning the semantics of proper names and indexical pronouns by defenders of both DR and Descriptivism.

1. Mill and Russell on Proper Names

The idea that proper names contribute precisely their referents to what is said by use of the sentences that contain the names could reasonably be taken as a piece of common sense. The idea has appeared in philosophical works as early as Plato's *Cratylus*. In more modern times, John Stuart Mill, in his *System of Logic* (1843), provided a plausible and thorough account of the semantics of singular terms (proper names and definite descriptions) and general terms (simple and complex predicates). It's clear I think that Mill would have endorsed DR as I've expressed it. He held that proper names have *denotations* (referents) but no *connotations* (semantic contents consisting of sets of attributes or properties), while general terms have both denotations and connotations. The denotation of a general term is the *class* of objects that satisfy the term's connotation. Mill also held that definite descriptions have both denotations and connotations, as long as there is a unique object that satisfies the description's connotation.

In his early work, *Principles of Mathematics* (1903), Russell discussed in some detail the semantics of the declarative sentences of natural languages as well as the constituents of such sentences, including singular terms (proper names and definite descriptions), predicates, and quantifier phrases. The fundamental concept used by Russell in this discussion is that of the *proposition*. Russell thought of propositions as abstract structured complexes that are the *meanings* of declarative sentences and whose structures and constituents correspond to the structures and constituents of the sentences that express the propositions. Each constituent of a proposition is also said to be the *meaning* of the corresponding constituent of a sentence that expresses the proposition.

Russell calls the meanings of proper names and definite descriptions *terms*, which are the objects or things that the propositions containing them are *about*. What counts as a term for Russell is anything that can be meaningfully *mentioned*, whether or not the thing exists. He held at this point of his career that whatever can be mentioned has *being*, even though it may not exist:

> Numbers, the Homeric gods, relations, chimeras, and four-dimensional spaces all have being, for if they were not entities of a kind, we could make no propositions about them. Thus being is a general attribute of everything, and to mention anything is to show that it is.
>
> (Russell 1903, 449)

The meanings of predicates Russell calls *non-denoting concepts*, where such a concept is a property or relation that is predicated or asserted of a term or terms by a given proposition containing the term or terms and the concept. Finally there are the meanings of quantifier phrases such as those of the forms *every F, all F, any F, an F, some F*, and *the F*, meanings which Russell calls *denoting concepts*.[4] Denoting concepts have denotations, but those denotations are not always constituents of the propositions expressed by use of these quantifier phrases.[5]

It is clear, I think, that Russell's semantic views in *Principles* logically imply the thesis of Direct Reference (DR). This may not be completely obvious since he calls the terms or constituents contributed to propositions by proper names, the names' *meanings*. But note that these contributed terms are also always the things or objects that the names *refer to*, or denote (in Mill's terminology). A similar issue arises concerning the properties and relations contributed to propositions by predicates. Russell says that such properties and relations are the *meanings* of the predicates. Would he also have allowed these properties and relations to be called the *referents* of the predicates? Perhaps, but perhaps not. I myself would prefer to say that predicates *express* or *predicate* properties and relations.

Russell's (1903) concept of a proposition's being an abstract complex entity that has the constituents and structure contributed by a corresponding sentence has had a revival among contemporary defenders of DR. This revival is largely due to the influence of David Kaplan, who endorsed the utility of Russell's concept in his seminal work on the semantics of indexical and demonstrative pronouns. [See Kaplan (1977, 194–197). Other prominent defenders of Russell's concept include Braun (1993), Salmon (1986), and Soames (1987)]. However, I should note that modern defenders of Russell's model reject the metaphysical extravagance of *The Principles* (as Russell eventually came to do as well), and they require that propositions and their constituents must *exist*.

There's no doubt that Russell's concept of a proposition has heuristic value. However, the theoretical utility of the concept may be limited. Representing the unique structure and constituents of the proposition expressed by a simple atomic sentence such as 'Socrates is wise' seems straightforward. We could do it this way:

<{Socrates}, [the property of being wise]>

Here, the curly brackets represent the proposition's subject position, while the square brackets represent the proposition's predicate position. We could then say that the proposition's *structure* can be represented as: < {}, [] >. Here it seems that we've correctly represented the proposition as having a unique structure and a unique set of constituents.

However, as Frege (1892b, 49) pointed out, it often happens that two different sentences that contribute different structures or constituents can express the same thought (proposition). Frege mentions the active/passive distinction as an example. So compare:

(1a). John loves Mary.   < {*John, Mary*}, [the relation of loving] >
(1b). Mary is loved by John.   < {*Mary, John*}, [the relation of being loved by] >

(Here I use asterisks to represent ordered pairs.) Given that the names 'John' and 'Mary' contribute specific persons as referents, (1a) and (1b) clearly express the same proposition, even though the propositions are represented as having different constituents. The representations contain different ordered pairs in subject position and different relations in predicate position.

Here's an example of two sentences that have different structures even though they express the same proposition:

(2a). John is bald, and John is tall.
     < CONJ(<{John}, [the property of being bald] >, <{John}, [the property of being tall] >) >
(2b). John is bald and tall.
     < {John}, [the property of being bald and tall] >

(Here, 'CONJ' represents conjunction.) (2a) and (2b) clearly have different structures. (2a) is a conjunction of two atomic sentences, while (2b) is an atomic sentence with a compound predicate. Yet obviously, given a specific referent for 'John', (2a) and (2b) express the same proposition. (For additional examples, see McKinsey 1999, 533–536.)

While it seems plausible to think of propositions as having constituents and structures, it also seems clear from these examples that propositions cannot always be *defined* in terms of a specific structure and set of constituents since the same proposition can be *correctly* characterized by other distinct structures and constituents. A defender of Direct Reference (like myself) can consistently endorse Russell's concept of propositions as understood in *Principles of Mathematics*, but such a defender is not required to do so. I myself would recommend acceptance of the Russell/Kaplan model of propositions because of its heuristic value, while also simply granting that a single proposition can be correctly described in terms of distinct models.

2. The Problem of Identity

We might say that Russell's semantic theory in *Principles of Mathematics* (1903), as well as in his later work, is *single-tiered*, even though the details of his semantic views changed considerably over time, as we shall see. However, some eleven years before Russell published *Principles*, Gottlob

Frege, in his seminal article 'On Sense and Reference' (1892a, 'Über Sinn und Bedeutung'), had given a powerful argument against single-tiered semantics and proposed a plausible alternative *double-tiered* view.

Frege's argument is based on what is often called 'the Problem of Identity', and it concerns referential theories of proper names and definite descriptions, all of which Frege called 'proper names'. The argument is based on the fact that there are identity sentences of the form '$a = b$' that are both true and informative. One of Frege's examples is

(3).   The Morning Star = The Evening Star.

(Here, I assume that the terms 'The Morning Star' and 'The Evening Star' are both proper names and not definite descriptions, though both names may have the *meaning* of a definite description. I also assume that both names refer to the planet Venus, even though Venus is not a star.) Since (3) is informative and in fact expresses a significant astronomical discovery (Frege's argument goes), (3) cannot express the same thought (that is, proposition) as the trivial and uninformative sentence

(4).   The Morning Star = The Morning Star

As Frege put it, (3) and (4) have different 'cognitive values'.

On the other hand, since (3) is true, the two names it contains must have the same referent. Thus if we follow DR and identify the propositional contributions of the two names with their referents, we would have to say that (3) and (4) do in fact express the same thought (proposition). But again (Frege's argument goes), it seems quite clear that these sentences do *not* express the same proposition. So it seems that a defender of DR cannot explain how it is possible for there to be identity sentences containing names that are both true and informative. It may even appear that DR *precludes* this possibility. This is the Problem of Identity.

To solve the problem, Frege adopts the hypothesis that while every meaningful term expresses a meaning or sense (*Sinn*), the sense of every term is distinct from any referent (*Bedeutung*) that the term might have. Rather, a term's sense *determines* which object, if any, is the term's referent. In the case of proper names and definite descriptions, Frege suggests, a term's sense determines its referent by providing a 'mode of presentation' of the referent (1892a, 57). For Frege, declarative sentences also have senses, where the sense of a sentence is the thought or proposition that the sentence expresses. Moreover, on Frege's view, the sense of a sentence is a function of the senses of its meaningful parts. Thus we can see how the senses of (3) and (4) – the propositions they express – can be different, even though the names they contain have the same referent, for the propositions expressed by (3) and (4) are determined by the *senses* of the names they contain and not by the names' referents. Therefore, since the senses of the names 'The Morning Star' and 'The Evening Star' are different, the propositions expressed by (3) and (4) can also be different. Thus we can see how (3) can express a true and informative proposition and hence be informative itself, even though (4) expresses a different and uninformative proposition. This is Frege's solution to the Problem of Identity.

Frege's solution is very plausible, but it is not conclusive. He infers from the fact that sentences (3) and (4) differ in 'cognitive value' that contrary to DR, the two sentences express different propositions. But there is good reason to suppose that even assuming that the sentences express the *same* proposition, ordinary speakers, at least before they become informed that (3) is true, would nevertheless have quite different psychological attitudes toward the sentences. For such a speaker would at first associate distinct bodies of information with the two names, so that upon being informed that (3) is true, the speaker would learn that both bodies of information are true *of the same object*. Thus, unlike sentence (4), sentence (3), if true, would provide new important information to our speaker. Note that this scenario explains how it is possible for sentence (3) to be both true and informative, independently of Frege's assumption that the names 'The Morning Star' and 'The Evening Star' have distinct descriptive meanings or senses.

Here's a simple illustration: Suppose that speaker S correctly believes that 'The Morning Star' refers to the heavenly body that appears brightest on the eastern horizon in the morning and that 'The Evening Star' refers to the heavenly body that appears brightest on the western horizon in the evening. Finally, assume that S comes to learn that sentence (3) is true. As a result, S also comes to learn that the heavenly body that appears brightest on the eastern horizon in the morning *is identical with* the heavenly body that appears brightest on the western horizon in the evening. This is of course an extremely important and interesting result! And again, note that nowhere in this scenario is it assumed or implied that 'The Morning Star' and 'The Evening Star' have distinct descriptive meanings or senses.[6]

Thus it is possible to explain how identity sentences like (3) and (4) can have different cognitive values for particular speakers, without assuming that these sentences express distinct propositions. We may conclude that Frege's main argument against the Direct Reference view of names is inconclusive.

3. The Problem of Substitution

Frege's two-tiered semantic theory contains two important principles of compositionality for complex expressions of language, one for senses and one for referents:

(5a). The sense of any complex expression is a function of (is determined by) the senses of its meaningful parts.

(5b). The referent of any complex expression is a function of (is determined by) the referents of its meaningful parts.

Frege discovered that, while both principles work for his mathematical logic, (5b) in particular is problematic when applied to natural languages. Since Frege held that the referent of a declarative sentence is always a truth value, it follows from (5b) that substitution of any sentence for another with the same truth value in a complex context must preserve truth value. However, this sort of substitution would seem to lead from truth to falsehood in sentences that contain verbs which take 'that'-clauses, such as 'said that', 'believes that', and many others. For instance, consider the inference

(6).   Columbus believed that the earth is round.

   The earth is round if and only if water is H_2O.

   ∴ Columbus believed that water is H_2O.

Since the second premise of this argument guarantees that the two sentences 'The earth is round' and 'water is H_2O' have the same truth value, Frege's principle (5b) would seem to guarantee that this argument is valid, even though it has true premises and a false conclusion. Or consider:

(7).   The ancients believed that The Morning Star appears in the morning.

   The Morning Star = The Evening Star.

   ∴ The ancients believed that The Evening Star appears in the morning.

Since the second premise of this argument implies that the names 'The Morning Star' and 'The Evening Star' have the same referent, Frege's principle (5b) would seem to guarantee that this argument is valid, yet it appears to have true premises and a false conclusion.

Frege's solution to this problem is to adopt the hypothesis that sentences which occur in 'that'-clauses, as well as their meaningful parts, do not refer to their *customary* (normal) referents, but rather to their normal *senses*, which Frege calls their 'indirect' referents (1892a, 59). Thus in argument (6), the *occurrences* of the sentences 'the earth is round' and 'water is H_2O' have different senses and hence different referents in the first premise and the conclusion, so the substitution of 'water is H_2O' for 'the earth is round' in the first premise is invalid. Similarly, in argument (7), the names 'The Morning Star' and 'The Evening Star' refer to different senses as they occur in the first premise and the conclusion, so the substitution of one name for the other is invalid. Note that Frege's suggestion amounts to a slight qualification of his principle of compositionality for referents, so it applies specifically to *occurrences* of complex expressions and their parts. So the principle now reads:

(5b*).   The referent of the occurrence of any complex expression is a function of (is determined by) the referents of the occurrences of its meaningful parts.

One of the main difficulties that faces Frege's solution to the problem regarding the compositionality of reference is that the solution seems to imply that every meaningful expression of any natural language must have an infinite hierarchy of senses, thus making that language unlearnable. (See Davidson 1964.) Such a hierarchy can be obtained by prefixing any sentence that begins with an operator that takes 'that'-clauses with another (or the same) such operator. For example, suppose that we prefix the first premise of argument (7) with the operator 'Frege imagined that', resulting in

(8). Frege imagined that the ancients believed that The Morning Star appears in the morning.

On Frege's proposal, the name 'The Morning Star', as it occurs in (8), would refer to the second-level sense that it has in the first premise of argument (7), thus requiring that 'The Morning Star' have a distinct third-level sense and so on, *ad infinitum*.

Many philosophers of language, including Russell and most contemporary defenders of DR, have agreed with Frege's basic idea that cognitive attitude verbs like 'believes' express relations that hold between persons and propositions.[7] But to preserve this idea while avoiding Frege's infinite hierarchy, it seems that we must abandon Frege's principle of compositionality for reference. For instance, we can suppose that in a sentence of the form 'S believes that p', the word 'that' is a term-forming operator such that, when prefixed to a sentence p, forms a term that refers to the proposition expressed by p. On such a proposal, note, the sentence p and its constituents retain their customary senses and referents. But the proposal simply violates compositionality of reference, for substitution of co-referring terms in a context of the form 'believes that p' can lead from truth to falsehood when the two terms have different senses.[8]

I argued earlier that the Problem of Identity does not provide a conclusive reason to reject DR, that is, to reject the proposal that proper names' sole contributions to the propositions expressed by sentences containing the names are the names' semantic referents. But the Problem of Substitution is much more difficult for DR to overcome. Consider again the argument (7):

(7). The ancients believed that The Morning Star appears in the morning.
   The Morning Star = The Evening Star.
   ∴ The ancients believed that The Evening Star appears in the morning.

Since the names 'The Morning Star' and 'The Evening Star' have the same referent (the planet Venus), DR implies that the two sentences 'The Morning Star appears in the morning' and 'The Evening Star appears in the morning' express the same proposition. Given this consequence and given the assumption that 'believes' expresses a relation between persons and propositions, it follows that the argument (7), as well as many other similar arguments, is valid, even though most speakers would have a strong intuition that such arguments can have true premises and a false conclusion. Again in Chapter 5, I will suggest a solution to the Problem of Substitution, a solution that is based on an important qualification to DR. According to this qualification, there is a small subclass of proper names that (following Gareth Evans), I call 'descriptive names' which are allowed (by an idiomatic convention of natural languages) to be used as short for descriptions in a small range of sentential context-types, including cognitive attitude ascriptions like the first premise of argument (7).

4. Russell's Theory of Descriptions

As Frege realized, his principle of compositionality for reference (5b*) implies that a sentence which contains a singular term that has no referent must be neither true nor false (Frege 1892a, 62–63). For the formalized languages of logic, mathematics, and science, Frege recommended choosing an arbitrary object (such as the null set) to be the referent of a term whose sense does not determine a referent. But for natural languages containing such terms, Frege just accepted the result that sentences containing non-referring terms have no truth value, counting reference failure as a defect of natural languages. However, this feature of Frege's semantics leads to serious problems, especially in the resulting interpretation of sentences containing definite descriptions (complex terms of the form 'the so-and-so'). For instance, consider positive and negative existence sentences containing non-referring definite descriptions, such as:

(9a).   The round square exists.
(9b).   The round square does not exist.

Since the description 'the round square' has no referent, Frege's official semantics counts both (9a) and (9b) as neither true nor false. But this is clearly wrong. (9a) is obviously false, and (9b) is obviously true. As I mentioned earlier (see note 4), DR is faced with a similar problem regarding the semantics of proper names, for which I will propose a solution in Chapter 5. The solution to the problem raised by non-referring definite descriptions was provided by Russell in his theory of descriptions, which he proposed in his seminal paper, 'On Denoting' (Russell 1905).

On Russell's theory, definite descriptions of the form 'The F', such as 'The present king of France', do not contribute a unit of meaning to the propositions expressed by sentences containing the description. He allowed that such descriptions have 'denotations', which are the objects (if any) that uniquely satisfy the descriptions' matrices, such as 'is a present king of France'; but he also held that a definite description never contributes its denotation to the proposition expressed by a sentence containing the description. Rather, Russell held that the propositions expressed by use of (large-scope) definite descriptions are general, quantified propositions, as opposed to singular propositions. Russell symbolized 'The F is G' as 'G($\imath x$)Fx', for which he gave the following contextual definition:

(TD) $G(\imath x)Fx =_{df} \exists x(\forall y(Fy \leftrightarrow y = x) \& Gx)$.

(Russell used the upside-down Greek letter iota to express the English operator 'the' so '($\imath x$)Fx' should be read as 'the x such that x is F'.) (TD) tells us that 'The present king of France is bald' expresses the general, quantified proposition that there exists one and only one present king of France and he is bald. A second part of Russell's theory is his definition of 'E!($\imath x$)Fx', which should be read as 'The x such that x is F exists':

(E) $E!(\imath x)Fx =_{df} \exists x\forall y(Fy \leftrightarrow y = x)$.

(E) tells us, for example, that 'The present king of France exists' expresses the general false proposition that there exists one and only one present king of France.

Note that Russell's theory of descriptions allows him to avoid (as of 1905) much of the metaphysical extravagance of his earlier semantic views in *Principles of Mathematics* (1903). For no longer is he committed to the Meinongian (1904) view that all definite descriptions contribute terms to propositions, even when those terms do not exist but only have being. Rather, on Russell's new theory, definite descriptions *never* contribute terms to propositions, so when a description has no referent or denotation, sentences containing the description will still express perfectly good propositions and thus be either true or false. For example, Russell's theory provides an elegant solution to Frege's problem of negative and positive existentials that contain a non-referring definite description, such as

(9a).   The round square exists.
(9b).   The round square does not exist.

If we let 'Rx' mean 'x is round' and 'Sx' mean 'x is square', Russell's analysis of (9a) is

(10a). $\exists x\forall y((Ry \& Sy) \leftrightarrow y = x)$.

(10a) says that there exists one and only one round square, which of course is straightforwardly false, as it should be. Meinong's (1904) view also makes (9a) false, but on that view, (9a) says falsely of the non-existent round square that it exists, thus assuming that in some sense, *there is* such a thing as the round square, an assumption that Russell's new theory neatly avoids.[9]

Russell's analysis of (9b) is simply the true negation of (10a):

(10b). $\sim \exists x \forall y((Ry \,\&\, Sy) \leftrightarrow y = x)$.

(10b) is straightforwardly true since it correctly denies that there exists one and only one round square. Russell's analyses (10a) and (10b) provide an extremely plausible explanation as to how positive and negative existentials containing non-referring definite descriptions can express true or false propositions, unlike Frege's view, and can do so without mentioning nonexistent objects, unlike the views of Meinong and the earlier Russell himself. (I will provide further discussion of Russell's theory of descriptions in Chapter 2, Sections 5 and 6.)

5. Russell's Descriptivism

Near the end of 'On Denoting' (Russell 1905), Russell introduced the epistemological principle that he would later call the 'Principle of Acquaintance' (in his article 'Knowledge by Acquaintance and Knowledge by Description' (Russell 1910–11)). Russell states the principle as follows (page 117):

(PA) Every proposition which we can understand must be composed wholly of constituents with which we are acquainted.

By 'acquaintance', Russell means a direct cognitive relation of awareness that persons can bear to themselves, to the ingredients of sensory experience such as sense data, and to abstract entities such as properties and relations. In effect, Russell uses (PA) to support a claim that for the most part, ordinary proper names must be used as short for definite descriptions since they cannot contribute their referents as constituents of propositions unless speakers are acquainted with those referents, and in general speakers are not acquainted (in Russell's sense) with ordinary physical things or other persons. Given (PA), Russell maintains that the only words of natural language that can be used as genuine, directly referring terms are such pronouns as 'I', 'this', and 'that', when used to refer to oneself or to one's fleeting sense data (Russell 1910–11, 121).[10] Of course, if Russell is right, the direct reference thesis DR is false since according to DR, when we use a proper name to refer to an ordinary thing, the name's referent will be a constituent of the proposition being expressed.

Unfortunately, Russell gives no argument for (PA), and so we are left to speculate as to why he believed it and especially as to why he thought that (PA) is so obvious that it requires no argument. I think it is likely that Russell believed (PA) in part because he took for granted a Cartesian assumption to the effect that one can always have direct, privileged, *a priori* knowledge of the propositional contents of one's own thoughts. This assumption has been the subject of recent debate, and a defender of DR could be expected to reject it. (See, for instance, McKinsey 2002, Section 3.)

It may be that (PA) was Russell's primary reason for endorsing Descriptivism regarding proper names, but it's clear that Russell was also motivated by Frege's problems of identity and substitution (see Russell 1905, 51–53). He was also motivated by the problem of truths containing empty names, a central problem addressed by both Meinong (1904) and Russell (1905, 54–55 and 1918, 242–243). In any case, the considerations raised by both Frege and Russell led to wide endorsement of Descriptivism regarding proper names that lasted for some forty years.

6. Kripke's Arguments Against Descriptivism

Following Nathan Salmon's (1981) useful proposal, we can classify Kripke's arguments against Descriptivism into three types: (1) modal arguments, (2) epistemological arguments, and (3) semantic arguments. In each case, an argument is given against a specific proposal to the effect that a certain name has the same meaning as a given description. It will then be clear that the argument about the specific proposal (when sound) can be generalized so as to refute a wide class of similar examples.

6.1 The Modal Arguments

The first modal argument was given by Searle (1958, 172). Later, Kripke (1972a, 278–279) endorsed the same sort of argument against Descriptivism, but in more detail and in a clearer and more general theoretical setting regarding modality. Consider the following sentences:

(a). Aristotle was not a philosopher.
(b). The last great philosopher of antiquity was not a philosopher.

[Here I assume that sentence (a) is being used in a given context to refer to the great philosopher of ancient Greece and that 'not' has smallest scope in both (a) and (b).]

Argument 1

(1). If 'Aristotle' means 'the last great philosopher of antiquity', then (a) and (b) express the same proposition. [Premise]
(2). (a) expresses a possible truth, while (b) expresses a necessary falsehood. [Premise]

∴ (3).   (a) and (b) do not express the same proposition. [By (2)]
∴ (4).   'Aristotle' does not mean 'the last great philosopher of antiquity'. [By (1) & (3)]

An analogous argument can be given to show an analogous conclusion regarding *any* proper name and *any* definite description whose matrix expresses a contingent property. A property Φ is *contingent* if and only if it is both possible for there to be an object that has Φ, and necessary that, if any object does possess Φ, then that object could fail to possess Φ and yet still exist.

Now it might be objected that the claim that (a) expresses a possible truth begs the question against Descriptivism. In reply to this complaint, I would emphasize, as Kripke did, that a crucial part of the intuition that sentence (a) 'Aristotle was not a philosopher' (in the assumed context) expresses a possible truth is the fact that, when we consider a possible situation in which Aristotle was not a philosopher, we are considering a situation in which *a certain individual*, namely, the man who is the referent of our use of the name 'Aristotle' *in the actual world*, was not a philosopher. As Kripke puts it (1972a, 279):

> we use the name 'Aristotle' in such a way that, in thinking of a counter-factual situation in which Aristotle didn't go into any of the fields and do any of the achievements we commonly attribute to him, still we would say that was a situation in which *Aristotle* did not do these things.
>
> [His italics]

Kripke's intuition, an intuition that I share, is that whether the proposition expressed by a simple sentence containing a proper name is true in a given possible situation depends on whether, in that situation, the actual referent of the name has or lacks the property predicated by the rest of the sentence. In particular, the proposition expressed by (a), the proposition that Aristotle was not a philosopher, would be true in any possible situation in which *Aristotle*, the actual referent of that name, as we are using it in this context in the actual world, was not a philosopher. Another way of putting the intuition, suggested by Gareth Evans (1979, 173), would be to say that in any possible world in which (a) is true, the state of affairs that makes it true is just that of *x's not having been a philosopher*, where *x* is the actual referent of 'Aristotle'.[11]

While it is one important part of a set of arguments that together can refute Descriptivism, we should note that the modal argument does not by itself show that proper names are never short for definite descriptions, only that names are never short for *contingent* descriptions. In particular, Kripke does not use the modal argument to support the view that names are directly referential. Rather he uses the argument to support a distinction between *rigid* and *non-rigid* designators, where he maintains that proper names are rigid and contingent descriptions are non-rigid. Again following Salmon's terminology (1981, 32–40), we can distinguish two main types of rigid designators: (1) singular terms that refer to the same object relative to every possible world in which that object exists and to nothing in worlds in which that object does not exist [these are called *persistently rigid* (or just *persistent*) *designators*]; and (2) singular terms that refer to the same object relative to every possible world, whether or not the object exists in that world [these are called *obstinately rigid* (or just *obstinate*) *designators*]. (Kaplan (1973) has forcefully argued that non-descriptional singular terms (proper names and indexical pronouns) are obstinately rigid.

6.2 *The Epistemological Arguments*

Consider the following sentences:

(d). If Aristotle existed, then Aristotle was a philosopher.
(e). If the last great philosopher of antiquity existed, then the last great philosopher of antiquity was a philosopher.

Argument 2

(1). If 'Aristotle' means 'the last great philosopher of antiquity', then (d) and (e) express the same proposition. [Premise]
(2). The proposition expressed by (e) is knowable *a priori*, but the proposition expressed by (d) is not knowable *a priori*, only knowable *a posteriori*. [Premise]
∴ (3). (d) and (e) do not express the same proposition. [By (2)]
∴ (4). 'Aristotle' does not mean 'the last great philosopher of antiquity'. [By (1) and (3)]

Clearly the proposition expressed by (e) is knowable *a priori*. To know it, one need only correctly deduce its consequent from its antecedent. But to know that the proposition expressed by (d) is true, one must have empirical evidence to the effect that Aristotle was the author of philosophical works, taught philosophy to students, or at least frequently indulged in thoughts about philosophy. But it might be that none of these things are true. (Works attributed to Aristotle were actually authored by someone else, etc.) Clearly this sort of epistemological argument, like the first modal argument, can also be used to show in general that no proper name means the same thing as any contingent description.

6.3 *Are Names Short for Rigid Descriptions?*

Examples of both the modal arguments and the epistemological arguments refute the hypothesis that a certain name (say, 'Aristotle') is short for a certain contingent, *non-rigid* definite description. But suppose that we instead consider the hypothesis that 'Aristotle' is short for a rigid, *world-indexed* description such as 'the *actual* last great philosopher of antiquity'. (See Linsky 1977 and Plantinga 1978.) This description is (persistently) rigid because it refers at every world in which Aristotle exists to the last great philosopher of antiquity *in the actual world* (namely, Aristotle). But with this change, the modal argument will not work. Suppose, for example, that in **Argument 1**, we replace (b) by

(b*).   The *actual* last great philosopher of antiquity was not a philosopher.

Unlike (b), (b*) expresses a possible truth, just as (a) does. For as we saw earlier, there are many possible worlds in which the *actual* last great philosopher of antiquity, namely Aristotle, was not a philosopher. Since both (a) and (b*) now express possible truths, premise (2) is now false, and the revised modal argument is now unsound.

Or consider the following modal argument that resembles Argument 2 except that it concerns the hypothesis that 'Aristotle' is short for 'the *actual* last great philosopher of antiquity'. Consider the following sentences:

(d).   If Aristotle existed, then Aristotle was a philosopher.
(e*).   If the *actual* last great philosopher of antiquity existed, then the *actual* last great philosopher of antiquity was a philosopher.

Argument 3

(1).   If 'Aristotle' means 'the *actual* last great philosopher of antiquity', then (d) and (e*) express the same proposition. [Premise]
(2).   The proposition expressed by (e*) is necessarily true, but the proposition expressed by (d) is possibly false. [Premise]
∴ (3).   (d) and (e*) do not express the same proposition. [By (2)]
∴ (4).   'Aristotle' does not mean 'the *actual* last great philosopher of antiquity'. [By (1) and (3)]

Sentence (e*) may *appear* to be necessarily true, but it's not. For there are many possible worlds in which the *actual* last great philosopher of antiquity (that is, Aristotle) existed, but in which the *actual* last great philosopher of antiquity (that is, Aristotle) was not a philosopher. Thus, there are possible worlds in which the antecedent of (e*) is true and its consequent is false. Thus, both (d) and (e*) express possible falsehoods, premise (2) of Argument 3 is false, and so this modal argument goes nowhere.

However, as Salmon (1981, 28) has pointed out, a slightly revised version of the *epistemological* Argument 2 that involves rigid descriptions still succeeds in refuting the short for rigid descriptions view. For (e*), even though it is possibly false, like (d) is nevertheless knowable *a priori*, while again, (d) is only knowable *a posteriori*.

Another type of persuasive argument against the idea that names are short for actual-world indexed descriptions was proposed independently by Fitch (1981, 30) and Soames (1998, 15). So far, we've been considering rigid descriptions of the form 'the *actual* F'. For the Fitch/Soames arguments, it will be useful to consider equivalent descriptions of the form 'the F in *the actual world*'. It is important to understand that a description of the form 'the actual world' is an indexical term, whose referent is always the world in which the term is being used. This indexicality is then inherited in the case of rigid descriptions of the form 'The F in the actual world'. With this in mind, consider the following argument(s) against the hypothesis that 'Aristotle' is short for the rigid world-indexed description 'The teacher of Alexander in the actual world'. (Note: the Fitch argument is the version that uses 'assert' and 'asserting', while the Soames argument uses 'believes' and 'believing'.)

Argument 4

(1). If 'Aristotle' means 'The teacher of Alexander in the actual world', then it is not possible to assert [believe] the proposition that is actually expressed by 'Aristotle was a philosopher' without asserting [believing] something about the actual world. [Premise]

(2). In some possible worlds, people do assert [believe] the proposition that is actually expressed by 'Aristotle was a philosopher' even though no one in those worlds has the capacity to either refer to or think of the actual world. [Premise]

Thus

(3). In some possible worlds, people assert [believe] the proposition that is actually expressed by 'Aristotle was a philosopher' without asserting [believing] something about the actual world. [By (2)]

Thus

(4). It is possible to assert [believe] the proposition that is actually expressed by 'Aristotle was a philosopher' without asserting [believing] something about the actual world. [By (3)]

Thus

(5). 'Aristotle' does not mean 'The teacher of Alexander in the actual world'. [By (1) and (4)]

Argument 4, though I think it is sound, is a bit tricky due to the indexicality of the term 'the actual world'. Keep in mind that when the argument is actually being considered or given (by you or me in this world), the term 'the actual world' refers to the actual world. But in another nonactual possible world *w*, even one that is almost exactly like the actual world, if

I or you were to give or consider what looks like the same argument, then the term 'the actual world' would refer to *w* and not to the actual world.

So far, we have seen that a combination of modal and epistemological arguments plus Argument 4 succeed in refuting both the hypothesis that names are short for contingent non-rigid descriptions and the hypothesis that names are short for rigid world-indexed descriptions. This does not conclusively prove that proper names are not short for or do not mean some other sort of rigid descriptions. But I have not found any other plausible candidates for rigid descriptions that work. So I think that the arguments we've considered so far provide very strong evidence that Descriptivism is false.

6.4 A Final Modal Example

While the Direct Reference thesis seems to be the consensus among philosophers of language, a significant minority endorses a form of description theory on which names are semantically equivalent to quotational descriptions of the form 'the bearer of "N"'.[12] This quotational view seems to have also gained considerable currency among linguists.[13] The main motivation for this view seems to be the fact that proper names have a predicative, as well as a referential, use, as in such sentences as 'Hundreds of John Smiths are listed in the white pages' and 'She is a McKinsey, born and bred'.[14] The idea is that if names have a predicative use, then it is plausible to suppose that their use as referring nouns is based on their predicative use, so a name such as 'John Smith' used as a noun would mean the same as the quotational description 'the bearer of "John Smith"'.

Of course, this quotational view is a species of description theory on which a name such as 'John Smith' means, or is short for, a certain contingent, non-rigid description, which in this case is 'the bearer of "John Smith"'. So it should be possible to refute this view by using a simple modal argument like **Argument 1**. Kent Bach (2002, 84–85) considers and rejects a different modal argument that is based on the following sentences:

(f).   Aristotle might not have been the bearer of 'Aristotle'.
(g).   Aristotle might not have been Aristotle.

(See also Abbott 2002.) Following the model of **Argument 1**, the argument based on (f) and (g) would look like this:

Argument 5

   (1). If 'Aristotle' means 'the bearer of "Aristotle"', then (f) and (g) express the same proposition. [Premise]
   (2). (f) expresses a truth, while (g) expresses a necessary falsehood. [Premise]

∴ (3).   (f) and (g) do not express the same proposition. [By (2)]

∴ (4).   'Aristotle' does not mean 'the bearer of "Aristotle"'. [By (1) & (3)]

Bach agrees that (g) has a reading on which it is necessarily false (when it means 'Aristotle might not have been identical with Aristotle'). But he correctly points out that on his quotational view, (g) also has a reading on which it expresses the same proposition as (f), so that Premise (2) of the argument is false, given this reading.

I am sympathetic with Bach's view that names can be used predicatively. However, the fact that this results in the ambiguity of (f) and (g) makes **Argument 5** a less-than-ideal form of modal argument. We can correct this defect by making slight revisions of (f) and (g):

(f*).   Aristotle might not have been identical with the bearer of 'Aristotle'.

(g*).   Aristotle might not have been identical with Aristotle.

The additional change to Premise 2 yields

(2*).   (f*) expresses a truth, while (g*) expresses a necessary falsehood.

The resulting modal argument seems compelling, especially the intuition that (g*) is false.[15]

Another convincing modal argument against Bach's view that any name N means 'the bearer of "N"', can be obtained by using **Argument 1** as a template and considering the following sentences:

(a*).   Aristotle was not a bearer of 'Aristotle'.

(b*).   The bearer of 'Aristotle' was not a bearer of 'Aristotle'.

Then using the premise that (a*) expresses a possible truth, while (b*) expresses a necessary falsehood, we may conclude that 'Aristotle' does not mean 'the bearer of "Aristotle"'. Thus it certainly seems that a simple version of the modal **Argument 1** conclusively refutes the quotational theory.

6.5 The Semantic Arguments

Kripke's semantic arguments are important because if correct, they seem to have the widest application of any of his arguments against various forms of description theory. (Donnellan 1970, independently proposed a similar type of semantic argument.) In particular, this sort of argument, if correct, not only refutes Descriptivism as the modal plus additional arguments show, it also refutes description theories on which a name use's semantic referent is *fixed*, or *determined*, either by a cluster of descriptions (as suggested by Searle 1958 and Strawson 1963) or by a single description. The latter sorts of description theory are consistent with both the Direct Reference thesis (DR) as well as with Kripke's thesis that names are rigid designators.[16] (I will explain Kripke's account of reference-fixing by description in Section 7.)

One of Kripke's semantic arguments is based on his Gödel-Schmidt example, in which the speaker's only substantive identifying belief about Gödel is that he was the man who discovered the incompleteness of arithmetic (Kripke 1972a, 294). Kripke is surely right to claim that the speaker's use of 'Gödel' would still refer to Gödel even if not Gödel, but an unknown Viennese named 'Schmidt' had discovered incompleteness. Kripke seems to infer from this consequence that the referent of the name 'Gödel' is in fact not determined by any description whatever. After describing the Gödel-Schmidt case and others like it, he says (where the φ's are the properties in a given cluster):

> Suppose that nothing satisfies most, or even any substantial number of the φ's. Does this mean the name doesn't refer? No: . . . you may have false beliefs that are true of absolutely no one. And these may constitute the totality of your beliefs.
>
> (Kripke 1972a, 295)

But this sweeping claim is simply not justified by the example. For one natural explanation of our intuitions about the Gödel-Schmidt case is that such a speaker would not primarily intend to refer to the discoverer of incompleteness, whoever that may be. Rather, desiring to communicate successfully with others and having so little knowledge about the referent of 'Gödel', the speaker would deferentially and primarily intend to refer to the man named 'Gödel' to whom she has heard others refer or to the man named 'Gödel' of whom she has heard that he discovered incompleteness. (See McKinsey 1978a and 1978b.)

So the Gödel-Schmidt example, like the other similar cases that Kripke describes, fails to show that in deferential uses of names, the name's referent is not determined by description. At most, such cases show that, contrary to the 'public' description theories of Strawson and Searle, names' referents are not always determined by publicly or *commonly associated* descriptions since the 'buck-passing' descriptions that appear to determine reference in deferential cases involve essential reference to the speaker. So Kripke's semantic arguments do not show that description theories are all false; rather these arguments show that only a description theory which allows privately associated descriptions to determine reference is in a position to give an adequate account of deferential name uses.

The fact that Kripke's semantic arguments against description theories are inconclusive is a matter of some importance since Kripke uses these arguments to motivate his influential suggestion that the referents of proper names' uses are typically determined, not by description, but by causal chains of communication that historically link the uses to initial baptisms of objects with the names in question. [See Kripke 1972a, 298–303; Donnellan (1970) made a similar suggestion. For an argument against Kripke's causal theory, see McKinsey 2010, 327–331.)]

7. Reference-Fixing by Description and the Semantics of Indexicals

It's important to note Kripke's point that in certain rare cases, the referent of a proper name may be fixed or determined by a single definite description, even though the name does not thereby acquire the same *meaning* as that description. Kripke gave as examples such descriptive names as 'Jack the Ripper', 'Hesperus', and 'Neptune' (1972a, 301 and 347, note 33; see Chapter 5, Section 1 for additional examples). The astronomer Le Verrier might have fixed the referent of 'Neptune' on the basis of a description of the form 'the planet that causes such-and-such discrepancies in the orbit of Uranus'. Kripke's suggestion is that the outcome would be that 'Neptune' becomes a (persistent) rigid designator of the planet that causes the relevant discrepancies in *the actual world*. This suggestion can be captured in the following form of reference rule:

(N)　For any object x, token α of 'Neptune', and possible world w, α is to refer to x at w if and only if in w, x = the planet that causes such-and-such discrepancies in the orbit of Uranus *in the actual world*.

Kripke's concept of reference-fixing by description has other significant semantic applications. In fact, he first introduced the concept in the course of providing a new explanation of how the Standard Meter can be used to *fix the property* that is ascribed by use of the predicate 'is one meter long' (Kripke 1972a, 273–275). Kripke's suggestion can be captured by the following semantic rule:

(SM)　For any token φ of 'is one meter long' and any property F, φ is to predicate F if and only if F is the property of having length L, where L is the length of the Standard Meter *in the actual world*.

[I have proposed that property-fixing rules analogous to (SM) can also be used to capture the semantic rules that determine the kinds, membership in which is predicated by natural kind terms such as 'water' and 'gold'. See McKinsey (1987)].[17]

As Kaplan forcefully pointed out in *Demonstratives* (1977, 518–520), one of the most important applications of reference-fixing by description is in the semantics of indexical and demonstrative pronouns. The reference rules for such pronouns as 'I', 'now', 'she', 'that', and 'that man' provide descriptive conditions that an object must satisfy to be the semantic referent of a use of the relevant pronoun. But, as Kaplan argues, these descriptive conditions are never constituents of the propositions expressed by use of the relevant pronouns, whose sole contribution is always simply the pronoun's semantic referent.

The chief difference between indexical pronouns and other singular terms such as proper names, the terms of mathematics, and definite descriptions is that the semantic referents of uses of indexicals are always determined in part by features of the context of utterance. Consider the pronoun 'I', for instance. Its linguistic meaning (or its 'character', in Kaplan's terms) can be expressed by the following semantic rule:

(11). For any use or token α of 'I', any object x, and any world w, α is to refer to x at w if and only if x is the speaker of α in the actual world.

In general, the semantic reference rule for any indexical can be expressed in terms of a two-place relation that the referent of any use or token of the term uniquely bears to *that use or token itself*.

Reichenbach (1947, 284) suggested that each token of an indexical pronoun is synonymous with the description that determines its referent. Thus, each token of 'I' would mean 'the speaker who utters this token'. But Kaplan (1977, 519) pointed out that this suggestion implies the following falsehood:

(12). If no one were to utter this token, then I would not exist.

The suggestion also implies the falsehood that no use of a simple atomic sentence of the form 'I am F' could be true at a world unless the speaker utters a token of 'I' at the relevant time in that world. This consequence is clearly false. If at a given time t I say 'I am tired' in the actual world, then what I've said is true at another world w if and only if I am tired at t in w; my use of 'I am tired' can be true in w even though I have uttered no token of any part of the sentence 'I am tired' at t in w.

We may conclude then that the condition that determines or fixes the referent of a given indexical does not provide a *synonym* for the indexical. So it is not the descriptive condition provided by a reference-fixing rule that is contributed to the proposition being expressed. Rather an indexical's contribution to the proposition being expressed is simply the indexical's *semantic referent*. In other words, like proper names, the semantic function of the use of an indexical is to directly refer to its referent, if it has one. I do want to say, however, that the reference-fixing rule that governs the use of a given indexical constitutes the indexical's *linguistic* meaning (its meaning in the language being spoken), while I call the referent of the use its *propositional* meaning.

(This distinction is very similar to Kaplan's distinction between *character* and *content*.)

According to Kaplan (1977, 489) there is a distinction between, on the one hand, the meanings of 'pure indexicals' such as 'I', 'you', 'here', and 'now', whose meanings do not require any demonstrative acts by the speaker (such as pointing to the intended referent), and, on the other hand, demonstrative indexicals such as 'this', 'that', 'she', 'he', and descriptive demonstratives of the form 'that F', which do require a demonstrative act. My own view is that uses of these demonstrative indexicals do not require any overt demonstrations by their speakers. Rather they simply require that *the speaker refers* to the intended semantic referent. Thus I might say 'He is a liar!' of a man whose image is on my TV screen and who has just asserted a blatant falsehood. Here, I need not have overtly demonstrated the man in order for him to be the referent of my use of 'he'. [See McKinsey 1983, 8 and 1984, 494. On the distinction between speaker's reference and semantic reference, see Kripke, (1977, 255–276)].[18]

Here are three examples of semantic rules for demonstratives, where in my view the reference condition requires that the speaker refer to the semantic referent:

(13). For any use or token α of 'that', any object x, and any world w, α is to refer to x at w if and only if the speaker of α refers to x with α in the actual world.

(14). For any use or token α of 'she', any object x, and any world w, α is to refer to x at w if and only if in the actual world: (i) the speaker of α refers to x with α (ii) x is female and (iii) x is neither the speaker nor the person being addressed.

(15). For any use or token α of 'that politician', any object x, and any world w, α is to refer to x at w if and only if in the actual world: (i) the speaker of α refers to x with α and (ii) x is a politician.

8. Conclusion

In this introductory chapter, I've reviewed the major nineteenth- and twentieth-century literature concerning semantic theories of proper names and indexical pronouns, their relations, and their problems. The two main views I considered were (i) the thesis of Direct Reference (DR), on which a name or indexical's sole semantic contribution to the propositions expressed by sentences containing such a term is simply the term's *semantic referent*, and (ii) Descriptivism, according to which names and indexicals always have the meaning of a definite description. In *Principles of Mathematics*, Russell clearly endorsed DR and provided a model of propositions as having structures and constituents corresponding to the structures and constituents of sentences that express those propositions. I cautioned that the models cannot be used to *define* their corresponding propositions since sentences with different structures and constituents can express the same proposition. I then discussed Frege's double-tiered semantics of sense and reference. I argued that Frege's argument for his semantics, based on the Problem of Identity, is inconclusive, but I conceded that the Problem of Substitution provides strong evidence for Frege's Descriptivism and against DR. I then described Russell's theory of descriptions, emphasizing that, unlike Frege's semantics, Russell's theory explains the fact that sentences containing non-referring descriptions can nevertheless be either true or false. Russell's form of Descriptivism regarding proper names became the dominant view for many years. But we saw that Kripke's modal and epistemological arguments (along with a form of argument suggested by Fitch and Soames) provide strong evidence that proper names do not have the meanings of either rigid or non-rigid descriptions, including (non-rigid) descriptions of the form 'the bearer of "N"'. We also saw that Kripke's semantic arguments, which seem designed to show that the semantic referents of proper names are not fixed by single descriptions or clusters of descriptions, are inconclusive. Finally we explained Kripke's notion of reference-fixing by description and the way this notion naturally applies to the semantics of indexical pronouns, as Kaplan pointed out.

The upshot so far: Kripke's modal and epistemological arguments plus the Fitch/Soames argument provide very strong evidence against Descriptivism and justify the current consensus among philosophers of language in favor of Direct Reference. However, both the problem of substitution and the problem of truths containing empty names still face DR, problems that I hope to solve in Chapter 5. Meanwhile, I will assume that DR is true, and in Chapters Two through Four, I will try to show in some detail that DR has important but rarely discussed consequences regarding the notions of logical truth and valid inference.

Notes

1. Russell is often said to have called such terms 'logically proper names', but I can find no use of this expression in Russell's work. The earliest use of the expression I've found is in P. F. Strawson's 'On Referring' (Strawson 1950, 90). In *Principles of Mathematics* (1903). Russell endorsed DR. But at least after 1910, if not before, Russell would have denied DR since by then he held that ordinary proper names are typically short for definite descriptions and so are not 'names in the logical sense'. (See Russell 1905, 55–56, and 1910–11, 121; also see Section 5 in this chapter.) The expression 'direct reference' is David Kaplan's. (See Kaplan 1977, 483.)
2. This idea, in turn, is equivalent to the idea that the result of replacing a genuine term in a sentence with another genuine term expresses the same proposition as the original sentence if and only if the two terms have the same referent.

3. It's an interesting fact that neither Searle nor Kripke endorsed DR for the case of names. But because of their arguments, as well as additional arguments by Keith Donnellan (1970) and Kaplan, DR has been explicitly endorsed by many prominent philosophers of language, including David Braun (1993), Donnellan, Kaplan, Gareth Evans (1982), Nathan Salmon (1986), and Scott Soames (1987), among many others.

4. Such quantifiers today are called 'restricted quantifiers'. For a discussion of restricted quantifiers and a defense of the view that definite descriptions are restricted quantifiers, see Chapter 2, Section 6.

5. Russell tries to explain what the relevant denotations would be, but his explanations are very difficult to follow. Soames (2014), Chapter 7, Section 4, provides a thorough general account of Russell's semantic views in *Principles of Mathematics*, including an ingenious solution to this problem about the denotations of denoting concepts.

6. My own view is that both 'The Morning Star' and 'The Evening Star' are 'descriptive names' whose referents are *fixed by description*, but neither of which has the *meaning* of a definite description. See the discussion of reference-fixing in Section 7.

7. However, I myself have argued at length against this idea. See McKinsey (1986, 1991, 1994, and 1999).

8. Contexts in which substitution of co-referring terms or sentences with the same truth values is valid are commonly called *extensional* contexts. In both classical and non-classical first-order predicate logics, all sentential contexts are extensional. Natural languages, however, are non-extensional, or *intensional*, since they contain many operators, like 'believes that' and 'it is necessary that', which form intensional contexts in which substitution of co-referring expressions can fail to preserve truth value. For further useful discussion of Frege's semantics, see Soames 2010, 15–20.

9. I will give a detailed criticism of Meinongian views in Chapter 4.

10. Unfortunately Russell does not give any clear or explicit argument based on (PA) for this conclusion. I think it is possible to give such an argument that is based on plausible assumptions, but the issue is complex.

11. There have been various attempts to refute Kripke's argument by claiming that proper names in modal contexts are always short for descriptions that have widest scope with respect to any modal operator or quantifier. See, for instance, Dummett 1973, Sosa 2001, and Nelson 2002. However, the modal **Argument 1** that I presented in the text contains no statements in which names or descriptions are either within or outside of the scope of a modal operator or quantifier. The argument does not concern the logical properties of modal sentences that contain names or descriptions; rather it concerns the modal properties of simple non-modal sentences such as sentences (a) and (b). This point was first made by Kripke himself (1972a, 279) and was also made with great clarity by Salmon (1981, 26, note 28); see also Hudson and Tye 1980. For other good criticisms of 'widescopism', see Soames 1998 and 2002, Everett 2005b, and Caplan 2005.

12. See, for instance, Bach 1987, 2002, Katz 1994, 2001, Recanati 1993, and Justice 2001.

13. See Geurts 1997 and the works cited there, as well as Elbourne 2005 and Matushansky 2008. For dissenting views (among linguists), see Abbott 2002, 2004, and Maier 2009.

14. See Bach 2002 for a thorough discussion of a variety of types of predicative uses of names.

15. I should confess here that in the semantics for modal logic that I propose in Chapter 3 (g*) is true. The reason is that in my view, one cannot be

self-identical in worlds where one does not exist. What is necessarily false in my system is not (g*), but rather:

> (g#)   Aristotle might have existed and yet not have been identical with Aristotle.

16. I have myself defended description theories of this sort. See McKinsey 1978a, 1978b, 1984, and 2010.
17. Here's an example of such a rule:

> (**W**)   For any token φ of 'is water' and any property F, φ is to predicate F if and only if there is a unique natural kind K such that (in the actual world) the watery stuff found in our environment belongs to K and F = the property of belonging to K.

Here, 'watery stuff' is a euphemism for a conjunction of surface qualities that ordinary speakers associate with 'water'.

18. Later Kaplan changed his view, so a demonstration is taken to be a 'directing intention' of the speaker (1989, 582–584). I will discuss demonstratives further in Chapter 4, Section 4.4.

2 From Direct Reference to Free Logic

1. When Direct Reference Fails

Perhaps the most important consequence of DR regarding reference failure is what I'll call (following David Braun 1993) the 'no proposition' view:

(NP1) Any sentence or use of a sentence that contains a non-referring name or indexical pronoun fails to express a proposition.

On DR, a name or indexical that fails to have a referent can make *no* semantic contribution to propositions expressed by sentences containing the name or indexical. As a result, it certainly seems, sentences containing such non-referring terms would express *no* propositions.

Now the apparent fact that DR entails (NP1) is commonly thought to be a problem for DR since (NP1) as stated may seem to be obviously false. The standard counterexamples to (NP1) consist of a range of fairly commonplace sentences that contain non-referring proper names but that certainly seem to succeed in expressing propositions. Consider for example:

(1). Santa Claus exists.
(2). Santa Claus does not exist.
(3). Sylvia believes that Santa Claus will bring her a doll for Christmas.
(4). Zeus is the most powerful of the Greek gods.
(5). Sherlock Holmes is a brilliant detective.

All of (1)–(5), as well as many other examples of the same sort, are counterexamples to (NP1) as stated. Positive and negative existence claims that contain non-referring names can sometimes express falsehoods, as does (1), and can sometimes express truths, as does (2). Also a cognitive ascription containing a small-scope non-referring name can nevertheless express a truth or falsehood, as in examples like (3). And finally, names from fiction and myth can be used to express truths about myth like (4) and truths about fiction like (5).

Some defenders of DR maintain that sentences like (1)–(5) do not in fact express any true or false propositions. (See, for example, Adams and Stecker 1994.) I think that this is wrong. (I'll discuss this issue at length in Chapter 5.) In my view, sentences like (1)–(5) can and sometimes do have meanings on which they semantically express true or false propositions. However, I hold that uses of names in sentences like (1)–(5) are relatively rare and unusual and that most such uses of names are *derivative* from their standard and more fundamental use as *genuine terms*. I have elsewhere suggested (McKinsey 1999) that there is a class of statistically rare names whose referents (if any) are epistemically remote from all speakers in the same way, so that all speakers have to base reference with such a name on the same narrow set of descriptive assumptions. Examples would include 'Jack the Ripper', 'Hesperus', 'Phosphorus', 'Zeus', 'God', 'Homer', 'Robin Hood', 'King Arthur', 'Vulcan', 'Santa Claus', 'Pegasus', and many others. Following Gareth Evans, I call these 'descriptive names'.[1] Those who believe that such a name has a referent will typically use the name as a genuine term. But because each such name is associated among speakers with a single description that fixes the name's referent, there is, I suggest, an *idiom* of natural language that allows the name to be used as short for the relevant description in certain types of context.[2] (Here, I am using 'idiom' to apply to any group of words whose meaning is not determined compositionally by the standard meanings of the words that make up the group, but is rather determined by a special convention.)

Among such contexts are existentials like (1) and (2), cognitive ascriptions like (3), and contexts regarding myth like (4). In such cases, I assume, the descriptions abbreviated by the names should be understood in accordance with Russell's (1905) theory of descriptions, so the failure of the description to refer will not prevent sentences like (1), (2), (3), and (4) from expressing true or false propositions [contrary to Frege's (1892a) theory of descriptions]. In contexts like (5) that involve talk about fiction, the names are similarly used as short for descriptions, but this requires another distinct idiom that applies specifically to uses of names from fiction. I will provide a full expression and defense of these suggestions in Chapter 5. I will also provide some important evidence for the basic idea in Chapter 3.

Given such examples as (1)–(5), we should express the Direct Reference thesis in a slightly qualified manner, as follows:

(DR)   The proper names and indexical pronouns (including demonstratives) of natural languages, *in their typical and most fundamental uses*, are used as genuine terms,

where we understand that when a term is used as a genuine term, its sole propositional contribution in that use is the term's semantic referent (if any). When a proper name is used in this typical and fundamental way, I will say that it is *used as a name*.[3] Thus, the names used in sentences like (1)–(5), when these sentences express true or false propositions, are in my view not really being *used as names* in these sentences, but in some other, derivative way (which again I will explain in Chapter 5). So we can state what I take to be a counterexample-free version of the no-proposition view as follows:

(NP)   Any sentence or use of a sentence that contains a non-referring proper name or indexical *that is being used as a genuine term* (and is not an E-type pronoun in the scope of mental anaphora) fails to express a proposition.[4]

2. Direct Reference and Failure of Bivalence

A defender of DR is, by definition, someone who is committed to the idea that propositions play a central role in semantics or at least in informal semantics. Indicative sentences typically express propositions, and because a sentence expresses a given proposition, that sentence can be used to say something true or false about the world, where the proposition in question is *what* the sentence can be used to say about the world. Moreover, it is by virtue of the truth or falsehood of the proposition expressed by a given sentence that the sentence itself is either true or false. (That is, propositions are standardly assumed to be the 'ultimate bearers of truth values'.)

But now suppose that we have a sentence that contains a genuine term which has no referent (such as a non-referring name that is used as a name in the sentence). Suppose for instance that a follower of the astronomer Le Verrier uses the name 'Vulcan' as a name in a sentence like 'Vulcan is smaller than Mercury'. Of course, the speaker is attempting to use 'Vulcan' as a name of the planet whose orbit is between the sun and Mercury. But since there is no such planet, this use of 'Vulcan' has no referent. Thus by (NP), the speaker's use of the sentence 'Vulcan is smaller than Mercury' expresses no proposition. But then the speaker's use of this sentence does not succeed in *saying* anything about the world. Hence, there is *no* way the world is that determines whether the sentence as used is either true or false: for there is *no* way the world is said to be by use of the sentence. Thus the sentence, in this use, can be neither true nor false. It is without truth value.

Thus we have another important consequence of DR, namely the failure of bivalence in the case of sentences containing non-referring names and indexicals:

(FBV)   Any sentence or use of a sentence that contains a non-referring name or indexical (when used as a genuine term that is not an

E-type pronoun in the context of mental anaphora) is a sentence
or use of a sentence that lacks truth value, that is, is neither true
nor false.

It is worth emphasizing the extreme generality as well as the logical significance of this nearly immediate consequence of the thesis of direct
reference. Given (FBV), absolutely *no* sentence of *any* language that contains a non-referring name or indexical pronoun (being used as a genuine
term in that sentence and not as an E-type pronoun in the context of
mental anaphora)[5] has a truth value, that is, is either true or false.[6]

Consider for instance any sentence containing a non-referring name
that also has the form of what in classical logic would be called a 'truth
functional tautology', such as 'Either Vulcan is a planet or Vulcan is not a
planet' ($Pv \lor \sim Pv$). Since the name 'Vulcan' has no referent, this sentence
[by (NP)] expresses no proposition and [by (FBV)], it has no truth value.
Thus, such a sentence is not a logical truth: such a sentence cannot be
a logical truth for the simple reason that it is *not true*. The same point
holds for every sentence that contains a non-referring genuine term. No
such sentence can be a logical truth since no such sentence is true.

Of course, in addition to truth functional tautologies containing
names, classical first-order logic also treats many other kinds of sentences containing individual constants (proper names) as logical truths
as well. A small but important selection would include identities of the
form $a = a$, existence claims of the form $\exists x(x = a)$, laws of identity such as
$a = b \rightarrow (Pa \rightarrow Pb)$, and laws of universal instantiation such as $\forall x Fx \rightarrow$
Fa, to mention a few. But many sentences of natural language that have
these same forms are not logical truths at all since they contain non-
referring genuine terms and so are neither true nor false.

I take this to be a defect of classical first-order logic. A first-order logic
should be applicable to (the first-order fragments of) natural languages so
as to provide a correct account of the logical properties of the sentences
and inferences that can be formulated in such languages. We have just
seen that classical first-order logic does not provide such an account.
Unlike classical logic, an adequate first-order logic should be able to tolerate both failure of reference and failure of bivalence. An adequate first-
order logic should, in other words, be a *free* logic.

Following Karel Lambert (2001), the varieties of free logic can be classified into three sorts: *positive*, *negative*, and *neutral*. *Positive* free logics are those that allow some atomic sentences containing non-referring
individual constants to be true; *negative* free logics are those on which
all such sentences are ruled false; and neutral free logics are those on
which all such sentences are ruled to be without truth value.[7] Given this
classification, it is already evident that only a neutral free logic is consistent with DR since, as we've seen, given DR, all atomic sentences (indeed
all sentences) containing non-referring individual constants are without

truth value. (I pointed this out in McKinsey 2006.) Here I'm assuming that the individual constants of first-order logic are to be understood as semantically analogous to proper names *when used as names*.

3. Some Inadequacies of Classical Logic

I'll discuss the differences between positive, negative, and neutral free logics further. But it's also worth noting the common ground shared by these logics in their opposition to classical logic. The main common ground is that all free logics allow models, or interpretations, on which individual constants may fail to refer. By contrast, on every classical interpretation, every individual constant is required to refer to a member of the domain of that interpretation. As a consequence, where a is any individual constant, the sentence $\exists x(x = a)$ (that is, 'there exists something that is identical to a') is counted as a logical truth in classical logic. This consequence is extremely counterintuitive, and when applied to natural language, the consequence is downright absurd.[8]

First, even if we restrict our attention to only those correlates in natural languages of individual constants – proper names – that in fact have existing referents, we obtain the absurd result that all sentences of the form 'a exists', where a has a referent, are logically true. So, for instance, the sentence 'Obama exists' would be counted logically true by classical logic since it is logically equivalent to a natural language translation of the first-order sentence $\exists x(x = \text{Obama})$, which is a classical logical truth. But of course the sentence 'Obama exists', though true, is certainly not logically true since it expresses a contingent proposition that is possibly false: while worlds in which Obama fails to exist are no doubt much deprived, some such worlds are certainly *possible*.[9] Since the proposition that Obama exists is neither true as a matter of logic nor knowable *a priori*, the sentence that expresses it, 'Obama exists', should clearly not be counted as a logical truth.

Second, when we also consider sentences of natural language that contain non-referring names, the proponent of classical logic faces a fatal dilemma. Either we go ahead and apply classical logic to such sentences or we don't. On the first horn of the dilemma, we obtain the absurd result that existence claims such as 'Vulcan exists' are logically true since their correlates in first-order classical logic are logically true. Thus, since $\exists x(x = \text{Vulcan})$ is true on every classical interpretation, the English correlate 'Vulcan exists' is also true on every classical interpretation and is thus a logical truth. But this is of course absurd. It is not implausible to suppose that 'Vulcan exists' is *false* (as it is held to be by all negative and positive free logics as well as by some neutral free logics[10]) or that it is neither true nor false (as it is held to be by the form of neutral free logic that I endorse). But to suppose that 'Vulcan exists' is not only true but *logically* true is just absurd.

So the proponent of classical logic is driven to accept the second horn of the dilemma: the proponent must *refuse* to apply classical logic to sentences of the first-order fragments of natural languages that contain non-referring names. One problem with this position, as Mark Sainsbury has pointed out, is that

> Applying classical logic to natural language would require a prior segregation of its proper names into those which have bearers and those which do not; only the former should be allowed to replace individual constants in the classical formalism.
>
> (Sainsbury 2005, 65)

But as Sainsbury goes on to say, this task of segregating referring from non-referring names requires factual *a posteriori* knowledge and so is beyond the capacity of logic alone, which is an *a priori* discipline.

Another related problem seems even more important. By accepting the second horn of the dilemma, the classical logician simply refuses to discuss or describe the logical properties of both sentences that contain non-referring names and the arguments that contain such sentences. Yet such sentences and arguments of natural language are perfectly meaningful, and the study of the logical properties of such sentences and arguments is surely a proper subject for logical investigation. If classical logic rules out the possibility of such investigation, then so much the worse for classical logic.

But the most serious problem with this alternative is that the proponent of classical logic can provide no plausible excuse or justification for refusing to apply classical logic to the natural language sentences which contain names that fail to refer. Again consider 'Vulcan exists'. This English sentence is logically equivalent to the sentence 'There exists an object that is (identical to) Vulcan', which in turn has the same logical form as a sentence of first-order logic, namely '$\exists x(x = \text{Vulcan})$'. Since it is a consequence of classical logic that any sentence of this form is a logical truth, it is also a consequence of classical logic that the English sentence 'Vulcan exists' is a logical truth, which again is absurd.

The only way that I can see for a proponent of classical logic to evade this simple argument is to insist that the alleged sentences of English containing 'Vulcan' are really *meaningless*.[11] Now of course I agree that classical logic should not be required to apply to meaningless strings that merely resemble English sentences. Consider something like 'All borogoves are borogoves' for instance (with apologies to Lewis Carroll). This meaningless string might resemble a sentence that has the logical form $\forall x(Fx \to Fx)$, instances of which are all logical truths. But of course we can't reasonably object to classical logic on the grounds that 'All borogoves are borogoves' is not logically true. After all, this string is not true (and hence not logically true) only because it is nonsense and not a sentence of English at all.

But this sort of evasion hardly works for sentences of English that contain non-referring names, sentences such as 'Vulcan exists', since such sentences are *perfectly meaningful*. It is true, in my view, that when in 'Vulcan exists', 'Vulcan' is being used as a name but has no referent, this sentence *expresses no proposition*, and so is neither true nor false. But to infer from this that 'Vulcan exists' is not meaningful in English or that it is not a sentence of English at all would be a serious error. To make such an inference is simply to confuse a sentence having a meaning in a language with the sentence expressing a proposition in that language, a confusion that was long ago persuasively and conclusively corrected, first by P. F. Strawson (1950) and later with even greater force and clarity by Richard Cartwright (1962).

So there really is no good excuse for refusing to apply classical logic to the first-order fragments of natural languages and hence to sentences that contain non-referring names. But since when so applied, classical logic leads to absurd consequences, a revised, more adequate form of first-order logic that avoids these consequences is required. The various forms of free logic are all reasonable and well-motivated attempts to provide such a revised and adequate logic.

4. Varieties of Free Logic

All forms of free logic agree in allowing interpretations on which individual constants fail to refer to existing objects. Typically this effect is accomplished by allowing interpretations that are *partial* on the individual constants. Thus, given an interpretation $I = <D, d>$, where D is a domain of objects and d is a denotation function for the predicates, function-names, and individual constants of the relevant language, $d(a)$ is allowed to be undefined with respect to constant a. But if $d(a)$ *is* defined, then $d(a) \in D$.[12]

Moreover, all free logics accept the standard objectual interpretation of the quantifiers '∀' and '∃' (which I have been assuming) on which these quantifiers, on every interpretation, range over that interpretation's domain of existing objects. Usually, but not always, free logics are also *universally* free, in the sense that they allow interpretations whose domains are empty. On such free logics, $\exists x(x = x)$ is not a logical truth, contrary to classical logic.

Since the quantifiers of free logic range over domains that contain only existing objects (when the domain is non-empty), the following theorem of classical logic is also a theorem of every free first-order logic with identity:

(6) $\forall x \exists y(x = y)$,

that is, it is a logical truth that everything exists. However, for no constant *a* is it a logical truth that

(7) $\exists y(a = y)$,

since if *a* does not refer to an existing object on a given interpretation, (7) is not true on that interpretation. While the inference from (6) to (7) is not valid in free logic, it is an instance of universal instantiation, which is counted as valid in classical logic. To block this form of inference, all forms of free logic place a restriction on universal instantiation, so that from a sentence $\forall x Ax$, inference to an instance Aa is not allowed without the additional premise $\exists x(x = a)$.

Beyond their general agreement that existence claims of the form (7) are not logical truths and that universal instantiation is invalid and needs restriction, however, the three forms of free logic exhibit many serious disagreements about truth, logical truth, and valid inference. Positive free logics, unlike negative and neutral free logics, allow there to be true atomic sentences that contain individual constants (names) that have no existing referents. A defender of negative free logic might say that such a sentence is not true since it says nothing true *of* any object. Thus, if we assume the principle of bivalence (that every sentence is either true or false), we must hold that such atomic sentences are false. (See Burge 1974, 313.) A defender of neutral free logic like me will agree that such a sentence says nothing true of anything, but will add that such a sentence indeed says nothing true *or false* of anything, and so such a sentence is neither true nor false, contrary to the principle of bivalence. (Bivalence is accepted by negative free logic, accepted by some though not all forms of positive free logic, and firmly rejected by neutral free logic.)

An important type of atomic sentence about which the three forms of free logic all disagree are identity sentences of the form *a = a*. Classical logic of course treats all such sentences as logical truths. Defenders of positive free logics agree, even when the instance of *a* fails to refer to any existing object, as in 'Pegasus = Pegasus'. By contrast, on negative free logic, the latter sentence is false, while on neutral free logic, it is without truth value; so on both of these two views, identities like 'Pegasus = Pegasus' are not true at all, let alone *logically* true. I find it difficult to understand the positive free logician's attitude regarding identity sentences that contain non-referring names. Yes of course all existing objects must be self-identical. So by all means we should accept the generalization $\forall x(x = x)$ as a logical truth (as do all forms of free logic). But an identity like 'Pegasus = Pegasus' fails to truly say of anything that it is self-identical, so surely we should not count such sentences as true, let alone *logically* true.

Bas van Fraassen (1966, 489) defended the logical truth of 'Pegasus = Pegasus' by correctly pointing out that if the true identity

'Cicero = Cicero' is logically true, then any sentence like 'Pegasus = Pegasus' that results from the former identity by substitution of singular terms for singular terms must *also* be logically true. However, given the implausibility of the view that 'Pegasus = Pegasus' is true, van Fraassen's true conditional provides equal justification for the conclusion (endorsed by both negative and neutral free logic) that 'Cicero = Cicero' (and all other identities of the same form) are simply *not* logical truths.

Besides identity sentences $a = a$ containing non-referring a, positive free logics also allow other atomic sentences containing non-referring names to be true (or false). Examples are sentences from fiction or myth such as

(8). Pegasus is a flying horse. (True)

and

(9). Pegasus is a flying cow. (False)

(Taking sentences like 'Pegasus = Pegasus' and (8) to be true requires the positive free logician to restrict existential generalization EG, so as to avoid commitment to the truth of such falsehoods as that there exists a flying horse or that Pegasus exists. So in positive free logic, a conclusion $\exists x P x$ is not derivable from an atomic premise $P(a)$ unless we add the additional premise $\exists x(x = a)$.

Sometimes sentences such as (8) and (9) are said to be true (or false) 'by convention' (Meyer and Lambert 1968, 19). But in fact there seems to be no sense in which such sentences are both atomic and true (or false) *simpliciter*. Rather, at best, such atomic sentences are true (or false) only *in the relevant story* (whether fiction or myth). But of course, being true *in a story* should not be confused with *being true*. If, say, (8) is counted as true *because* it is true in the relevant story, then we'd be committed to also counting it true that

(10). Pegasus exists,

since, after all, (10) is *also* true in the relevant story.

As Burge (1974) pointed out, if we take a sentence like (8) as true merely because it is true in a certain story, then we are taking such sentences as prefixed by an implicit intensional 'story' operator of the form 'In the story (fiction, myth) S'. But so taken, such sentences are not atomic at all, and since such an intensional operator cannot by definition be in the vocabulary of a first-order language, there is simply no basis for counting a sentence like (8) as both atomic and true (or false in my view) under any first-order interpretation on which the relevant name in the sentence fails to refer. Thus, I can see no reasonable basis for endorsing a positive free logic on which some atomic sentences containing non-referring constants can be true.

As noted previously, the defender of negative free logic is motivated by the correct idea that an atomic sentence *Pa* containing a non-referring name *a* can be used to say nothing true about anything, and so *Pa* is not true. Assuming bivalence, the defender of negative free logic goes on to infer that *Pa* is false. The defender of neutral free logic agrees that if *a* has no referent, then *Pa* is not true, but demurs regarding the assumption of bivalence, on the grounds that *Pa* says nothing false of anything either.

Defenders of negative free logic tend to provide very little, if any, reason to endorse bivalence and tend to just *assume* the principle. [As Lehmann (2002, 226) has pointed out.] The one argument that I've seen to support the idea that atomic sentences containing non-referring names are false (as opposed to being neither true nor false) was given by Sainsbury (2005). He points out that hypotheses expressed by sentences containing non-referring names such as 'Vulcan is at least 1000 miles in diameter' can be *refuted* by observational evidence since the sentence can be a premise of a proof that leads to consequences that are inconsistent with the evidence. Here, Sainsbury seems to assume that refutation of the hypothesis-sentence must amount to showing that the sentence is false. But this assumption seems unmotivated. Why not say instead, following neutral free logic, that the refutation consists in showing merely that the hypothesis-sentence is *not true*? In the present case, the proof would show that the premise 'Vulcan is at least 1000 miles in diameter' is not true since if it were true, then the relevant (false) consequence would also be true. But to assume that such a proof would thereby show that the premise is *false* is to just assume bivalence once again. So Sainsbury's argument is inconclusive at best.

Taking atomic sentences containing non-referring constants to be false, negative free logic rejects the logical truth of identities of the form $a = a$ since such sentences are false on interpretations where *a* does not refer. A related difference between negative and positive free logic is that the former, unlike the latter, holds that existential generalization (EG) on the occurrences of individual constants in atomic sentences is valid since such sentences cannot be true unless the constants refer. However, in negative free logic, EG is not valid in general since complex, non-atomic sentences containing non-referring constants such as ~(Pegasus = Pegasus) can be true. An important example of this type would be negative existentials containing non-referring names, such as $\sim\exists x(x = \text{Pegasus})$, which both positive and negative free logic would count as true and from which we obviously should not be allowed to use (unrestricted) EG to infer the contradiction $\exists y\sim\exists x(x = y)$. By contrast, EG is quite generally valid on the form of neutral free logic that I endorse, according to which *no* sentence containing individual constants, including $\sim\exists x(x = \text{Pegasus})$, is either true or false unless the constants refer.[13] (I will discuss the vexed questions of EG and negative existentials at greater length in both Chapter 3 and Chapter 5.)

An important feature shared in common by positive and negative free logics is that, in these free logics, all classical truth functional tautologies remain logical truths. Typically, this just results from the common assumption of bivalence, rejected by neutral free logic. However, van Fraassen (1966) showed how, even when bivalence is denied, one can use his semantic method of supervaluations to define a notion of logical truth for positive free logic on which the logical truth of truth functional tautologies is preserved [as well as the logical truth of $a = a$ and $a = b \rightarrow (Pa \rightarrow Pb)$]. But in my view, if we really take failure of bivalence seriously, then we should *not* take supervaluations seriously in this context. Consider a tautology of the form $Fa \lor \sim Fa$, where a has no referent. On the method of supervaluations, this sentence is logically true and hence true, even on interpretations on which neither of its parts Fa and $\sim Fa$ has a truth value. But this means that the truth value of $Fa \lor \sim Fa$ is not a function of the truth value of its parts, which in turn means that the disjunction symbol '$\lor$' is not consistently being treated as a truth functional connective.[14] It also means that the language of our first-order positive free logic is not extensional. For instance, substitution of another truth valueless sentence, Fb for Fa in $Fa \lor \sim Fa$, takes us from truth to absence of truth value.[15] Given these simple points, it is difficult – I think impossible – to explain what it is, according to supervaluational semantics, that is supposed to *make* a tautology like $Fa \lor \sim Fa$ true when both of its parts are without truth value. It is certainly not made true by any truth table!

The only attempted explanation that I know of is given by Bencivenga (1986). On supervaluational semantics, a sentence S is *supertrue* on a partial interpretation I just in case it is true on every classical completion I′ of I. A classical completion of I is (roughly) an interpretation I′ that preserves the truth values, if any, that are provided for atomic sentences by I and which also provides referents for the constants that do not refer on I. (An atomic sentence that is without truth value on I remains without supertruthvalue on I since it will be true on some classical completions and false on others.) Obviously, $Fa \lor \sim Fa$ will be true on every classical completion I′ of any partial interpretation I so that $Fa \lor \sim Fa$ will be logically true with respect to supervaluational semantics (in the sense of being supertrue on every partial interpretation I). Bencivenga defends this idea by what he calls a 'counterfactual theory of truth' (1986, 406): a sentence whose constants do not refer, he says, nevertheless *is* true just in case it *would be* true on any way of providing referents for its constants. Lehmann (2002, 233) has responded with the following decisive objection:

> Why should truth, which is ordinarily regarded as *correspondence to fact*, be reckoned in terms of what is *contrary to* fact? Why should we reckon that 'Pegasus is Pegasus' is true because it *would be* true if, *contrary to fact*, 'Pegasus' did refer?

I think that Lehmann's point is clearly correct. Given a sentence S whose constants don't refer on a given partial interpretation I, the fact that S *would be* true on every one of a class of closely related but *different* interpretations on which the constants in S *do* refer just seems utterly irrelevant to determining the truth value of S on the initial interpretation I. In the absence of any account that plausibly explains the alleged relevance, I take it that this application of the method of supervaluations in this context is *ad hoc* and without any rational motivation. (I don't take a strong desire to preserve as many classically logical truths as possible to be a rational motivation since acting on this motivation alone merely begs the question against my basic argument for neutral free logic.)

Again, from the point of view of Direct Reference, a classical truth functional tautology that contains a non-referring genuine term should not be counted as a logical truth, for the simple reason that it is not true (or false). Such a sentence is neither true nor false because it can be used to say nothing, not even anything tautologous, and so there is no fact about the world, not even a logical fact, that could make the sentence true (or false). Nevertheless, truth functional tautologies containing genuine terms are very important to logic since they *cannot be false* on any interpretation. In fact, as we shall see in Chapter 3, on interpretations on which the genuine terms in such sentences do refer, the sentences express *necessary truths*. As we shall also see, such tautologies are typically only knowable *a posteriori*, and so, when true, they constitute a new and important type of *a posteriori* necessity.

5. Definite Descriptions in Free Logic

So far, I have argued against classical logic as well as the treatments of sentences containing non-referring terms that are provided by positive and negative free logics and in favor of the treatment of such sentences found in neutral free logic. In these arguments, I have assumed that the relevant terms, individual constants, should be understood as *names*, and so should be thought of as genuine terms whose only relevant semantic features (at least in the context of a first-order logic) are their referents.

However, free logics have been constructed on which some of the singular terms of the relevant first-order language are complex definite descriptions, some of which are treated as individual constants. Such a language will contain a description operator ⅂ and the formation rule: if A is any formula, $⅂xA$ is a term. The semantics for, say, a negative free logic would then include the following reference rule for descriptions, where under any interpretation I and assignment a to the free variables:

(11). If some individual α of D uniquely satisfies A, then $⅂xA$ refers to α; otherwise, $⅂xA$ does not refer.

(See Lehmann 2002, 245.)[16] When *A* contains no free variables other than *x*, then any referent of ɿ*xA* under **I** and *a* will be a member of *D* that is independent of assignment *a*, so ɿ*xA* may be treated as an individual constant (Lehmann 2002, 238).

Burge's (1974) negative free logic is in fact designed for first-order languages whose only terms other than variables are definite descriptions. (See p. 311.) The resulting account of the truth conditions of atomic sentences containing (closed) descriptions is equivalent to Russell's (1905) account of the same sentences on his theory of descriptions. As Burge points out (p. 314), his logic has the following Russell equivalence as a theorem:

(12). $B\text{ɿ}xAx \leftrightarrow \exists x(\forall y(Ay \leftrightarrow x = y) \ \& \ Bx),$

where *B* is atomic. Of the various forms of free description theories that have been proposed (on all of which closed descriptions are treated as individual constants), the form I prefer is Burge's since I endorse Russell's theory and Burge's negative form of free description theory is the only form that is consistent with Russell's theory (at least with respect to the truth conditions of sentences containing descriptions).

As (12) indicates, it is a hallmark of both Burge's and Russell's theories that an atomic sentence containing a non-referring description is false, so that its negation is counted as true. This feature allows Russell's theory to have the great virtue of allowing sentences containing descriptions to express given propositions and to have definite truth values, independently of whether or not the descriptions refer. I say that this is a virtue because I think it is clearly correct and because, as Russell (1905) argued, it provides a preferable alternative to the theories of descriptions of both Frege (1892a) and Meinong (1904).

For instance, consider Russell's nice example (1905, 47) in which the King in the *Tempest* might truly say

(13). If Ferdinand is not drowned, then Ferdinand is my only living son.[17]

As Russell points out, (13) is true whether or not its antecedent is true, and so it is true whether or not the description 'my only living son' has a referent (at the time of use). If the antecedent is true, then the term 'my only living son' continues to refer to Ferdinand, and so the consequent is true. But if the antecedent is false, then 'my only living son' has no referent, and so the consequent would be false. But (13) would still be true.

By contrast, if (13)'s antecedent is false, so that 'my only living son' has no referent, both Frege (1892a) and Strawson (1950) are committed to both (13) and its consequent being neither true nor false. This result is obviously false since again (13) is obviously true whether or not 'my only living son' has a referent. On Meinong's view, when (13)'s antecedent is false, the description 'my only living son' would refer not to Ferdinand, but to an object that exists at no time. This results in a bizarre interpretation of (13)'s consequent, on which it is false because it falsely implies that Ferdinand is identical with a certain object that never exists in reality. This preserves the truth of (13), but at the cost of maintaining that descriptions that fail to refer to existing objects end up referring to nonexistent objects (objects that never exist in reality). As we saw in Chapter 1, Russell's theory is preferable to both Frege's and Meinong's views since it allows sentences containing non-referring descriptions to express true (or false) propositions while it avoids having to allow nonexistent objects into our semantic ontology.

While Burge's negative free logic agrees with Russell's theory regarding the truth conditions of sentences containing definite descriptions, it disagrees with Russell regarding the logical form of such sentences. Like other free description theories, Burge's theory treats closed descriptions as primitive, undefined singular terms with their own semantic clauses that determine their reference, namely instances of (11). By contrast, descriptions on Russell's theory are not singular terms at all. Rather descriptions are introduced by means of contextual definitions of the sentences that contain them. On these contextual definitions, all sentences containing definite descriptions are mere abbreviations of purely general quantified sentences that do not contain the descriptions at all. (See Russell 1905 and especially Russell and Whitehead 1910, 67–84.) In effect, on Russell's theory, descriptions have no semantic features of their own; rather all the semantic features of sentences containing descriptions are determined by the semantic features of the parts of the quantified sentences for which defined sentences containing descriptions are abbreviations.

So while Burge's and Russell's theories agree on the truth conditions and the propositions expressed by sentences containing descriptions, they disagree on *how* these sentences come to have these truth conditions and express these propositions.[18] Regarding the disagreement, I side with Burge and other free description theorists and agree with them that descriptions have their own semantic features and so are not introduced into natural language *via* contextual definitions of the sort that Russell used to introduce descriptions into *Principia*. The hypothesis that descriptions are introduced by such definitions is not impossible of course, but it does seem to be an extremely unlikely hypothesis about natural language.

For one thing, this hypothesis forces us to concede that, as Russell maintained, simple sentences of the form 'The F is G' have a surface grammatical form that is exceedingly misleading as to logical form. Yet Russell provides no real reason to believe this. We can agree with him that a sentence of the form 'The F is G' expresses the same proposition as a sentence of the form 'There exists exactly one object that is F and it is

G', without agreeing that these sentences have the same logical form. It is far more plausible to suppose that the surface structure of sentences of the form 'The F is G' is precisely their logical structure, so that the proper units of meaning of such a sentence are the noun phrase 'The F' and the predicate 'is G'. Thus it is more plausible to suppose that descriptions in natural language have separate meanings on their own, that is, to suppose that the semantic conventions of natural language apply directly to descriptions and determine their semantic features.[19]

But while I agree that descriptions are primitive and are provided with their semantic properties directly rather than by definition, I disagree with the view that (closed) descriptions are singular terms that have semantic referents and that can be treated as individual constants. I once did endorse this view (McKinsey 1979), but I have since been persuaded that descriptions are in fact *quantifiers* rather than singular terms.[20]

6. Definite Descriptions Are Quantifiers

The most plausible view is that definite descriptions are not singular terms but quantifiers. In particular, definite descriptions are one of a vast assortment of quantifiers in natural language, which are the subject of a well-developed field in both logic and linguistics known as *generalized quantifier theory*. Here I will rely on Stephen Neale's (1990) straightforward and intuitive discussion.[21]

Natural languages contain a plethora of *determiners*, such as 'all', 'some', 'no', 'every', 'at least one', 'most', 'exactly one', 'each', 'few', 'between three and five', 'the', and many, many, others. On one treatment, these determiners can combine with formulae or predicates to form *restricted* quantifiers. For instance, 'all', 'some', 'most', and 'exactly one' can form such restricted variable binding quantifiers as

[all x: men x]; [some x: men x]; [most x: men x]; [exactly one x: man x]

Such a restricted quantifier can then be combined with a second formula to form an additional formula, such as:

[all x: men x](mortal x) – All men are mortal.
[some x: men x](mortal x) – Some men are mortal.
[most x: men x](mortal x) – Most men are mortal.
[exactly one x: man x](mortal x) – Exactly one man is mortal.[22]

Similarly, definite descriptions can also be treated as variable binding quantifiers. For instance, Russell's (1905) example, 'the present king of France is bald', can be represented as having the form:

[the x: present king of France x](bald x)

or more formally

$$[\eta x K x](B x).$$

Note the significant difference between this representation and the representation provided by both Russell and the 'individual constant' view, which is: $B[\iota x K x]$. [See Prior (1963), who calls the Russell/individual constant form 'quite misleading' (p. 198).]

On this view, sentences containing descriptions understood as quantifiers have exactly the same truth conditions (and intuitively express exactly the same propositions) as on Russell's theory. For instance, for a first-order language extended by adding such descriptions as quantifiers, the semantics will imply the following truth condition for formulae of the form $[\eta x \phi] \psi$ for any interpretation I and assignment a:

(14). $[\eta x \phi] \psi$ is true under I and a iff (1) there is exactly one object $d \in D$ such that ϕ is true under I and $a(d/x)$ and (2) ψ is also true under I and $a(d/x)$,

where ϕ and ψ are any formulae containing x free and $a(d/x)$ is the assignment exactly like a except that it assigns object d to x.

Note first that unlike Russell's theory and like the individual constant view, the descriptions-as-quantifiers view both preserves the surface structure of description-containing English sentences as reflecting logical form, and it allows descriptions to be primitive, rather than defined, expressions that have independent meanings provided by the semantic rules of the language in question. In this respect, the quantifier view satisfies the main (and as far as I can tell, the only) consideration in favor of the individual constant view. Of course, the quantifier view shares with Burge's version of the individual constant view the advantage of coinciding with Russell's theory of the truth conditions of sentences containing descriptions. [I briefly argued in Section 5 of this chapter that this is a distinct advantage. For more extensive defenses of Russell's theory, see Mates (1973) and Neale (1990).]

Thus, the view that descriptions are quantifiers is *at least* as plausible as the individual constant view. Are there reasons for *preferring* the quantifier view? I think that, though they are perhaps not conclusive, there are persuasive reasons for holding that descriptions are quantifiers rather than true singular terms. First, as Evans (1979, 170) pointed out, is the fact that treating natural language descriptions as quantifiers allows for the plausible generalization that sentences constructed by use of descriptions are built up (both syntactically and semantically) in the same way as the vast number of other types of quantified sentences. Thus sentences of the form 'The F is G' are clearly analogous in structure to 'Every F is G', 'Some Fs are G', 'Most Fs are G', 'No Fs are G', and so on. In other words, the hypothesis that descriptions are quantifiers fits nicely with generalized quantifier theory, for which there is overwhelming linguistic evidence.

But perhaps the strongest evidence for the quantifier view is the ease with which the view accounts for the phenomenon of scope ambiguities in natural language sentences containing descriptions and other operators, as compared to the difficulty for the individual constant view that is raised by the same phenomenon.

Consider, for instance, Russell's (1905) famous example:

(15). The present king of France is not bald.

As Russell pointed out, this sentence has two readings, depending on the relative scopes of 'The present king of France' and 'not'. On the quantifier view, the two readings on which the description has small and large scope, respectively, are perspicuously represented by

(15S) $\sim [\imath x K x](B x)$; and

(15L) $[\imath x K x] \sim (B x)$

Since there is no unique present king of France, $[\imath x K x](B x)$ is false, and so its negation (15S) is true. But since (15L) implies that there is a unique present king of France (who is not bald), (15L) is false. Note the similarity of this account to that provided by generalized quantifier theory of the ambiguities found in such sentences as the Shakespearean example:

(16). All that glisters is not gold,

whose two readings are perspicuously rendered as:

(16S). $\sim$[all x: glisters x](gold x) – (true)
(16L).   [all x: glisters x]$\sim$(gold x) – (false)

Thus on the quantifier view of descriptions, scope ambiguities in sentences of natural language containing descriptions can be understood as simply an instance of the common and widespread phenomenon of quantifier scope ambiguity in English and other natural languages.

But by contrast, the individual constant view of descriptions faces a serious difficulty in explaining scope ambiguities involving descriptions. For if they are individual constants, then descriptions can only attach directly to atomic predicates (in first-order logic), and so they must always have smallest scope. (Burge 1974, 313, notes the problem.) To handle wide scope descriptions, special devices of some sort must be added to the relevant language. Lehmann (2002, 245–246) notes a suggestion by Scales (1969, 11), on which complex predicates $\lambda y \Psi$ are formed from perhaps complex formulae Ψ, from which sentences are then formed by attaching descriptions [$\imath x\phi$] as individual constants. This provides representations of wide scope readings, such as the following representation of Russell's (15L):

(15L*) $\lambda y(\sim By)\imath xKx$

Of course, a representation like this can succeed in *expressing* the large scope reading of (15). But this fact hardly explains *how* (15) *could have such a reading*. English, note, does in fact have a complex predicate-forming operator analogous to Scales's λ, namely the 'such that' operator. Using this operator, we can easily express the large scope reading of (15) by writing:

(15st).   The present king of France is such that he is not bald.

But of course (15) itself does not have this grammatical structure since if it did, it would not be ambiguous. To get an explanation of (15)'s ambiguity, we'd have to suppose in addition that there's a possible structure of (15) on which it contains an implicit 'such that' operator or something of the sort. But there seems to be no good reason to believe this.

On the other hand, if the description 'the present king of France' is a quantifier, then it can of course attach to complex predicates or open sentences like 'is not bald', and given that this is one of the two structures that (15) can have if its contained description is a quantifier, it is easy to see how (15) can have a large scope reading. The simplest and most intuitively obvious hypothesis is that the ambiguity in a sentence like (15) is a *scope* ambiguity, as Russell himself saw. The individual constant view of descriptions is simply not consistent with this obvious hypothesis, and so this view of descriptions is wrong.

The ease with which the quantifier view deals with structural scope ambiguities in sentences containing definite descriptions provides, I think, the strongest argument that descriptions are quantifiers and not singular terms.

The final advantage of the quantifier view of descriptions that I want to mention was emphasized by Evans (1979). The advantage is that if descriptions are treated as quantifiers, then we may take the relation of semantic reference to be the simple two-place relation between singular terms and referents that it seems to be. But if we take descriptions to be referring singular terms, then reference must rather be taken to be a much more complex *five*-place relation that holds between terms and objects, *relative to* possible worlds, times, and assignments.

Kripke (1972a) famously and persuasively argued that while names are rigid designators, that is, are terms that refer to the same object at every possible world, contingent definite descriptions are not rigid but rather may refer to different objects relative to different possible worlds. Thus Kripke assumed that the reference relation must be relativized to possible worlds. But Evans (1979) made the important point that the sole motivation for relativizing reference to worlds is the desire to treat (non-rigid) descriptions as singular terms (p. 179). If instead we treat them as quantifiers, then there is no motivation at all for relativizing reference to worlds. For all *other* terms, including names, indexical pronouns, and demonstratives, never vary in their reference from world to world, and so we can treat them as simply referring to their (actual) referents. The truth value at a given world w of a sentence containing a name, for example, is then simply determined by the features that the *actual* referent of the name has or lacks in w. This of course is consistent with Kripke's correct point that a name's referent never varies from world to world. (See McKinsey 1984, 494, and Chapter 1 of this book.)

Evans also pointed out that descriptions as singular terms must also have their reference relative to times since they can occur in tensed sentences and so may have different referents at different times. And since descriptions may contain free variables (unbound pronouns), their reference must also be relativized to assignments of objects to variables. (Closed descriptions would then refer to objects relative to *every* such assignment.) But again, other (genuine) terms do not require such kinds of relativized reference.

So by taking descriptions to be quantifiers, we obtain a much simpler and intuitively straightforward conception of reference as a two-place semantic relation. We also obtain a theoretically satisfying distinction in our semantic theory that adequately captures the vast semantic difference between definite descriptions on the one hand and the genuine terms (names, indexicals, and demonstratives) on the other, a difference emphasized first by Russell and later by Kripke (1972a), Donnellan (1970), and Kaplan (1977).

This vast semantic difference is theoretically enshrined in Russell's way, by treating descriptions solely as expressions of generality (as quantifiers), while true (genuine) terms are taken to be expressions of singularity, being the only kind of expression that can *refer* to single objects in the world. Moreover, given Direct Reference, the concept of reference on this kind of view takes on added semantic significance. For on this view, again, the referent of a true term not only determines the truth value of sentences containing the term, but it does so by being the term's sole contribution to what is said (the proposition expressed) by use of those sentences. Giving this degree of semantic significance to the reference relation was of course Russell's original idea.

7. Is There a Problem With Partial Interpretations?

Maria Lasonen-Aarnio (2008) has claimed that defenders of Direct Reference (DR) like me should not endorse any form of free logic that allows interpretations on which individual constants can fail to refer. (This would in fact rule out *all* forms of free logic: positive, negative, and neutral.)[23] Lasonen-Aarnio's contention seems to be that the proponent of DR who appeals to the notion of an interpretation that is partial on the individual constants is involved in some sort of inconsistency (p. 539). For, she seems to be saying, a partial interpretation that fails to assign a referent to a given term also provides the term with no semantic value, leaving both the term and sentences containing it, as she puts it, 'without interpretations'. I am not sure why this is supposed to be a problem for proponents of Direct Reference like me. Indeed if it is a problem for me, then it must *also* be a problem for the proponents of all forms of free logic (positive, negative, and neutral), whether or not they also endorse DR. For there is no *other* form of semantic value provided for non-referring terms by these logics since all of them allows interpretations to be partial.[24]

But what exactly is the problem supposed to be? Is there supposed to be something intrinsically *wrong* with the idea of a partial interpretation that leaves some terms without semantic values? To merely make this claim just begs the question against free logic in general and in favor of classical logic. Remember, the free logicians have given powerful arguments in favor of a first-order semantics that allows interpretations to be partial on the individual constants (so that such constants can fail to refer on an interpretation of the language). Without use of such partial interpretations, names are required to refer on every interpretation, and we are again saddled with the absurdities of classical logic: positive existence claims using either referring or non-referring names are absurdly counted as logical truths; invalid inferences in natural languages from true universal generalizations to untrue instances containing non-referring terms are absurdly counted as valid. Far from being intrinsically wrong, partial interpretations are both useful and *required*, if we are to avoid the absurd consequences of classical logic.

Yet we still have no inkling of what Lasonen-Aarnio's *argument* might be. Maybe she is saying that partial interpretations are bad (or somehow inadequate) because they provide no *meanings* ('interpretations') for some singular terms and the first-order sentences that contain them. This perhaps resembles the excuse considered earlier (in Chapter 1, Section 3) that a classical logician might give for refusing to apply classical logic to (allegedly) meaningless sentences of natural languages that contain non-referring terms. But the objection that I'm now imagining is different. It's not an objection to *applying* formal semantics to certain sentences of natural language. Rather it's an objection to the *formal semantics* for first-order logic that the free logicians are proposing. But I think that this objection is misguided.

Consider the kinds of semantic values that are provided for terms, predicates, and sentences on interpretations by the standard formal semantics for first-order logic (whether classical or free). Individual constants are provided with referents from the domain of interpretation, n-place predicates are assigned sets of n-tuples from the domain, and sentences are assigned either truth or falsehood. But none of these – referents, sets of n-tuples, and truth values – are properly called either 'meanings' or 'interpretations'. Rather they are of course properly called the *extensions* of the relevant expressions. In formal semantics, the word 'interpretation' (and equivalently 'model') is a technical defined expression that applies only to a set-theoretic entity that itself applies to (is 'of') only an entire language. It does *not* apply properly to the words and sentences of a language, which do not have 'interpretations' in this technical sense. A classical, bivalent, first-order semantics differs from the various forms of free semantics in that it requires interpretations to provide an extension for every constant, predicate, and sentence of a given language, while free semantics allow interpretations that fail to provide an extension for every constant and perhaps also fail to provide extensions for every sentence when the semantics are not bivalent.

But it is important to understand that the interpretations of *neither* classical *nor* free first-order semantics provide *meanings* (as opposed to extensions) for the types of expression in question. Consider individual constants in particular. In *actual* languages, on their *actual* interpretations, in the *actual* world, singular terms such as names, indexicals, and demonstratives can have linguistic meanings which together with facts about the world typically provide referents for these terms. In other words, *meaning* (typically) determines *reference* (extension), as Frege (1892a) taught us.[25] A singular term's meaning in a language always provides a condition that an object must uniquely satisfy in order to be the referent of the term or a contextual use of the term. But these conditions are typically *contingent*: in the end, it is contingent facts about the world that determine which object, if any, is a term's referent.[26] But since these conditions are contingent, it sometimes happens, due to facts about the world, that *no* object satisfies the relevant condition so the relevant term, though it is perfectly meaningful, *has no referent* (extension). It is this kind of reference failure by meaningful terms that the partial interpretations of free logic are intended to model. The interpretations of neither classical nor free semantics can actually *provide* meanings (as opposed to referents) for individual constants. Rather, we might say, the simple extensional semantics for first-order logics *presuppose* that on each interpretation the constants have meanings (of some sort or other) which, together with the (also presupposed) *possible situation* represented by the interpretation, determine the referents (if any) of the constants in question on that interpretation.[27] The denotation function of a given interpretation simply *assigns* extensions to the individual constants and predicates of the language in question. But this in effect collapses into a *single* function what in real language is the sum of all the meanings of all the constants and predicates of the language *plus* a possible world, which are all being presupposed for the sake of simplicity and mathematical clarity. Of course in more complex intensional logics, these implicit dual roles of meaning and possible world can be, and have been, made explicit. (See, for instance, Kaplan's 1977 formal semantics for his logic of demonstratives.)[28]

Failure of reference of meaningful terms is an actual phenomenon that occurs in the actual first-order fragments of natural languages like English. To model in first-order semantics this kind of real reference failure, we need to use the notion of a partial interpretation. The fact that such an interpretation provides no extension ('semantic value') for some terms is not a *defect* of the interpretation. Rather it's the *whole point* of using such interpretations in first-order semantics. Nor is the fact that such interpretations fail to provide *meanings* (intensions) for some terms any kind of defect since no semantics for first-order logic, whether classical or free, provides such meanings for terms.

So I can see no relevant or plausible reason why a proponent of DR is somehow rationally precluded from rejecting classical logic and instead endorsing free semantics that permit interpretations that are partial on the constants. Indeed I believe that I showed earlier that proponents of DR are rationally required to endorse a non-bivalent neutral free logic that permits such interpretations.

8. Conclusion

In this chapter I have argued that the Direct Reference thesis (DR) implies the no-proposition view that sentences containing genuine terms that fail to refer do not express propositions, and as a further consequence, sentences of natural language that contain such non-referring genuine terms are neither true nor false. Since natural languages do in fact contain such terms, the only form of first-order logic that is adequate for application to natural language must be a *free logic* which, unlike classical first-order logic, can tolerate both failure of reference and failure of bivalence. I described the relevant defects of classical logic, defended my view that they *are* defects, and explained how the various forms of free logic can be used to remedy these defects (in various ways). I described the features of the varieties of free logic, including positive, negative, and neutral free logic, and I argued that only neutral free logic is consistent with DR. (I also argued on independent grounds against the various forms of positive free logic, including the form based on supervaluations that tolerates failure of bivalence.) I discussed free description theories on which (closed) definite descriptions are treated as individual constants. While a negative free logic like Burge's shares many of the advantages of Russell's theory of descriptions and while unlike Russell's theory it preserves the surface structure of natural language sentences that contain descriptions, I argued for the view that definite descriptions in natural languages are best thought of as quantifiers rather than as individual constants. The quantifier view of descriptions, I argued, not only preserves surface structure like the individual constant view, but it also has some decisive theoretical advantages over the individual constant view. Finally I defended the semantics of free logics that utilize partial interpretations against a recent objection by Lasonen-Aarnio. I argued that Lasonen-Aarnio provides no cogent reason why partial interpretations should not be used, and I defended and motivated the use of such interpretations in the formal semantics of free logic.

Notes

1. Kripke's (1972a) famous 'Gödel'/'Schmidt' case shows that *most* names are not like this since it shows that the referents of most names are not determined by the descriptions that are *commonly associated* with the names. But the names I've mentioned here are *exceptions* to this fact.
2. A referee asked whether or not a descriptive name like 'Homer' remains (semantically) a name when used as short for a description in one of the relevant allowed contexts. Good question. My answer is 'no'. We can say that the expression 'Homer' when used descriptively is syntactically the same as the name 'Homer' when used as a genuine term, but it is not semantically a name at all when used descriptively. In effect, my idiom hypothesis makes uses of descriptive names ambiguous when they occur in one of the relevant types of context. Such an occurrence can be understood either as a directly referring use of a genuine term, or it can be understood as short for a given definite description. As in all cases of ambiguity, disambiguation is accomplished by the intentions of the speaker.
3. I provide a detailed account of what it is for an expression to be used as a proper name in McKinsey (2010).
4. The exception in parentheses concerns a philosophically important linguistic construction in which a type of anaphoric pronoun [called 'E-type' by Gareth Evans (1977a)] occurs. An E-type pronoun is an indexical genuine term whose reference is fixed by the descriptive content of the pronoun's antecedent quantifier phrase. I have argued elsewhere at some length that when such a pronoun occurs in the scope of a cognitive operator and where the pronoun's quantifier antecedent *also* occurs in the scope of a cognitive operator such as 'assumes that', then the entire sentence in which the pronoun occurs can express a true proposition, even when the pronoun fails to refer. I call such constructions 'mental anaphora'. An example would be 'Oscar assumes that just one fish got away from him, and Oscar wishes that he had caught *it* (that very fish)'. Such constructions were discovered by Peter Geach (1967), though the semantic interpretation of them just described is my own. (See McKinsey 1986 and 1994.)
5. Unless noted otherwise, I will leave out this parenthetical qualification and assume that the names and pronouns being discussed are being used as genuine terms and are not E-type pronouns in a context of mental anaphora.
6. At least one defender of DR, David Braun (1993), nevertheless continues to endorse bivalence, in spite of the previous argument. Braun holds that atomic sentences containing non-referring names nevertheless express propositions, which he calls 'gappy' propositions, where these gappy propositions are held to be false (for no reason that I can detect). This view violates the

fundamental idea of DR, namely the idea that the proposition expressed by use of a name is a *function* of the name's semantic referent. I will argue in Chapter 4 that the gappy proposition view is false.

7. The following are some of the earliest and most important works on free logic: on positive free logic, Lambert (1963a, 1963b), van Fraassen (1966), and Meyer and Lambert (1968); on negative free logic, Schock (1968) and Burge (1974); on neutral free logic, Smiley (1960) and Lehmann (1994). A useful short survey is Lambert (2001). My discussion of free logic in this chapter and especially in Chapter 3 is hugely indebted to the very useful and thorough survey by Lehmann (2002).

8. I am here assuming the standard objectual understanding of the quantifiers of first-order logic, according to which these quantifiers range over existing objects in the relevant domain of interpretation. This is the view of the quantifiers endorsed by most philosophers and logicians, including Frege, Russell, Tarski, and Quine. This standard view has been challenged by followers of Alexius Meinong like Richard Routley (1966), who allow domains of interpretation to contain nonexistent objects. It has also been challenged by some defenders of substitutional quantification such as Alex Orenstein (1978, 1990). I will discuss these alternative views of the quantifiers in Chapter 4.

9. Here I am assuming the 'Rule of Necessitation', a standard axiom or rule of systems of modal logic, on which if p is a theorem (or logical truth) of the system, then so is $\Box p$ (that is, Necessarily, p').

10. It is counted false on Lehmann's (1994, 2002) neutral free logic.

11. Russell may well have had such a response in mind for cases in which 'Pegasus' is used as a genuine term. See Russell (1918, 242–243).

12. Positive free logics are sometimes provided with 'outer domain' semantics on which the (non-empty) domain D is the union of two subdomains, an 'inner' domain D_i over which the quantifiers range and an 'outer' domain D_o containing possible but nonexistent objects. On these semantics, $d(a)$ is defined for every constant a, and so interpretations are not partial: if $d(a) \notin D_i$, then $d(a) \in D_o$.

13. Thus, on my neutral free logic, on every interpretation on which $\sim\exists x(x =$ Pegasus) has a truth value, it is false, so it is true on *no* interpretation. Thus trivially, on every interpretation on which it is true, its contradictory generalization $\exists y \sim \exists x(x = y)$ is also true. (So even in this case, EG is valid.) Of course, this does *not* imply that $\sim\exists x(x =$ Pegasus) is itself a contradiction since it is not false on every interpretation either. If it were, then $\exists x(x =$ Pegasus) would be a logical truth, as in classical logic. These considerations make it easy to see how Russell might have reasonably thought that when a is a genuine term, $\sim\exists x(x = a)$ could not be true, and so perhaps this might also explain why someone like Russell who endorses bivalence could end up with the mistaken idea that $\exists x(x = a)$ is a logical truth!

14. Lehmann (1994, 331) has pointed this out.

15. This is pointed out by the defenders of supervaluations themselves. See p. 42 of Bencivenga, Lambert, and van Fraassen (1991), which is a very useful source for supervaluational semantics. See also van Fraassen (1966), Bencivenga (1986), and Lehmann (1994, 330–334, and 2002, 227–233).

16. Theories of descriptions have also been provided in the context of positive free logics. See, for instance, Lambert (1963b, 1964), Scott (1967), and van Fraassen and Lambert (1967).

17. Here I have taken the liberty of adding the word 'living' to the description 'my only son' in Russell's example. I do this because Russell wants the description 'my only son' to fail to refer if the antecedent of (13) is false. But I've argued elsewhere that terms involving kinship relations like 'my only

son', 'my mother', 'my paternal grandfather', and so on can still refer after their referents have ceased to exist. (See McKinsey 2005, 162–163.)

18. This disagreement corresponds to an important distinction that Kaplan (1970) pointed out.

19. As Evans (1982, 57) so aptly put it, 'One thing is sure: there is absolutely no need for the butchery of surface structure in which Russell so perversely delighted.'

20. I was first persuaded of this by Gareth Evans (1979), though my friend Richard Sharvy (1969) had earlier proposed the same idea.

21. As far as I know, A. N. Prior (1963, 198) was the first to suggest the idea that definite descriptions are quantifiers (though of course the idea is certainly suggested by Russell's theory). Later the idea was also (independently) proposed by Sharvy (1969) and Grice (1969) and developed by Evans (1977b, 1979). Montague (1970) seems to have been the first to suggest the idea in the context of a general theory of quantifiers in natural language. [See also Evans (1977a), Wiggins (1980), and Davies (1981)]. Especially important for generalized quantifier theory are the seminal papers by Barwise and Cooper (1981) and Higgenbotham and May (1981). For a nice basic account of generalized quantification in natural language, see Larson and Segal (1995, Chapter 8). For more technical surveys of generalized quantifiers in both logic and linguistics, see Westerståhl (2001) and Glanzberg (2006).

22. This is the approach of Sharvy (1969), Barwise and Cooper (1981), Higgenbotham and May (1981), and Neale (1990). An alternative approach, which seems to have become standard in the literature, is to take determiners themselves to be binary quantifiers that form formulae from pairs of formulae. Thus, 'all men are mortal' would be represented by '[all x](men x, mortal x)'. This is the approach suggested by Prior (1963), Evans (1977a), Wiggins (1980), Davies (1981), Larson and Segal (1995), Westerståhl (2001), and Glanzberg (2006).

23. Positive free logics, including both those given supervaluational semantics and those given 'story' semantics, allow failure of reference. Positive free logic has also been given 'outer domain' semantics on which all individual constants refer (on every interpretation). See note 12 in this chapter.

24. Again with the exception of outer domain semantics.

25. But take care. As Kaplan (1977) correctly pointed out, Frege's notion of meaning or *Sinn* is a conflation of two different notions of meaning, one of which Kaplan calls 'character' (or linguistic meaning), the other of which he calls 'content' (proposition expressed or component of proposition expressed). On Kaplan's view, which I share, the referent of a term is typically determined by the term's linguistic meaning (or character), while the term's content just is its referent. (Though in my view, determination of a proper name's referent is a much more complicated matter. See McKinsey 2010.)

26. For discussion and specific views regarding the reference conditions for names, indexicals, and demonstratives, see, for instance, Kaplan (1977), Perry (1977, 1979, 1997), and McKinsey (1978a, 1984, and 2010).

27. Lehmann (2002, 212) plausibly suggests that formal interpretations represent possible situations.

28. It may be that some, perhaps including Lasonen-Aarnio, have been misled by the word 'direct' in Kaplan's expression 'direct reference'. As a result, they may have made the mistake of thinking that on DR, the referent of a genuine term is not determined, or mediated by, any other semantic properties that the term might have (such as a descriptive linguistic meaning or character), so that, absent a referent, the term would have no semantic features whatever,

and so would be meaningless. (Again, Russell himself may have believed this. See his 1918, 242–243.) This idea is quite wrong and not at all what Kaplan meant, as he himself has made quite clear. (See Kaplan 1977, 483 and 1989, 568–569.) DR is simply not a view about how the referents of genuine terms are determined. Rather it is a view about the kind of proposition that is expressed by use of such terms; again the view is that the proposition (content) expressed by a sentence containing a name, indexical, or demonstrative is functionally determined directly by the term's referent and not (as on Frege's view) by some descriptive *Sinn* that the term might have that in turn determines the term's referent. For instance, on Kaplan's view (and mine), indexical and demonstrative pronouns are directly referential in his sense. However, the referent of such a term (in a particular context) is mediated or determined by a descriptive reference rule which Kaplan calls the term's character and which I call the term's linguistic meaning. (See Kaplan 1977, 505–507 and McKinsey 1984, 491–498, and 512, note 13.)

3 From Neutral Free Logic
to *a posteriori* Necessity

In this chapter, I will begin by describing, explaining, and defending the main features of the semantics for neutral logic that I prefer, which I will call 'NuFL'. This discussion will occur in Sections 1 and 2. Details of the semantics will be found in Appendix 1 at the end of the chapter. My semantics for NuFL is largely derived from the semantics proposed by Scott Lehmann (2002) and will differ from his solely in its treatment of the quantifiers ∀ and ∃. This difference in turn derives from the different motivations that Lehmann and I have for endorsing neutral free logic, as I will explain. I will then go on in Section 3 to motivate and propose a new semantics for quantified modal logic that is based on neutral free logic. An interesting feature of this modal semantics is that, while truth functional tautologies and many other logical truths of classical logic that contain individual constants (names) cease to be logical truths in neutral free logic, they plausibly re-emerge as *a posteriori* necessary truths in modal logic, under interpretations where the constants refer. Details of the modal semantics will be found in Appendix 2 at the end of the chapter.

1. Motivations for Neutral Free Semantics

Only a few philosophers have publicly endorsed, or at least made serious use of, a form of neutral free logic: Timothy Smiley (1960), Peter Woodruff (1970), Scott Lehmann (1994, 2001, 2002), James Pryor (2006), and McKinsey (2006).[1] Of these, Smiley, Woodruff, and Lehmann are motivated by Fregean assumptions, while Pryor and I are motivated by semantic and metaphysical considerations based on Direct Reference.[2]

As we discussed in Chapter 1, Frege (1891, 1892a) held a principle of extensionality to the effect that the referent of any complex expression of language is a function of the referents of the expression's meaningful parts. In the case of sentences, this implies (on Frege's view) that the *truth value* of a sentence is a function of the referents of its meaningful parts. As Frege (1892a, 62) pointed out, this means that indicative sentences of natural language are sometimes neither true nor false since such sentences sometimes contain non-referring singular terms. (This consequence of Frege's view was much later famously endorsed by P. F. Strawson 1950.)

Frege thought that failure of reference by singular terms and the resulting failure of bivalence for sentences are defects of natural language, and so he stipulated successful reference in the case of all terms and sentences of his formal logic (1892a, 70). But the desire to have a form of first-order logic that is applicable to natural language plus an appreciation for Frege's principle of extensionality provides a strong motivation for developing forms of neutral free semantics of the sort first proposed by Smiley (1960) and later by Lehmann (1994). Lehmann (1994) also provided a sound and complete proof theory for his version of neutral free logic.

It is an extremely interesting, even surprising,[3] fact that Frege's functional semantic theory, based in part on his principle of extensionality and the Russellian notion of a genuine term which forms the basis of the DR-thesis, should both equally well provide motivations for neutral free semantics and the resulting radically non-classical concepts of logical truth and logical consequence. In Chapter 2, we saw in effect that the truth value of a natural language sentence containing a genuine term (when used as such) is a function of the term's referent since the proposition expressed by the sentence is a function of the referent and the sentence's truth value is determined by the proposition it expresses. So on both Fregean and Russellian principles, a first-order logic that permits terms without referents should also require sentences containing such terms to lack truth value: such a logic, that is, should be a neutral free logic.

In particular, an *atomic formula* of a first-order language is without truth value on interpretations on which one or more of the terms in the formula fail to refer. Where s and t are any terms (variables or individual constants) and P is any n-place predicate, the truth values of atomic formulae under interpretations $I = \langle D, d \rangle$ and assignments f are the following:[4]

(v1). If each t_i refers, then $Pt_1 \ldots t_n$ is true if $\langle \alpha_1 \ldots \alpha_n \rangle \in d(P)$ and $Pt_1 \ldots t_n$ is false if $\langle \alpha_1 \ldots \alpha_n \rangle \notin d(P)$, where t_i refers to α_i; otherwise $Pt_1 \ldots t_n$ lacks truth value.

(v2). If s and t refer, then $s = t$ is true if $\alpha = \beta$ and $s = t$ is false if $\alpha \neq \beta$, where s refers to α and t refers to β; otherwise $s = t$ is without truth value.

In the case of truth functionally compound formulae, the truth value of such a compound is computed as usual by the classic truth tables when all of its components have truth value. But when a truth functional compound has any component that lacks truth value, both Frege's extensionality principle and the DR-thesis require that the whole compound lack truth value. Thus a negation ~A lacks truth value if A lacks truth value; any disjunction A ∨ B, conjunction A & B, or conditional A → B will lack truth value if either A or B lacks truth value. The non-classical tables for computing truth values this way are called the *weak* truth tables (after Kleene 1950, 334). The *strong* Kleene truth tables permit some compounds to have truth values even though they have components without truth values. Thus, while negations are treated the same as on the weak tables, a disjunction A ∨ B is counted true if one of A and B is true, whether or not the other has truth value; thus a conditional A → B, being equivalent to ~A ∨ B, is true as long as A is false or B is true, whether or not the other has truth value; a conjunction is counted false if at least one conjunct is false.

Again, both of the motivations provided by Frege and Direct Reference obviously require truth value assignments to truth functional compounds that are in accord with the *weak* truth tables. (For details, see Appendix 1.) For Frege of course, the truth functions named by the connectives must have the truth values T or F as *arguments* in order to have either T or F as *values*. So lack of truth value by any component will result in a truth functional compound's also lacking truth value. As Lehmann (2001, 147) aptly puts it, in Fregean functional semantics, 'where there is no input, there is no output'. On the DR-thesis, the proposition expressed by a truth functional compound is a function of the referents of any terms contained in the components. So if any such term lacks a referent, the compound (as a whole) will fail to express a proposition and so will lack truth value (though one or more components of the compound may express propositions and have truth values). Again, lack of a referent as input results in a lack of truth value as output.

Whether we adopt the weak or strong truth tables, we already have the consequence that such classical logical truths as $t = t$, $Pt ∨ ~Pt$, and $s = t → (Ps → Pt)$ have no truth value if s and t do not refer. (See Lehmann 2002, 228.) Thus such formulae are not logical truths in neutral free logic, given the standard conception of logical truth as truth under every interpretation and assignment, the conception I endorse. (For further discussion of logical truth and logical consequence in neutral free logic, see Appendix 1.)

2. Quantifiers in Neutral Free Logic

It remains to provide valuation rules for quantified formulae. On this matter, there is a serious difference of opinion between me and other defenders of neutral free logic (with the exception of Woodruff 1970, 138). In my view, motivated by the DR-thesis, quantified sentences containing non-referring constants should all be without truth value since like other sentences containing genuine terms that lack referents, such quantified sentences express no propositions and thus can be used to say nothing true or false about the world. In effect, on my neutral free semantics NuFL, the quantifiers are 'trivalent'. But on the systems proposed by Lehmann (1994, 2002), Smiley (1960), and Pryor (2006), all quantified sentences are 'bivalent', always being either true or false, even when they contain non-referring constants.[5]

I will begin by giving some negative arguments against the two proposals by Lehmann (1994, 2002) that provide different bivalent interpretations of the quantifiers. Then I will provide some positive arguments in favor of my trivalent interpretation. In brief, my main positive argument will be based on the claim that there are only two ways of interpreting individual constants, either (1) as closed definite descriptions or abbreviated definite descriptions understood according to Russell's theory of descriptions or (2) as genuine terms that are semantically analogous to the proper names and indexical pronouns of natural language. On alternative (1) quantified sentences containing individual constants (that are descriptions or abbreviated descriptions) will be bivalent all right, but so will every other sentence containing only such constants, whether they refer or not. In this case, there really is *no* motivation for neutral free logic (contrary to the Fregean view); rather as we saw in Chapter 2, a Russellian negative free logic will suffice. On alternative (2), neutral free logic still has a motivation, but this motivation has the consequence that quantified sentences containing non-referring constants can be used to say nothing true or false about the world, and so are themselves without truth value.

2.1 Some Negative Arguments

In his (1994) Lehmann took the existential quantifier ∃ as primitive and the universal quantifier ∀ to be defined as usual, so $\forall x A$ means $\sim\exists x \sim A$. His valuation rule for $\exists x A$ under interpretation I and assignment f can be stated as follows:

(L1).　$\exists x A$ is true if for some $\alpha \in D$, A is true under $f(\alpha/x)$; otherwise $\exists x A$ is false.

[Where $f(\alpha/x)$ is the assignment exactly like f except that it assigns $\alpha \in D$ to x. See Lehmann 1994, 327 and 2002, 234–235.] If A is, for instance, an atomic formula Pxa where a does not refer, then Pxa will be truth-valueless on every assignment to x, and so for no $\alpha \in D$ is Pxa true under $f(\alpha/x)$. Thus on (L1), $\exists x Pxa$ will be false. Similarly, where a does not refer, $\exists x(x = a)$ will be false, and so $\sim\exists x(x = a)$ will be true. Lehmann interprets the former sentence as meaning 'a exists' and the latter as meaning 'a does not exist', so that whenever a does not refer, the former is false, and the latter is true. These consequences regarding positive and negative existentials containing names will no doubt seem plausible to many. Yet (L1) plus the definition of $\forall x A$ as $\sim \exists x \sim A$ implies that if a fails to refer in a formula Pxa, then $\forall x Pxa$ will be *true* [as Lehmann (2002, 235) points out]. Since Pxa will be truth-valueless under any assignment to x, so will $\sim Pxa$, and so for no $\alpha \in D$ is $\sim Pxa$ true under $f(\alpha/x)$; hence, by (L1), $\exists x \sim Pxa$ is false, and so by definition of $\forall x A$, $\forall x Pxa$ is true.

Thus it follows from Lehmann's (1994) view of the quantifiers that since Pegasus doesn't exist, so nothing is identical with Pegasus, it nevertheless also follows that everything *is* identical with Pegasus after all! For on Lehmann's semantics, we have

$$(1) \quad \sim \exists x (x = \text{Pegasus}) \vDash \forall x (x = \text{Pegasus}).$$

If the premise of (1) is true on I, then 'Pegasus' does not refer on I; but then, as we've seen, the conclusion of (1) must also be true on I, given Lehmann's semantics. But surely, no correct semantics should allow such an argument to both have a true premise and be valid, since the conclusion $\forall x (x = \text{Pegasus})$ should be counted as either false or without truth value when 'Pegasus' fails to refer, except perhaps when the domain is empty. Moreover, given Lehmann's semantics, it appears that on any interpretation I on which 'Obama' refers and 'Pegasus' does not, it will turn out that both '$\forall x (x = \text{Pegasus})$' and '$\exists y (y = \text{Obama})$' are true on I. Thus, given only the standard free logic restriction on UI, it would follow that 'Obama = Pegasus' is true, provided only that 'Obama' refers and 'Pegasus' does not. Since it also follows on Lehmann's semantics that 'Obama = Pegasus' is without truth value and hence *not* true when 'Pegasus' does not refer, Lehmann's (1994) semantics requires some additional restriction on UI.

But it seems to me that no such further restriction is required. For it just seems obvious that the following argument is valid:

$$(2) \quad \begin{array}{l} \forall x (x = \text{Pegasus}) \\ \underline{\exists y (y = \text{Obama})} \\ \therefore \text{Obama} = \text{Pegasus} \end{array}$$

Surely, given an interpretation I on which both 'Everything is identical with Pegasus' and 'Obama exists' are true, 'Obama is identical with Pegasus' would also be true on I! Since on my trivalent semantics of the quantifiers, '$\forall x (x = \text{Pegasus})$' can be true on an interpretation only if 'Pegasus' refers on that interpretation, (2) counts as valid on my semantics without restriction. The fact that Lehmann's (1994) semantics for the quantifiers has the consequence that arguments like (2) are invalid is, I think, a good reason to reject that semantics.

In his (2002, 234–235), Lehmann provides a different semantics for bivalent quantifiers. There, he retains rule (L1) for $\exists x A$ but does not define $\forall x A$ as $\sim\exists x\sim A$. Instead like $\exists$, he takes $\forall$ as primitive and provides it with a new valuation rule, according to which, under I and f,

(L2). $\forall x A$ is true if for every $\alpha \in D$, A is true under $f(\alpha/x)$; otherwise $\forall x A$ is false.

Given (L2), problems such as those raised by results like (1) no longer arise. Thus, when 'Pegasus' fails to refer, it no longer follows that '$\forall x(x = \text{Pegasus})$' is true. On the contrary, since '$x = \text{Pegasus}$' will be truth valueless on every assignment, '$\forall x(x = \text{Pegasus})$' will be *false*, provided that the domain is not empty.

However, as Lehmann points out (2002, 234–235), given (L1) and (L2), $\exists x A$ and $\sim\forall x\sim A$ cease to be equivalent. [When a fails to refer, $\exists x Pxa$ will be false on (L1), but on (L2), $\sim\forall x\sim Pxa$ will be *true* (in a non-empty domain) since $\forall x\sim Pxa$ will be false.] But it seems to me that this failure of quantifier equivalence is a serious drawback of Lehmann's (2002) semantics since it violates our intuitive understanding of the quantifiers. Even the standard relations of the modern square of opposition are violated. For instance, given that 'Pegasus' fails to refer, (L1) implies that it is false that some persons are identical with Pegasus [$\sim\exists x(Px \ \& \ x = p)$, where '$Px$' means '$x$ is a person' and 'p' = 'Pegasus'.] But this certainly seems equivalent to saying that no persons are identical with Pegasus [$\forall x(Px \to x \neq p)$]. Yet the latter would be false given (L2). Thus on Lehmann's semantics, Aristotelian I-propositions of the form 'Some As are Bs' are not in general the contradictories of their corresponding E-propositions 'No As are Bs' since both can be false. Similarly of course for 'Some As are not Bs' and 'All As are Bs' which can also both be false on Lehmann's semantics.

Lehmann could of course respond by correctly pointing out that failure of the standard equivalences between $\exists$ and $\forall$ occurs only in cases where the quantified sentences contain non-referring constants: where reference does not fail, the standard equivalences hold. Fair enough. But I still have a serious problem with Lehmann's (2002) quantifiers. It is just this. Under interpretations on which 'Pegasus' does not refer, Lehmann counts 'Pegasus does not exist', symbolized as '$\sim\exists x(x = \text{Pegasus})$' as *true*. But he also counts 'No existing object is Pegasus', symbolized as '$\forall x(\exists y(y = x) \to x \neq \text{Pegasus})$', as *false* (in a non-empty domain). Here, I think, Lehmann's (2002) semantics makes a distinction without a difference. It just seems obvious that the English sentences in question ('Pegasus does not exist' and 'No existing object is Pegasus') are logically equivalent (in the sense that on every interpretation, they are true, false, or truth valueless together), and if they expressed propositions (on interpretations where 'Pegasus' refers), they would express precisely the same (false) proposition.

Consider the following argument (in English on the left, symbolized on the right):

	All horses exist.	$\forall x(Hx \rightarrow \exists y(y = x))$
(3)	Pegasus does not exist.	$\sim \exists y(y = \text{p})$
	∴ Pegasus is not a horse	$\therefore \sim Hp$

On Lehmann's semantics (both the 1994 and the 2002 versions), argument (3) is *invalid* since the truth of the second premise alone guarantees that the conclusion lacks truth value. Still, the argument certainly *appears* valid, and I think that most who would accept the premises as true (as would, say, a defender of negative free logic) would also accept the conclusion. [On my trivalent semantics for the quantifiers in NuFL (see Section 2.2), (3) is *trivially* valid since its second premise is true on *no* interpretation, being false when 'Pegasus' refers and lacking truth value when 'Pegasus' does not refer.]

Now compare (3) with the apparently equivalent argument:

	All horses exist.	$\forall x(Hx \rightarrow \exists y(y = x))$
(4)	No existing object is Pegasus.	$\forall x(\exists y(y = x) \rightarrow x \neq \text{p})$
	∴ No horse is Pegasus	$\therefore \forall x(Hp \rightarrow x \neq \text{p})$

While (3) and (4) certainly appear to be the same argument, expressed in slightly different ways, Lehmann's (2002) semantics treats (3) as invalid but (4) as *valid*. (4) is trivially valid, since on Lehmann's semantics, its second premise is true only on interpretations whose domain is empty, which guarantees that the conclusion is trivially true as well. [NuFL (Section 2.2) also counts (4) as trivially valid, but for a different reason: its second premise, like the second premise of (3), is true on no interpretation.]

In English, arguments (3) and (4) are equivalent, having premises and conclusions that are logically equivalent. So these arguments should both be counted as valid or invalid together. (Both are valid in my view.) By treating the second premises of the arguments as nonequivalent, Lehmann, in his (2002) semantics, is giving a meaning to the universal quantifier that it does not have in natural language, and so this semantics cannot be accurately applied to natural language. The standard assumption that $\exists x A$ and $\sim \forall x \sim A$ (as well as $\forall x A$ and $\sim \exists x \sim A$) are equivalent should be accepted as correct.

2.2 A Simple Positive Argument

Here is a simple argument that merely for the sake of consistency, advocates of neutral free logic should hold that, as in the case of atomic sentences, quantified sentences containing non-referring constants are neither true nor false. It is not unusual for some formulations of positive free logic to contain a primitive one-place predicate constant 'E!' understood to mean 'exists', where of course on every interpretation, 'E!' is true of every member of the relevant domain so that '∀xE!x' is a logical truth. With identity '=' added to such a system of positive free logic, the biconditional

(5) $E!a \leftrightarrow \exists x(x = a)$

is also derivable, as Hintikka (1959) showed. Of course in neutral free logic, this biconditional is not a logical truth since 'E!a', being an atomic sentence, should have no truth value when a fails to refer. Yet surely, 'E!a' and '∃x(x = a)' should, on any interpretation, be held true, false, or truth valueless together. After all, these sentences certainly seem to have, or are at least *close* to having, the same meaning and at any rate are clearly logically equivalent: 'E!a' means 'a exists', while '∃x(x = a)' means 'a is identical with some existing object'. But again, since neutral free logic treats all atomic sentences that contain non-referring constants as without truth value, it must also treat 'E!a' as without truth value when a does not refer. So by parity of reasoning, '∃x(x = a)' should be treated the same way, and so it too should be treated as without truth value when a does not refer.[6] To accommodate this fact then, neutral free semantics should hold that quantified sentences containing non-referring constants lack truth value.

For the reasons so far given (and for an additional major reason to be given in Section 2.3), I prefer a form of neutral free logic whose quantifiers are 'trivalent', where Lehmann's (L1) and (L2) are replaced by the following, so that under any interpretation I and assignment f:

(v5). If each constant and free variable (other than x) in A refers, then $\forall x$A is true if for every $\alpha \in D$, A is true under $f(\alpha/x)$, and A is false if for some $\alpha \in D$, A is false under $f(\alpha/x)$; if some constant or free variable (other than x) in A does *not* refer, then $\forall x$A lacks truth value.

(v6). If each constant and free variable (other than x) in A refers, then $\exists x$A is true if for some $\alpha \in D$, A is true under $f(\alpha/x)$, and $\exists x$A is false if for every $\alpha \in D$, A is false under $f(\alpha/x)$; if some constant or free variable (other than x) in A does *not* refer, then $\exists x$A lacks truth value.

(We may take either ∀ or ∃ as primitive and define the other in the usual way.)

2.3 Another Positive Argument

Many philosophers who write about these matters share Lehmann's point of view to the effect that when a meaningful constant a fails to refer, the sentences 'a exists' and 'a does not exist' are false and true, respectively.[7] Such philosophers seem to take it to be a virtue of any semantic account of singular terms that it has this consequence. I think that this point of view is seriously mistaken. Following Russell (1918, 242–243), my view is that, if a given term *t* fails to refer and yet the sentences '*t* exists' and '*t* does not exist' are false and true respectively, then *t* is either a definite description or is being used as short for a description. By contrast, if *t* is being used as a genuine term, semantically analogous to the names and indexicals of natural language, then the sentences in question, since they express no propositions, are without truth value.

Philosophers, who without hesitation endorse the view that when constant *a* fails to refer '*a* exists' and '*a* does not exist' are false and true respectively, are, I think, over-exaggerating the significance of ordinary existence claims involving non-referring names, claims that do seem obviously to be either true or false. I mentioned these kinds of cases early on in Chapter 2 (p. 2), cases like

(6). Santa Claus does not exist,

And

(7). Homer existed.

I will shortly argue that typically, in cases like this, the proper names are used as short for descriptions, and in Chapter 5 I will explain how this is both possible and consistent with the fact that the use of names as genuine terms is the basic and most typical way of using names in natural language, while their use as abbreviated descriptions is derivative and idiomatic. Here my goal is the narrower one of providing further evidence that to have a clear and well-motivated system of first-order neutral free logic, we must treat the individual constants as analogous to the genuine terms of natural language so that quantified sentences, as well as atomic and truth functional ones, should fail to have truth values when they contain non-referring constants, as my rules (v5) and (v6) stipulate.

When thinking about the semantics of positive and negative existentials containing names like (6) and (7), it is important to be clear about the contrast between the meaning of such sentences when the names in them are being used as genuine terms, on the one hand, and their meaning when used to state some interesting factual discovery or to address the topic of some controversial debate about existence on the other. Alvin Plantinga was, I believe, the first to clearly explain this contrast (1974, 137–148). My discussion will be based in part on his. Consider Plantinga's examples:

(8). Socrates does not exist.
(9). Socrates exists.

First, suppose that I utter (9) assertively, using 'Socrates' as a name, as a genuine term. In doing so, I would be asserting a singular proposition about Socrates to the effect that he has (or at least had at some time) the property of existence. This is of course a perfectly fine proposition, but using (9) out of the blue to assert this proposition would normally be a peculiar thing to do. For in using (9) this way, I would be presupposing its truth; in using 'Socrates' in (9) to refer to Socrates, I would presuppose his existence in order to (redundantly) predicate existence of him. On the other hand, as Plantinga points out (p. 145), there are other cases involving this same singular proposition where its expression, as opposed to its assertion, seems quite natural, as in

(10). It is necessarily true that if Socrates teaches Plato, then Socrates exists.

For my purposes though, the most important fact about sentences of the form '*a* exists', where *a* is used as a name, is that unless they are true, such sentences can be used to say nothing at all and thus have no truth value. Thus such sentences *cannot be false* on any first-order interpretation. This is why it is pointless to use such sentences assertively.[8]

Assertive uses of negative existentials like (8) are even more peculiar, given that the names they contain are being used as names. It would of course be absurd to refer to Socrates with his name, only to go on to falsely claim that he does not exist. Here the important fact is that unless (8) is false, it can be used to say nothing at all, and so would be without truth value. So such sentences *cannot be true* on any first-order interpretation. This is why it is not just pointless, but pragmatically inconsistent, to use such sentences assertively.[9] Once again, though it would be absurd to use a sentence like (8) assertively, (8) expresses a perfectly good (though false) singular proposition. And again, like (9), there are many contexts in which use of sentence (8) to express this proposition is quite natural, as in

(11). Though Socrates in fact exists, it is possible that Socrates does not exist.[10]

I will say that existentials like (8) and (9), wherein the contained name is used as a genuine term, are *pointless*, in the sense that they either cannot be used to assert anything true [as in (8)] or they cannot be used to assert anything false [as in (9)].

As Plantinga points out, there is an enormous contrast between (1) the meaning of existentials like (8) and (9) in which the names are used as genuine terms so that the existentials are assertively pointless and (2) the meaning of existentials of the same grammatical forms when they are used to express genuine discovery or disagreement regarding existence. Plantinga says the following about a case of the latter type:

> Suppose a pair of classicists have a dispute as to whether or not Homer existed; it would be incorrect, I think, to represent them as referring to the same person – namely, Homer – and disagreeing as to whether that person had the property of existing. The one who takes the affirmative, I think, is not singling out or specifying a person by use of the name 'Homer' and then predicating existence of him; his opponent is not using that name to specify a person of whom he then goes on to predicate nonexistence.
>
> (1974, 141)

I think that there can be no serious doubt that Plantinga is right about this. It is especially obvious that no supporter of a negative existential of the form 'a does not exist', where a is a name, would be absurdly attempting to assert nonexistence of a's referent.[11] But then the supporter of 'a exists' would also not be trying to (pointlessly) predicate existence of the referent of a since in doing so, the supporter would not be asserting what her opponent is denying.

In short, in serious discussions or disputes about existence, where the issue being discussed or disputed is expressed by using a proper name, the name is not being used *as* a name, as a genuine term. How then *is* the name being used? Plantinga discusses three different views, those of Russell, Searle, and Donnellan, according to which the names in such contexts are in effect being used as short for various sorts of definite description.[12] Plantinga endorses none of these views, but he does suggest that some such view must be correct.[13] I think that Plantinga is right about this since there in fact seems to be no reasonable alternative, as I shall argue further in Chapter 4. It is clear that when a given name a is being used in a serious discussion or dispute about existence, the existence of the name's referent is *not* being presupposed, as would be the case if the name were being used as a genuine term. The best hypothesis would thus seem to be that the name a is being used as short for a description understood according to Russell's, rather than Frege's, theory of descriptions. Understood this way, positive and negative existentials such as 'Homer existed' and 'Homer did not exist' will both express propositions that are either true or false, whether or not the name 'Homer' refers. Again, in Chapter 5, I will provide an account of how, given the holding of certain relatively rare conditions, names may be used in certain specific forms of sentence as abbreviated definite descriptions, even though names are standardly, in most types of sentences, used as genuine terms.

Now let's return to the main topic of this section, that of whether or not the quantifiers of neutral free logic should be treated as bivalent. We have seen that when a constant a is treated as semantically analogous to the names and indexicals of natural language, that is, when it is treated as a genuine term, negative existentials containing *a* of the forms $\sim\exists x(x = a)$ and $\sim E!a$ *cannot be true* on any first-order interpretation; for either *a* refers so that these negative existentials are false or *a* does not refer, so they lack truth value.

We have also seen that the one and apparently only way in which a negative existential of the form $\sim\exists x(x = a)$ can be true is when the constant *a* is treated as a definite description or as short for a description, understood in Russell's way. Treating constants as Russellian descriptions will result in existentials of the form $\exists x(x = a)$ being false and their negations $\sim\exists x(x = a)$ being true when *a* fails to refer, just as Lehmann and many other philosophers and logicians desire. I argued in Chapter 2 that (closed) descriptions should not be treated as individual constants but rather as quantifiers. But even if we waive those arguments, treating individual constants as descriptions or as short for descriptions eliminates all need or motivation for neutral free logic. For as we also saw in Chapter 2, Russell (1905) showed that the truth values of sentences containing definite descriptions are *not* in general a function of the descriptions' referents. He provided various examples of sentences containing non-referring descriptions that are nevertheless either true or false. His nice example

(12). If Ferdinand is not drowned, then Ferdinand is my only living son,

can intuitively be true whether or not the description 'my only living son' has a referent, showing that the truth value of (12) is simply *not* a function of the description's referent. (For several other nice examples which show the same thing, see Mates 1973.) So if we assume that the individual constants of first-order logic should be understood as semantically analogous to (closed) definite descriptions, then quantified sentences containing non-referring constants will be bivalent all right. But since Frege's principle of extensionality fails to accurately apply to such constants, the assumption that all constants are descriptions implies that our first-order language will be bivalent *in general*, so that a neutral free logic will not be applicable to such a language. As we saw in Chapter 2, the correct logic for such a language will be a *negative* free logic of the sort proposed by Schock (1968) and Burge (1974).

The only other alternative is that the individual constants of first-order logic should be understood as semantically analogous to the proper names and indexical pronouns of natural language, that is, such constants should be understood as genuine terms, or 'names in the logical sense'.[14] As I mentioned earlier, the DR-thesis, that the individual constants of a first-order language are genuine terms, implies the Fregean thesis that the truth value of any sentence containing an individual constant is a function of the constant's referent. So the DR-thesis provides a strong and coherent motivation for neutral free logic. But to apply Frege's thesis in a manner consistent with Direct Reference, we have to consistently apply this thesis to *all* sentences across the board, not just to atomic sentences and truth functional compounds but to quantified sentences as well. So on the only plausible motivation for neutral free logic, that provided by the DR-thesis, we should treat quantified sentences that contain non-referring constants as lacking truth value.

This concludes my argument in favor of a semantics for neutral free logic on which the quantifiers are 'trivalent', that is, on which quantified sentences that contain individual constants which fail to refer must lack truth value, including positive and negative existentials of the form $\exists x(x = a)$ and $\sim\exists x(x = a)$.

But before moving on, I think it is important to point out that along the way we have also seen that there is a significant tension in Frege's seminal work on the semantics of singular terms. On the one hand, Frege took definite descriptions as his model of singular terms, a fact which led him to propose his famous theory of sense and reference, on which all meaningful singular terms have descriptive senses that determine the terms' reference, and on which the propositions (thoughts, *Gedanke*) expressed by sentences that contain such terms are a function of the terms' senses and are *not* a function of the terms' referents. But on the other hand, Frege also thought that a term's referent (if any) was always a semantically important characteristic of the term, an idea embodied in his principle that the truth value of a sentence containing singular terms is a function of the terms' referents.

But again, Russell showed that the truth values of sentences containing definite descriptions are *not* a function of the descriptions' referents. This in turn has the effect of showing that on Frege's theory of sense and reference, the truth value of *no* sentence-containing terms is a function of the terms' referents since on Frege's theory, *all* singular terms are of the same semantic type as definite descriptions. Thus Russell's point about definite descriptions has the effect of showing that Frege's theory of sense and reference *is in conflict with* his principle of extensionality. It also shows that Frege's overall semantic view does not provide a coherent justification for neutral free logic. By contrast, Russell's concept of a genuine term, when coupled with the thesis of Direct Reference (which Russell denied), provides a strong justification both for Frege's principle of extensionality as well as for neutral free logic.

Given Frege's adamant rejection of Russell's concept of a genuine term, it is somewhat ironic that by endorsing his principle of extensionality for singular terms (a principle that holds for Russell's genuine terms), Frege showed that his concept of a singular term was much closer to Russell's concept of a genuine term than Frege himself realized.[15]

3. From Logical Truth to *a posteriori* Necessity

We've seen that certain first-order sentences containing genuine terms which classical logic classifies as logical truths are in fact not logical truths since given the DR-thesis, these sentences have no truth value under interpretations where the terms fail to refer. Examples of such sentences include all truth functional tautologies containing names, such as sentences of the forms $(Pa \lor \sim Pa)$ and $(Pa \rightarrow Pa)$, identity sentences such as $(a = a)$ and $(a = b \rightarrow (Pa \rightarrow Pb))$, and existentials of the form $\exists x(x = a)$. While sentences of these forms, whether in formal or natural languages, are not logically true, they are still of logical importance. First, these sentences *cannot be false* on any first-order interpretation. But second – and what is more important – when the constants contained in truth functional tautologies as well as in many other classical logical truths, all refer on a given modal interpretation I, then (as we shall see) these sentences express on I true propositions that could not be false of any possible world, and so are *necessarily true* on I. But (as we shall also see) the same does not hold for sentences of the forms $(a = a)$ and $\exists x(x = a)$. While such sentences cannot be false in fact (in the actual world), such sentences are possibly false on modal interpretations, and so are *not* necessarily true, provided that the referent of a is a contingent object.

I will shortly outline and defend a semantics for quantified modal logic that is based on my neutral free logic NuFL and that has the features just described, so that truth functional tautologies and many other classical logical truths, all of whose constants refer on an interpretation I, are also necessarily true on I. But first I want to stress the important fact that the singular necessary truths expressed by such sentences can only be known *a posteriori*, when the objects they are about are contingent.

3.1 *Singular Classical 'Logical Truths' Are Typically* a posteriori

Consider for instance such singular propositions as

(10). Either Socrates was wise or Socrates was not wise.

Let us abbreviate this proposition as $(Ws \lor \sim Ws)$. Could anyone know this proposition *a priori*? That is, could anyone know this proposition independently of perceptual experience or empirical investigation? It surely seems that, except for Socrates himself, no one could know *a priori* that $(Ws \lor \sim Ws)$ since such knowledge requires knowledge that *Socrates exists* and no one but Socrates can know this *a priori*. In general, all that one can know *a priori* that is relevant to knowledge of a tautological singular proposition is the *universal closure* of the tautology, which in the present case would be $\forall x(Wx \lor \sim Wx)$. But as we've seen, we cannot infer any *instance* of such a universal logical truth such as $(Ws \lor \sim Ws)$, absent the required additional existence assumption, $\exists x(x = s)$. Once the relevant existence assumption is known, then the instance $(Ws \lor \sim Ws)$ can also be known. But this knowledge would be *a posteriori* since it would be based both on the *a priori* knowledge that $\forall x(Wx \lor \sim Wx)$ and the *a posteriori* knowledge that $\exists x(x = s)$.

So if I am right that truth functional tautologies and various other classical logical truths containing individual constants express necessary truths under interpretations where the constants all refer, then we have discovered a new large class of *a posteriori* necessities, a class that is quite different from the *a posteriori* necessities discovered by Kripke (1972a) and Putnam (1970).

One interesting objection to my view that there are *a posteriori* necessities of this kind is based on the suggestion that there are two distinct levels of interpretation needed in order to know that a sentence is true. In the case of a truth functional tautology such as 'Either Socrates was wise or Socrates was not wise', we have to first come to understand the meanings of the words in the sentence, that 'or' expresses a certain truth function, that 'Socrates' has a referent that once existed, and so on. On this level, knowledge of what the words of the sentence mean is *a posteriori*. But then, given this knowledge, no more empirical investigation is needed at the second level to come to know that the tautology is true, in contrast to our *a posteriori* knowledge, say, that Socrates was wise.

Here, the objection seems to imply that, in an interesting sense, truth functional tautologies containing names are knowable *a priori*, contrary to my view. My response would begin by suggesting that our knowledge that a given name has a referent is not in general something that we have to know at the first level of interpretation. All we can know at that level about a name such as 'Socrates' is that it is a meaningful name, not that the name has a referent. Note that on both the neutral free logic NuFL and the modal system MNFL that I defend here, no sentence containing a proper name or individual constant can be a logical truth since there will always be interpretations on which the constant fails to refer, so the relevant sentence will have no truth value and thus will not be true on that interpretation. Thus no truth functional tautology containing a name can be true as a matter of logic: for such a sentence to be true, the name must actually refer, and that is not in general a matter of logic (or meaning) alone.

Here's a simple argument that truth functional tautologies containing names are not in general knowable *a priori*. Suppose for *reductio* that I can know *a priori* that either Socrates was wise or Socrates was not wise. On my system NuFL of neutral free logic, under every interpretation on which it is true that either Socrates was wise or Socrates was not wise, it is also true that Socrates once existed. Hence, that either Socrates was wise or Socrates was not wise logically implies that Socrates once existed. Hence, by a simple valid deduction, I can correctly infer from a premise that (by assumption) I know *a priori*, to the conclusion that Socrates once existed. Thus, I can come to know *a priori* that Socrates once existed, which is absurd. Hence, by *reductio*, I cannot know *a priori* that either Socrates was wise or Socrates was not wise. Thus, such knowledge is *a posteriori*.

The situation regarding singular identity propositions of the form $(a = a)$ is both similar to and different from the situation regarding singular tautologies. A person who knows *a posteriori* that, say, Venus exists, could also come to know that Venus = Venus in part on the basis of *a priori* knowledge that $\forall x(x = x)$. But the resulting knowledge is *a posteriori* since it is also based in part on the *a posteriori* knowledge that Venus exists. (See McKinsey 2006, 450.) However, unlike singular tautological propositions, identity propositions expressed by sentences of the form $(a = a)$, where *a* refers to a contingent object, are not necessarily true since (as I will argue in Section 3.3) such identities are true only of worlds in which the referent of *a* exists. And needless to say, existence claims of the form $\exists x(x = a)$ are neither logically true nor necessarily true on interpretations where *a* refers to a contingent object.

3.2 A Modal Semantics MNFL Based on NuFL

Kripke (1963) famously and persuasively argued that a correct possible world semantics for quantified modal logic should allow that different worlds have different domains of objects over which the quantifiers range at those worlds, as opposed to requiring that there be a single, fixed domain of objects for all worlds. But by now, it is widely accepted that to be adequate, a modal logic that accepts Kripke's world-relative domains should also be based on a *free*, rather than a classical, form of first-order logic. For, as James Garson (1984, 1991) has pointed out, a modal logic based on classical logic has consequences that in effect block the advantages of world-relative domains and so conflicts with the motives for introducing such domains in the first place. (For details, see Garson 1991, 113–115.) By contrast, free logics have the resources to block these consequences. Garson, for instance, bases the modal systems he discusses on a minimal form of positive free logic, while Robert Stalnaker (1994) bases the form of modal logic he proposes on negative free logic. And the modal semantics I will propose here is of course based on neutral free logic.

To obtain a modal language from our first-order language, we simply add the logical constants '□' and '◊' as sentence operators, where '□' means 'it is necessary that' and '◊' means 'it is possible that'. We'll take '□' as primitive and define '◊φ' as '~□~φ'. In addition, it will be useful to have an actuality operator '*A*' meaning 'it is actually the case that'.

An *interpretation* I for our modal language is a quintuple $<W, w_0,$ $D, Q, V>$, where W is a set of possible worlds; w_0 is a distinguished member of W (the 'actual' world of W); D is a non-empty domain; and Q is a function that assigns to each member w of W a (possibly empty) subset $Q(w)$ of D so that $Q(w)$ is the set of objects that *exist* in w; and V is a denotation function that assigns values to the individual constants and predicates of the modal language. (Note the absence in the interpretations of any 'accessibility' relation R between worlds. This is because the semantics is intended to provide models for a version of quantified S5 on which every world is universally accessible from every other so there is no need to include other equivalence relations in the models. See, for instance, Hughes and Cresswell 1968, 74, Menzel 1990, 356, note 11, and Garson 2006, 105.)[16]

In the semantics for modal logics, the valuation rules for assigning truth values to formulae (under interpretations I and assignments f) are similar to the rules for first-order logic, except that truth and falsehood (under I and f) are always relative to worlds $w \in W$. The additional major difference is of course that we must also add new valuation rules for modal formulae of the forms '$\Box A$' and 'AA'. In MNFL, these new rules are:

$(v_M 1)$. $\Box A$ is true$_{I,f}$ at w if for every world $w' \in W$, A is true$_{I,f}$ at w', and $\Box A$ is false$_{I,f}$ at w if for some w', A is false$_{I,f}$ at w'; if A is neither true$_{I,f}$ nor false$_{I,f}$ at w, then $\Box A$ is neither true$_{I,f}$ nor false$_{I,f}$ at w.

$(v_M 2)$. AA is true$_{I,f}$ at w if A is true$_{I,f}$ at w_0 and AA is false$_{I,f}$ at w if A is false$_{I,f}$ at w_0; if A is neither true$_{I,f}$ nor false$_{I,f}$ at w_0, then AA is neither true$_{I,f}$ nor false$_{I,f}$ at w.

The rules for the truth functional connectives ~ and → are the same as in NuFL, except for the relativization of truth$_{I,f}$ and falsehood$_{I,f}$ to worlds. (See Appendix 2.) The rule for quantified formulae of the form $\forall x A$ is:

$(v_M 3)$.   If each constant and free variable (other than x) in A refers$_{I,f}$, then $\forall x A$ is true$_{I,f}$ at w if for all d in $Q(w)$, A is true$_{I,f(d/x)}$ at w, and $\forall x A$ is false$_{I,f}$ at w if for some d in $Q(w)$, A is false$_{I,f(d/x)}$ at w; if some constant or free variable (other than x) in A does *not* refer$_{I,f}$, then $\forall x A$ is neither true$_{I,f}$ nor false$_{I,f}$ at w, where $f(d/x)$ is the assignment that is exactly like f except that it assigns d to x.

One slightly unusual feature of the modal semantics of MNFL is that only objects in the domain of the *actual world* w_0 of the relevant interpretations are allowed to be referents of individual constants. That is, the denotation function V of an interpretation is allowed to be partial on the individual constants (as in NuFL), but if V is defined at constant a, then $V(a) \in Q(w_0)$. (See Appendix 2.) This has the effect of requiring the individual constants to be (obstinately) rigid designators, even though reference is not relativized to worlds. Here I'm following the suggestion of Gareth Evans (1979) that was discussed and defended earlier in Section 6 of Chapter 2.[17] Of course, if a constant *a* has no referent on a given interpretation I, then no sentence containing *a* has a truth value under I, and as before, no sentence of the modal language that contains an individual constant can be a logical truth in MNFL.

N-place predicates of the modal language are assigned extensions relative to worlds, where the extensions are sets of *n*-tuples of objects from the domain of the world in question. That is, for each *n*-place predicate *P* and world $w \in W$, $V(P,w)$ is an *n*-place relation in $Q(w)$. This is the standard way of treating predicates in modal semantics, but it is worth emphasizing that this treatment implies that an *n*-place predicate *P* can be satisfied at a world *w* by an *n*-tuple $<\alpha_1,\ldots,\alpha_n>$ only if each of the α_i *exists* in *w*.

Under interpretations I and assignments f, the truth values of *atomic formulae* with respect to a world *w* are determined as follows:

($v_M 4$). If each term t_i refers$_{I,f}$, then $Pt_1 \ldots t_n$ is true$_{I,f}$ at *w* iff $< \alpha_1,\ldots,\alpha_n > \in V(P,w)$, where t_i refers$_{I,f}$ to α_i and $Pt_1 \ldots t_n$ is false$_{I,f}$ at *w* iff $<\alpha_1,\ldots,\alpha_n> \notin V(P,w)$; otherwise $Pt_1 \ldots t_n$ is neither true$_{I,f}$ nor false$_{I,f}$ at *w*.

($v_M 5$). If *s* refers$_{I,f}$ to α and *t* refers$_{I,f}$ to β, then $s = t$ is true$_{I,f}$ at *w* iff $\alpha \in Q(w)$, $\beta \in Q(w)$, and α is β, while $s = t$ is false$_{I,f}$ at *w* iff either α is not β or $\alpha \notin Q(w)$ or $\beta \notin Q(w)$; if either *s* or *t* fails to refer$_{I,f}$, then $s = t$ is neither true$_{I,f}$ nor false$_{I,f}$ at *w*.

3.3 A posteriori *Necessities in MNFL*

We are now in a position to see why, where a truth functional tautology φ contains only individual constants that refer on a given interpretation, φ will be a necessary truth on that interpretation. The basic reason is very simple: when all of the constants in a truth functional tautology refer on I, then all of the sentential components of the tautology will be bivalent on I, and since a tautology is true no matter what the truth value of its components are, the tautology will be necessarily true on I.

To take a simple case, consider a tautology of the form $(Fa \lor {\sim}Fa)$, where *F* is a one-place predicate. Given an interpretation I on which *a* refers and a world *w* in which the referent α of *a* exists, α will either be, or will not be, a member of *F*'s extension at *w*. In either case, $(Fa \lor {\sim}Fa)$ will be true on I at *w*. If the referent α of *a* does *not* exist in *w*, then of course α will not be in the extension of *F* at *w*, so that by rule ($v_M 4$), *Fa* will be false on I at *w*, ${\sim}Fa$ will be true on I at *w*, and again $(Fa \lor {\sim}Fa)$ will be true on I at *w*. Thus, for any world *w*, whether the referent of *a* does or does not exist in *w*, $(Fa \lor {\sim}Fa)$ will be true on I at *w*, and so $\Box(Fa \lor {\sim}Fa)$ will be true on I at any world *w*.[18]

It is worth emphasizing that on MNFL there are *two* different ways in which an object can fail to be in the extension of a predicate P at a world **w**. For instance, when P is one place, an object α that exists in **w** can simply fail to be in $V(P,w)$. Or α can fail to be in $V(P,w)$ simply by not existing in **w**, that is, by failing to be a member of $Q(w)$. In both cases, $\sim Pa$ would be true at **w**, where a refers to α. (See Menzel 1991, 353.)

On some other systems of modal logic, as in MNFL, terms are allowed to refer to objects that fail to exist in various worlds, but in these systems, unlike MNFL, sentences containing such terms lack truth value at worlds in which the terms' referents fail to exist. (See Hughes and Cresswell 1968, 177 ff. and Gabbay 1976, 75 ff.) In my view, this type of semantics is counterintuitive. Consider a sentence such as 'Clinton is a politician', where the name 'Clinton' in fact refers to Bill Clinton. Now consider a possible world **w** in which Clinton does not exist. Would Clinton be a politician in **w**? Clearly not, since only an object that *exists* in a world could be a politician in that world. Thus the proposition C that Clinton is a politician would be *false* (not truth valueless) of **w**. And since the sentence 'Clinton is a politician' expresses C, it too should be counted false with respect to **w**, and its negation should be counted true.[19]

The treatment of the identity predicate '=' in MNFL is different from the treatment it is given in many other systems of modal logic. It is common to treat sentences of the form $(a = a)$ as logical truths, so $\square(a = a)$ is also treated as logically true. Of course in MNFL $(a = a)$ is not a logical truth, for the by now familiar reason that $(a = a)$ has no truth value under interpretations where a has no referent. But in MNFL, even under interpretations on which a does refer, $\square(a = a)$ will typically have instances that are not true at any world. This is simply because on MNFL, $(a = a)$ is held to be *false* at worlds in which the referent of a fails to exist. [See rule $(v_M 5)$.] In turn, my reason for endorsing this treatment is that the identity predicate, like any other atomic predicate, should hold at a world **w** only of objects that *exist* in **w**. As Stalnaker nicely puts it: "self-identity, like all properties, entails existence" (1994, 27, note 14). Thus the principle of the necessity of identity, $\forall x \forall y (x = y \rightarrow \square(x = y))$, fails to hold in both Stalnaker's (1994) system and in MNFL. Rather as Stalnaker puts it (p. 21), what holds is the *essentiality* of identity, $\forall x \forall y (x = y \rightarrow \square(E!x \rightarrow x = y))$. Also, in both systems the necessity of distinctness, $\forall x \forall y (x \neq y \rightarrow \square(x \neq y))$, is a logical truth. (See Stalnaker 1994, 22.)

In addition to truth functional tautologies containing individual constants, many other sentences containing constants that are classical logical truths fail to be logical truths on MNFL but are necessary truths on interpretations where the constants all refer. For example, partial universal closures of tautologies that contain more than one referring constant, such as $\forall x (Rxb \lor \sim Rxb)$, are necessarily but not logically true. Other non-tautological examples would include such sentences as $(Fa \rightarrow a = a)$, $(a = a \leftrightarrow \exists x(x = a))$, $(Fa \rightarrow \exists x(x = a))$, and the law of identity $(a = b \rightarrow$

$(Fa \rightarrow Fb))$, where F is a one-place predicate. And again, the singular propositions expressed by such sentences are both necessarily true and only knowable *a posteriori*.

All of the various sorts of necessities containing individual constants that hold on interpretations on which the constants all refer are valid consequences in MNFL of premises to the effect that the referents of the constants exist in the actual world. The cases we've mentioned thus correspond to the following inferences that are valid in MNFL (where 'X $\vDash$ A' means that A validly follows from the set of premises X):

(a). $A(\exists x(x = a)) \vDash \Box(Fa \vee \sim Fa)$.

(b). $A(\exists x(x = b)) \vDash \Box\forall x(Rxb \vee \sim Rxb)$

(c). $A(\exists x(x = a)) \vDash \Box(Fa \rightarrow \exists x(x = a))$.

(d). $A(\exists x(x = a)) \vDash \Box(a = a \leftrightarrow \exists x(x = a))$.

(e). $A(\exists x(x = a)) \vDash \Box(Fa \rightarrow a = a)$.

(f). $A(\exists x(x = a)), A(\exists x(x = b)) \vDash \Box(a = b \rightarrow (Fa \rightarrow Fb))$.

Again, all of these various types of sentence [in the scope of '$\Box$' in (a) – (f)] express singular necessary truths that are only knowable *a posteriori*, when the objects referred to are contingently existing objects. But *a posteriori* necessities of this kind are quite different from the kind of *a posteriori* necessities identified by Kripke (1972a) and Putnam (1970), both in the reason for their necessity and in the reason why they are *a posteriori*. The Kripke/Putnam examples, such as 'Water is H_2O' are necessary if true because their truth is determined by the essential *natures* of the kinds of substances or objects picked out by the natural kind terms involved, while their being *a posteriori* is due to the fact that these natures themselves can only be discovered by *a posteriori* empirical investigation.

But the *a posteriori* necessities that I've identified here are quite different. For their necessity is not due to the natures of the objects referred to; rather their necessity is due solely to facts about *logic* (which perhaps explains why these necessities have in the past been confused with logical truths). And their *a posteriority* of course also has nothing to do with knowledge of the natures of the objects involved; rather it has to do with the fact that the necessities are *singular propositions* that are typically about contingent objects whose existence can only be known *a posteriori* (except perhaps by the objects themselves). Such propositions cannot be known without knowing that the contingent objects they concern exist, and the latter sort of knowledge can only be obtained by *a posteriori* methods.

This completes my argument for, and explanation of, my positive view regarding what I take to be the significant logical and metaphysical consequences that follow from reference failure, given the thesis of Direct Reference. But before ending this chapter (and going on to defend my view against various objections and alternatives), I need to explain some additional important implications for the notions of logical truth and logical consequence that are suggested by MNFL.

3.4 *Validity in MNFL*

The definitions of truth under an interpretation I (truth$_I$) at a world w and of truth under I (truth$_I$) *simpliciter* are standard (where a *sentence* is understood to contain no free variables):

(TIW)   A sentence A *is true$_I$ at w* iff for every assignment **f**, A is true$_{I,f}$ at **w**.
(TI)   A sentence A *is true$_I$* iff A is true$_I$ at w_0.

But when it comes to defining logical truth and logical consequence, there is a difficult choice to be made between what are standardly called *real-world* validity (logical truth) and *general* validity (logical truth). (This terminology was first suggested by Crossley and Humberstone 1977.) For reasons to be given shortly, I have chosen *general* validity for MNFL. The relevant definitions of general validity are

(GLT)   A sentence A is *logically true* ($\vDash A$) if on every interpretation $I = \langle W, w_0, D, Q, V \rangle$ and for every world $w \in W$, A is true$_I$ at **w**.
(GV)   Where X is a set of sentences and A is a sentence, A *validly follows from* X ($X \vDash A$) if, on every interpretation $I = \langle W, w_0, D, Q, V \rangle$ and for every world $w \in W$ such that each member of X is true$_I$ at **w**, A is also true$_I$ at **w**.

On these definitions, the fundamental notion used is that of truth on an interpretation I *at a world w*. By contrast, the fundamental notion that is used in the corresponding definitions according to *real-world* validity is just that of truth on an interpretation, that is, truth on an interpretation I *at w_0*, the *actual* world of I. These definitions are:

(RLT)   A sentence A is *logically true* ($\vDash A$) if on every interpretation I, A is true$_I$.
(RV)   Where X is a set of sentences and A is a sentence, A *validly follows from* X ($X \vDash A$) if, for every interpretation I such that each member of X is true$_I$, A is also true$_I$.

In many modal systems, these two pairs of definitions are simply equivalent to each other, and so for these systems it doesn't matter whether we choose (GLT) and (GV) or (RLT) and (RV). (For a proof sketch of this, see Davies 1981, 223.) But in systems containing the actuality operator A and in MNFL, with or without A, the two pairs of definitions have significantly different consequences.

In MNFL, the problem of which of these pairs of concepts to use arises primarily in the case of arguments. Should the validity of arguments be determined by (GV) or by (RV)? In my neutral free semantics NuFL, for example, existential generalization (EG) is valid on *every* sentence containing constants, however complex that sentence may be. This is simply because *no* sentence that contains a constant a can be true on a (first-order) interpretation I unless a refers on I to an existing object in the domain of I. But when we consider a modal semantics based on NuFL, it becomes clearly counterintuitive to suppose that unrestricted EG is valid.

For as we saw earlier, on MNFL there are, for instance, interpretations I on which an atomic sentence Fa is false at a world $\mathbf{w}$ simply because the referent of a does not exist in $\mathbf{w}$ so $\sim Fa$ is true on I at $\mathbf{w}$. But then, it surely should not be taken to follow from the fact that $\sim Fa$ is true at $\mathbf{w}$ that $\exists x \sim Fx$ is also true at $\mathbf{w}$ since it is perfectly consistent with the referent of a's failure to exist at $\mathbf{w}$ that $\forall x Fx$ be true at $\mathbf{w}$. So it surely seems that in MNFL, unrestricted EG should *not* be counted valid. Otherwise, we would have to count any argument of the form

$$(\mathrm{EG_U}) \quad \underline{\varphi(a)}$$
$$\therefore \exists x \varphi(x / a)$$

as valid, even though there are possible worlds at which the argument's premise is *true* and its conclusion is *false*.[20]

As I mentioned, $(\mathrm{EG_U})$ is valid in NuFL. It would also be valid in MNFL if we adopted the (RV) definition of logical consequence. But again, if we do this, we are forced to accept the counterintuitive consequence that some arguments are valid, even though it is possible for their premises to be true and their conclusions false. Since in my view such a consequence would be undesirable, I will adopt (GV) rather than (RV) for MNFL. (I will further defend this choice in Section 3.5.) On (GV), only a restricted version of EG is valid:

$$(\mathrm{EG_R}) \quad \varphi(a), \exists x(x = a) \vDash \exists x \varphi(x / a).$$

However, EG is valid without restriction on atomic sentences so we also have:

$$(\mathrm{EG_A}) \quad Pt_1 \ldots t_n \vDash \exists x_i P x_i,$$

where x_i replaces t_i at one or more occurrences in $Pt_1 \ldots t_n$.

The reason why $(\mathrm{EG_U})$ has to be counted as valid in NuFL is that in first-order logic, the notion of truth can only be relativized to interpretations (and languages, of course). This is not a drawback of NuFL as compared to other extensional first-order logics since all such logics have this drawback. We might say that the validity of inferences in first-order logic amounts to a limited kind of 'real-world' validity since truth on an interpretation amounts to truth *in the actual world* on an interpretation. When we advance to a modal logic, where truth is relativized to both interpretations *and* worlds, then in my view we achieve a more adequate way of understanding the validity of inferences, by way of the definition (*GV*). In the end, we can think of validity in first-order logic as a special case of general validity, as in (*GV*). For instance, using the actual world operator A, we can express what we might call 'real world EG':

$$(\text{EG}_{\text{RW}}) \qquad A\varphi(a) \vDash A\exists x\varphi(x \mid a),$$

which holds in MNFL, given (*GV*).

Similarly, the following argument is valid in both NuFL and in MNFL + (*RV*):

$$(\text{E}) \qquad \frac{\varphi(a)}{\therefore \exists x(x = a)}$$

But since again in MNFL there will be possible worlds at which a sentence of the form $\varphi(a)$ is true while $\exists x(x = a)$ is false, accepting (*GV*) forces us to reject the validity of (E). In MNFL + (*GV*) we instead have

$$(\text{E}_{\text{RW}}) \qquad \varphi(a) \vDash A\exists x(x = a).$$

Another important contrast between both validity in NuFL and modal validity given (*RV*) on the one hand and MNFL + (*GV*) on the other can be seen by considering inferences of the form

$$(\text{C}) \qquad \frac{\sim \exists x(x = a)}{\therefore (\varphi \ \& \sim \varphi)}$$

where φ contains no constants. As we saw earlier in Section 2.3, the premise of this argument is true on *no* interpretation in NuFL since it is either false (when *a* refers) or without truth value (when *a* does not refer). So all arguments of this form are trivially valid in NuFL. But intuitively, this form of argument is not really valid since there are *modal* interpretations on which it is clearly *possible* for an argument of this form to have a true premise and a false conclusion. For example, while there is no interpretation on which $\sim\exists x(x = \text{Obama})$ is true with respect to *the actual world*, there certainly are interpretations on which $\sim\exists x(x = \text{Obama})$ is true with respect to *some world*. Of course, at any such world, $(\varphi \ \& \sim\varphi)$

will be false. So if (*GV*) is used in MNFL, arguments of the form (C) will be counted invalid, as I think they should be. But we do have that

$$(C_{RW}) \qquad A \sim \exists x (x = a) \vDash (\varphi \,\&\sim \varphi)$$

holds in MNFL. If instead of (*GV*) we used (*RV*), not only would (C_{RW}) hold, but (C) would be valid, a bad result, I take it.

3.5 Zalta's Objection

Edward Zalta (1988) contends that *real-world* validity, that is, (RLT) rather than (GLT), provides the correct account of logical truth for modal logic. [See also Nelson and Zalta (2012)]. He also endorses various radical consequences of this contention, including the consequence that some logical truths are *contingent* rather than necessary and that, therefore, the rule of necessitation (that if $\vDash \varphi$, then $\vDash \Box\varphi$) is incorrect. [This rule holds in MNFL + (GLT).] For instance, given (RLT), every instance of the following schema would be a logical truth:

$$(A) \qquad A\varphi \to \varphi.$$

For on any interpretation **I**, any instance of (A) will be true on **I**, that is, will be *true in the actual world* w_0 on **I**.[21] But as Zalta points out (1988, 63), an instance of (A) will be *contingent* on an interpretation **I**, provided that the relevant instance of φ is both true and contingent on **I**. In this case, there will be a world w at which the antecedent of the instance of (A) is true but the consequent is false. Thus the instance of (A) will not be necessary on **I**.

If Zalta is right, then the motivations that I gave for including the definition (*GV*) in MNFL are wrong. For if (RLT) is the correct definition of logical truth, then (*RV*) must be the correct definition of logical consequence since on any view, I take it, a sentence is a logical truth if and only if it is a logical consequence of every set of premises, including the null set. My motivation for endorsing (*GV*) and (GLT) is that I take it to be obvious that all inferences of the forms (EG_U), (E), and (C) are *invalid* in MNFL since in MNFL there are interpretations and worlds where the premises of arguments of these forms are true and their conclusions are false. But Zalta would reject this reasoning since if he is right, (*RV*) is the correct account of valid inference, and given (*RV*), all inferences of the forms (EG_U), (E), and (C) are *valid* in MNFL, *even though* it is possible for their premises to be true and their conclusions false.

I of course think that Zalta is wrong about this. But what is his *argument* that (GLT) and hence (*GV*) are incorrect? The only grounds that he gives are these:

(1) the most important semantic definition for a language is the definition of truth under an interpretation, and the alternative method,

in which no world is distinguished as the actual world, has no means of defining this notion; and (2) the semantic notion of logical truth is properly defined in terms of the semantic notion of truth, and the alternative definition of logical truth [i.e., (GLT)] is the wrong one because it fails to do this.

(1988, 66)

Objection (1), however, does not apply to MNFL since on this semantics, on every interpretation, exactly one world w_0 is distinguished as the actual world, and so on MNFL, truth under I *simpliciter* can be defined as truth under I at w_0. [See definition (TI).]

Objection (2) is unconvincing, in part because there is a clear sense in which general validity (GLT) *does* define logical truth in terms of 'the semantic notion of truth'. In the formal semantics for any formal language, truth is always construed as being relative to various things, including at least the language in question and interpretations of the language. So truth in formal semantics is at least a three-place relation between a sentence, a language, and an interpretation. In the semantics of both propositional and quantified modal logic, truth is of course relativized further to possible worlds as well, thus becoming a four-place relation. Truth on I *simpliciter* can of course then be defined as truth on I at the actual world w_0. This allows us to see how the notion of truth as the three-place relation that is used in the semantics of extensional first-order logic can be defined and so understood in terms of the four-place relation used in the semantics of modal logic. From this point of view, it is *truth on I at w* that is the more conceptually fundamental notion, and so it is both natural and plausible that our definition of logical truth should be based on this concept rather than on the defined notion of *truth on I*. In fact, Zalta himself defines *truth on I* in the standard way by appealing to the notion of *truth on I at w*, and so he himself seems to presuppose that the latter notion is the fundamental one.

Of course, Zalta claims instead that the three-place relation of truth that is found in first-order semantics and that is definable in modal semantics is somehow the more important and more conceptually fundamental notion of truth, and so it is *this* relation that should be used to define logical truth and logical consequence in modal semantics. But as far as I can tell, this is just a claim for which Zalta gives no good reason.

Zalta even goes so far as to accuse the proponents of general validity (like me) of proposing what is a 'conflation of the semantic notion of validity and the metaphysical notion of necessity' (1988, 66). But no such conflation is suggested by (GLT). At most, (GLT) implies that all logical truths are metaphysically necessary but does not imply the converse. This no more 'conflates' logical truth and metaphysical necessity than the plausible view that all metaphysical necessities are physically necessary 'conflates' metaphysical and physical necessity.

Note that the view that being logically true implies being metaphysically necessary (though not conversely) is equivalent to the innocent and plausible view that what is metaphysically possible is also logically possible (that is, *consistent*). But as Zalta points out (1988, 73), on his view there are sentences (and hence propositions) that are metaphysically possible but logically false. For instance, as we've seen, on his view, conditionals of the form $(A\varphi \rightarrow \varphi)$ are logically true, so instances of the form $(A\varphi \;\&\; \sim\!\varphi)$ are logically false, even though instances of $\Diamond(A\varphi \;\&\; \sim\!\varphi)$ are true on some interpretations (where φ is contingent).

It is this last feature of Zalta's view that bothers me the most since it corresponds to a notion of logical implication or consequence that seems obviously defective. On his view, valid inferences are those which on every interpretation preserve truth merely *in the actual world*: they need not, and sometimes will not, preserve truth at other possible worlds. But again, this seems a defective notion of logical implication. When a given sentence or proposition P logically implies another sentence or proposition Q, we normally take P to imply Q in every possible situation, circumstance, or world, whether that situation, circumstance, or world is actual or not. In everyday planning and decision-making, we constantly consider various alternative possible actions and scenarios, and we reason about what would be true in those alternatives without ever assuming that any of them are *actual*. If we know or believe that P logically implies Q and we take P to be true in a given possible scenario, then we thereby take Q to be true in that same scenario, and we act or decide accordingly. But if Zalta is right, such an inference might very well be mistaken since valid arguments invariably preserve truth only in the actual world, not always in other possible worlds. But this seems obviously wrong and inconsistent with the way we normally reason about possibilities.

So contrary to what Zalta says (1988, 73), I think that we are in fact correct when we teach our students that an argument is valid only if it is impossible for its premises to be true and its conclusion false.

4. Conclusion

Beginning in Chapter 2, I argued that defenders of the DR-thesis are committed by the facts of reference failure to neutral free logic and thus to the consequence that no sentences of the first-order fragments of natural language that contain proper names and indexical pronouns (when used as genuine terms) are logical truths. In this chapter, I first motivated, explained, and defended the form of semantics for neutral free logic that I think is correct, NuFL. In particular, I argued against one of the main features of Lehmann's neutral free logic, namely his treatment of quantified sentences as bivalent, even when they contain non-referring individual constants. I gave some negative arguments that raised some serious problems for Lehmann's semantics. But in my main positive argument,

I contended that the only way in which quantified sentences containing non-referring constants can be plausibly understood as bivalent is by construing the constants as being either (closed) definite descriptions or as being short for such descriptions. But then, as Russell showed, the truth values of sentences of the relevant language will not be a function of the constants' referents, and so all motivation for neutral free logic is lost. But if, on the other hand, we treat the constants as genuine terms, then the DR-thesis requires that *all* sentences, including quantified ones, must lack truth value when they contain non-referring constants.

I then went on to motivate and explain a semantics for modal logic MNFL that is based on my neutral free logic NuFL. This modal semantics enabled me to explain how many classical logical truths containing constants, such as truth functional tautologies, while they are not logical truths in either NuFL or MNFL, nevertheless turn out to express *a posteriori* necessary truth on interpretations where the constants refer (to contingent objects). This new type of *a posteriori* necessity is quite different from the type discovered by Kripke and Putnam since the relevant types of propositions are necessary solely on the basis of logic, while their being *a posteriori* is due to their being *singular* propositions about contingent objects whose existence can typically only be known *a posteriori*. Finally I explained why I prefer to understand logical truth and logical consequence in MNFL in terms of *general* validity, as opposed to *real-world* validity, and I defended my view against Zalta's contentions to the contrary.

Appendix 1

Semantics for Neutral Free Logic (NuFL)

Let $\mathcal{L}$ be any first-order language whose logical vocabulary includes the identity predicate =, the universal quantifier $\forall$, negation ~, and the material conditional $\rightarrow$. Additional truth functional connectives including disjunction $\lor$, conjunction &, and the biconditional $\leftrightarrow$ may be defined in terms of ~ and $\rightarrow$ as usual. Also the existential quantifier $\exists$ may be defined using ~ and $\forall$ as usual. The non-logical vocabulary of $\mathcal{L}$ includes individual variables and constants (the terms of $\mathcal{L}$) and n-place predicates.

The following neutral free semantics closely follows Lehmann's (2002) presentation, except for the following clauses (v5) and (v6) regarding the quantifiers $\forall$ and $\exists$. (See especially Lehmann 2002, 223, 227, 228, 234, and 235.)

An *interpretation* I of $\mathcal{L}$ is a pair $< D, d >$, where D is a set (the *domain* of I) and d is a function (the *denotation* function of I) such that

(i1). D may be empty;
(i2). d may be partial on the individual constants of $\mathcal{L}$, but if $d(a)$ is defined, where a is an individual constant, then $d(a) \in D$;
(i3). if P is an n-place predicate of $\mathcal{L}$, $d(P)$ is an n-place relation in D;

An *assignment function f* is a perhaps partial function which maps variables x of $\mathcal{L}$ to members of D, so if $f(x)$ is defined, then $f(x) \in D$. $f(\alpha/x)$ is the assignment exactly like f, except that it assigns object $\alpha \in D$ to x.

Under I and f, terms (constants and variables) of $\mathcal{L}$ *refer* to individuals in D according to the following reference rules.

(r1). If $f(x)$ is defined, then x refers to $f(x)$; otherwise x does not refer.
(r2). If $d(a)$ is defined, then a refers to $d(a)$; otherwise a does not refer.

Where P is any n-place predicate, s and t are any terms, and A and B are any formulae, truth values of formulae under I and f are determined by the following valuation rules:

(v1). If each t_i refers, then $Pt_1 \ldots t_n$ is true if $< \alpha_1 \ldots \alpha_n > \, \in d(P)$ and $Pt_1 \ldots t_n$ is false if $< \alpha_1 \ldots \alpha_n > \, \notin d(P)$, where t_i refers to α_i; otherwise $Pt_1 \ldots t_n$ lacks truth value.

(v2). If s and t refer, then $s = t$ is true if $\alpha = \beta$ and $s = t$ is false if $\alpha \neq \beta$, where s refers to α and t refers to β; otherwise $s = t$ is without truth value.

(v3). ~A is true if A is false; ~A is false if A is true; ~A lacks truth value if A lacks truth value.

(v4). A → B is false if A is true and B is false; A → B is true if either A is true and B is true, or A is false and B is true, or A is false and B is false; A → B lacks truth value if either A or B lacks truth value.[22]

(v5). If each constant and free variable (other than x) in A refers, then $\forall x$A is true if for every $\alpha \in D$, A is true under $f(\alpha/x)$, and A is false if for some $\alpha \in D$, A is false under $f(\alpha/x)$; if some constant or free variable (other than x) in A does *not* refer, then $\forall x$A lacks truth value.

Given a definition of $\exists x$A as meaning ~$\forall x$~A, we also have the derived valuation rule for $\exists x$A:

(v6). If each constant and free variable (other than x) in A refers, then $\exists x$A is true if for some $\alpha \in D$, A is true under $f(\alpha/x)$, and $\exists x$A is false if for every $\alpha \in D$, A is false under $f(\alpha/x)$; if some constant or free variable (other than x) in A does *not* refer, then $\exists x$A lacks truth value.

Note that if a formula A in $\forall x$A contains any constant or free variable (other than x) that fails to refer under I and f, then A will lack truth value under I and f. The valuation rules (v5) and (v6) say in effect that when A lacks truth value under these circumstances, so do $\forall x$A and $\exists x$A.[23]

As noted in the text, many forms of sentence-containing individual constants that are logically true in classical logic, such as $\exists x(x = a)$, $a = a$, $Pa \vee$ ~Pa, and $a = b \rightarrow (Pa \rightarrow Pb)$, are not logically true in neutral free logic. This holds on the standard conception of logical truth on which a sentence A is logically true ($\vDash$ A) if and only if A is true under any interpretation I and assignment f.

As Lehmann points out (2002, 234), we could perhaps ameliorate this situation by adopting a *weaker* sense of logical truth on which a sentence A is logically true if and only if A is *not false* under any interpretation and assignment. This results in all sentences of the forms $\exists x(x = a)$, $a = a$, $Pa \vee$ ~Pa, and $a = b \rightarrow (Pa \rightarrow Pb)$ being logical truths since such sentences are always either true or without truth value (on my semantics outlined previously in this chapter). But it also has the counterintuitive consequence that some sentences that are not in fact true are nevertheless logical truths. Thus such sentences as 'Pegasus = Pegasus' and '$\exists x(x = a)$', while they are in fact without truth value (on my semantics), would count as logical truths since they are false on no interpretation and assignment. And in general, all sentences of the form $\exists x(x = a)$ would be logical truths, including contingently true instances such as '$\exists x(x = \text{Obama})$'. But as I argued in Chapter 2, such instances should not count as logical truths since they are not *necessary* truths. So in my view, we should adopt the standard strong sense of logical truth on which A is logically true if and only if A is true under every I and f.

Similarly, as Lehmann also points out (2002, 235), logical consequence may also be defined in various ways. But again I will endorse the standard definition, on which logical consequence is necessarily truth-preserving, so a sentence A is a logical consequence of a set of sentences X ($X \vDash A$) if and only if for every interpretation I and assignment f, if every sentence in X is true under I and f, then A is true under I and f. (It is an interesting fact, again pointed out by Lehmann, that on this standard definition of logical consequence as truth preservation, transitivity holds in neutral free logic but not contraposition. For instance, $a \neq a \vDash Pb$ holds trivially since $a \neq a$ cannot be true on any interpretation. But $\sim Pb \nvDash a = a$ since $\sim Pb$ may be true on an interpretation on which a fails to refer, so $a = a$ lacks truth value.

One of the most important facts about neutral free logic, in all its forms, is that neither conditional proof nor *reductio* are valid without restriction. For example, while $Pa \vDash \exists x(x = a)$ holds, $\vDash Pa \rightarrow \exists x(x = a)$ does not. Under every I on which Pa is true a refers, so $\exists x(x = a)$ is also true on I. But $Pa \rightarrow \exists x(x = a)$ is not true on every I since it has no truth value under interpretations on which a fails to refer. However, in a situation similar to the standard free logic restriction on universal instantiation, a restricted version of conditional proof is also available, as follows:

(CP1).   If A is a sentence containing no individual constants, then if X, $A \vDash B$, then $X \vDash A \rightarrow B$.

(CP2).   If A is a sentence that contains constants $t_1 \ldots t_n$, then if X, $A \vDash B$, then X, $\exists x_1 \ldots \exists x_n(x_1 = t_1 \ldots x_n = t_n) \vDash A \rightarrow B$.

(A similarly restricted version of *reductio* is of course also available in my semantics.)

Other inferences that are valid in classical logic but invalid in neutral free logic also must be supplied with similar existence restrictions. For instance, the rule of addition is invalid in neutral free logic since when B contains one or more individual constants not contained in A, there are interpretations on which A is true but $A \vee B$ is truth valueless. The restricted rule of addition would be:

(RA).   If B contains no constants $t_1 \ldots t_n$ not contained in A, then $A \vDash A \vee B$; otherwise A,

$$\exists x_1 \ldots \exists x_n \left(x_1 = t_1 \ldots x_n = t_n \right) \vDash A \vee B.$$

Like other forms of universally free logic, neutral free logic permits interpretations whose domains are *empty*. Because of this, many inferences based on the classical laws of confinement turn out to be invalid in universally free logics.[24] For instance, the following equivalences are logically true in classical logic, but not in neutral free logic, where x does not occur free in B:

(1). $\forall x(B \,\&\, Ax) \leftrightarrow (B \,\&\, \forall xAx)$

(2). $\exists x(B \vee Ax) \leftrightarrow (B \vee \exists xAx)$

(3). $\exists x(B \to Ax) \leftrightarrow (B \to \exists xAx)$

(4). $\exists x(Ax \to B) \leftrightarrow (\forall xAx \to B)$

Consider (1), for instance, and let B be false on I, where the domain D of I is empty and Ax contains no terms that fail to refer. On the clause (v5) for quantification, $\forall x(B \,\&\, Ax)$ is trivially true on I since there is *no* $\alpha \in D$. But since B is false on I, so is $(B \,\&\, \forall xAx)$. So we have $\forall x(B \,\&\, Ax) \nvDash (B \,\&\, \forall xAx)$. Here, a restriction on which the domain is assumed to be non-empty is required:

(R1) $\forall x(B \,\&\, Ax), \exists x(x = x) \vDash (B \,\&\, \forall xAx)$.

Inferences based on the right-to-left directions of (2), (3), and (4) must be similarly restricted.

Appendix 2
A Semantics for Modal Logic MNFL

[Based on Neutral Free Logic]

$\mathcal{L}_M$ is a modal language that has all the same non-logical vocabulary as the first-order language $\mathcal{L}$ described in Appendix 1, plus the additional logical constants '□', '◊', and '𝒜'. Each of these logical constants is a sentence-forming operator, so if ϕ is a formula, □ϕ, ◊ϕ, and 𝒜ϕ are also formulae. '□' is taken to be primitive and is understood to mean 'it is necessary that' or 'necessarily'; '◊' is understood to mean 'it is possible that' or 'possibly' and is defined thus: $◊\phi =_{df} {\sim}□{\sim}\phi$. '𝒜' is also taken as primitive and is understood to mean 'it is actually the case that' or 'actually'.

A. Interpretations

An *interpretation* I for a modal language $\mathcal{L}_M$ is a quintuple $<W, w_0, D, Q, V>$, defined as follows:

(1). W is a non-empty set; intuitively W is a set of possible worlds;
(2). w_0 is a distinguished member of W; intuitively w_0 is the 'actual' world of W;
(3). D is a non-empty domain of objects;[25]
(4). Q is a function that assigns to each member w of W a (possibly empty) subset Q(w) of D; intuitively Q(w) is the set of objects that *exist* in w; and
(5). V is a function that assigns values to the individual constants and predicates of $\mathcal{L}_M$ as follows:

    (a). V may be partial on the constants, but if V is defined at constant a, then $V(a) \in Q(w_0)$;
    (b). for any n-place predicate P and world $w \in W$, $V(P, w)$ is an n-place relation in Q(w).

B. Assignments to Variables and the Reference of Terms

(1). An *assignment* to the variables of $\mathcal{L}_M$ is a perhaps partial function f which maps variables x to members of $\mathbf{D}$, so $f(x) \in \mathbf{D}$ given that f is defined at x; $f(d/x)$ is the assignment that is exactly like f except that it assigns object d to x.

(2). Given any interpretation I and assignment f, terms (constants and variables) of $\mathcal{L}_M$ *refer*$_{I,f}$ to members of $\mathbf{D}$ in accordance with the following reference rules:

  (a). if f is defined at variable x, then x refers$_{I,f}$ to $f(x)$; otherwise x does not refer$_{I,f}$;

  (b). if V is defined at constant a, then a refers$_{I,f}$ to $V(a)$; otherwise a does not refer$_{I,f}$.

C. Truth$_{I,f}$ With Respect to a World w (A is true$_{I,f}$ at w)

Formulae are true and false under I and f with respect to a world $\mathbf{w} \in \mathbf{W}$ (true and false under I and f *at* $\mathbf{w}$), in accordance with the following valuation rules:

(1). If each term t_i refers$_{I,f}$, then $Pt_1 \ldots .t_n$ is true$_{I,f}$ at $\mathbf{w}$ if $< \alpha_1, \ldots, \alpha_n > \in$ $V(P,\mathbf{w})$, where t_i refers$_{I,f}$ to α_i, and $Pt_1 \ldots t_n$ is false$_{I,f}$ at $\mathbf{w}$ if $<\alpha_1, \ldots, \alpha_n>$ $\notin V(P,\mathbf{w})$; otherwise $Pt_1 \ldots .t_n$ is neither true$_{I,f}$ nor false$_{I,f}$ at $\mathbf{w}$.

(2). If s refers$_{I,f}$ to α and t refers$_{I,f}$ to β, then $s = t$ is true$_{I,f}$ at $\mathbf{w}$ if $\alpha \in$ $Q(\mathbf{w})$, $\beta \in Q(\mathbf{w})$, and α is β, while $s = t$ is false$_{I,f}$ at $\mathbf{w}$ if either α is not β or $\alpha \notin Q(\mathbf{w})$ or $\beta \notin Q(\mathbf{w})$; if either s or t fails to refer$_{I,f}$, then $s = t$ is neither true$_{I,f}$ nor false$_{I,f}$ at $\mathbf{w}$.

(3). $\sim A$ is true$_{I,f}$ at $\mathbf{w}$ if A is false$_{I,f}$ at $\mathbf{w}$, and $\sim A$ is false$_{I,f}$ at $\mathbf{w}$ if A is true$_{I,f}$ at $\mathbf{w}$; if A is neither true$_{I,f}$ at $\mathbf{w}$ nor false$_{I,f}$ at $\mathbf{w}$, then $\sim A$ is also neither true$_{I,f}$ nor false$_{I,f}$ at $\mathbf{w}$.

(4). $A \to B$ is false$_{I,f}$ at $\mathbf{w}$ if A is true$_{I,f}$ at $\mathbf{w}$, and B is false$_{I,f}$ at $\mathbf{w}$; $A \to B$ is true$_{I,f}$ at $\mathbf{w}$ if either A and B are both true$_{I,f}$ at $\mathbf{w}$, or A is false$_{I,f}$ at $\mathbf{w}$ and B is true$_{I,f}$ at $\mathbf{w}$, or A and B are both false$_{I,f}$ at $\mathbf{w}$; if either A or B is neither true$_{I,f}$ nor false$_{I,f}$ at $\mathbf{w}$, then $A \to B$ is neither true$_{I,f}$ nor false$_{I,f}$ at $\mathbf{w}$.

(5). If each constant and free variable (other than x) in A refers$_{I,f}$, then $\forall x A$ is true$_{I,f}$ at $\mathbf{w}$ if for all d in $Q(\mathbf{w})$, A is true$_{I, f(d/x)}$ at $\mathbf{w}$; and $\forall x A$ is false$_{I,f}$ at $\mathbf{w}$ if for some d in $Q(\mathbf{w})$, A is false$_{I,f(d/x)}$ at $\mathbf{w}$; if some constant or free variable (other than x) in A does *not* refer, then $\forall x A$ is neither true$_{I,f}$ nor false$_{I,f}$ at $\mathbf{w}$.

(6). $\square A$ is true$_{I,f}$ at $\mathbf{w}$ if for every world $\mathbf{w}' \in \mathbf{W}$, A is true$_{I,f}$ at $\mathbf{w}'$; and $\square A$ is false$_{I,f}$ at $\mathbf{w}$ if for some $\mathbf{w}'$, A is false$_{I,f}$ at $\mathbf{w}'$; if A is neither true$_{I,f}$ nor false$_{I,f}$ at $\mathbf{w}$, then $\square A$ is neither true$_{I,f}$ nor false$_{I,f}$ at $\mathbf{w}$.

(7). AA is true$_{I,f}$ at $\mathbf{w}$ if A is true$_{I,f}$ at $\mathbf{w}_0$, and AA is false$_{I,f}$ at $\mathbf{w}$ if A is false$_{I,f}$ at $\mathbf{w}_0$; if A is neither true$_{I,f}$ at $\mathbf{w}_0$ nor false$_{I,f}$ at $\mathbf{w}_0$, then AA is neither true$_{I,f}$ nor false$_{I,f}$ at $\mathbf{w}$.

D. Truth on an Interpretation I (truth$_I$) at a World

Where A is a sentence of $\mathcal{L}_M$, A *is true$_I$ at w* iff for every assignment $\mathbf{f}$, A is true$_{I,f}$ at $\mathbf{w}$.

E. Truth on an Interpretation I (truth$_I$)

Where A is a sentence of $\mathcal{L}_M$, A *is true$_I$* iff A is true$_I$ at $\mathbf{w}_0$.

F. Logical Truth

Where A is a sentence of $\mathcal{L}_M$, A is *logically true* ($\vDash A$) iff on every interpretation $I = <\mathbf{W}, \mathbf{w}_0, \mathbf{D}, \mathbf{Q}, \mathbf{V}>$ and for every world $\mathbf{w} \in \mathbf{W}$, A is true$_I$ at $\mathbf{w}$.

G. Validity

Where X is a set of sentences of $\mathcal{L}_M$ and A is a sentence of $\mathcal{L}_M$, A *validly follows from* X ($X \vDash A$) iff, on every interpretation $I = <\mathbf{W}, \mathbf{w}_0, \mathbf{D}, \mathbf{Q}, \mathbf{V}>$ and for every world $\mathbf{w} \in \mathbf{W}$ such that each member of X is true$_I$ at $\mathbf{w}$, A is also true$_I$ at $\mathbf{w}$.

Notes

1. Needless to say, there are still plenty of seats available on this slow-moving bandwagon!
2. Pryor's (2006) use of neutral free logic is in the service of providing a solution to a problem raised by "object-dependent" thoughts for the apriroicity of self-knowledge regarding one's thoughts. As I explained in Chapter 2, my use of neutral free logic is motivated by what I have always assumed is implied by the conjunction of Direct Reference and reference failure, namely the failure of bivalence. (See, for instance, McKinsey 1978a, 180–181; 1984, 500; 1986, 170; 1994, 313; and 1999, 542–543.)
3. The surprise stems from the fact that for Frege, Russell's concept of a directly referring genuine term was anathema. (See Frege 1904, for instance.) I'll contend that the semantic importance that Frege placed on the notion of reference shows that Frege's concept of a singular term was much closer to Russell's than Frege himself realized.
4. (v1) and (v2) follow Lehmann's v_1 and v_2 (2002, 227–228).
5. Pryor (2006) adopts the semantics for bivalent quantifiers of Lehmann 1994. Smiley's quantifiers are quite close to being bivalent, differing from Lehmann's only in a rare sort of case. (See Lehmann 2002, 235.)
6. In his (1994, 327), Lehmann writes, 'Since $\ulcorner \exists v = vt \urcorner$ is true if t refers, $\ulcorner \exists v = vt \urcorner$ may be read as $\ulcorner t$ exists$\urcorner$, taking U to represent what there is (according to I).' But in a footnote to part of this sentence "$\ulcorner \exists v = vt \urcorner$ may be read as $\ulcorner t$ exists$\urcorner$",

Lehmann says 'Strictly, $\ulcorner r(t)$ exists$\urcorner$', where $r(t)$ is the reading of t' (1994, 335, note 7.) If by 'reading' Lehmann means 'referent' here, then he may be indicating that he wants $\ulcorner \exists v = vt \urcorner$ to be given a *metalinguistic* interpretation. If so, then Lehmann would be introducing an ambiguity into his first-order semantics on which terms t would be sometimes used and sometimes mentioned in atomic formulae. This seems to be a mistake.

7. See, for instance, Donnellan (1974) and Braun (1993) as well as the work of both the positive and negative free logicians we've cited so far, including van Fraassen (1966), Meyer and Lambert (1968), and Burge (1974).

8. Though as we'll see in this chapter, sentences like (9) can be false on *modal* interpretations since they will be false at possible worlds in which the actual referent of the relevant name fails to exist.

9. Though again, on *modal* interpretations, such sentences can be true at worlds in which the actual referent of the relevant name fails to exist. It's worth noting that Russell comes close to saying what I'm saying about sentences like (8) and (9) when the relevant name is being used as a genuine term. He says that when a name is used this way, such sentences 'could not be even significant' unless the relevant term's referent existed. (Russell 1918, 242; except for the words in quotes, I've paraphrased Russell's sentence so as to avoid possible use/mention confusions.) I think that by 'significant', Russell here means 'expresses a proposition', and if so, he was saying exactly what I'm saying.

10. This is similar to a valuable point first made by G. E. Moore about the significance of 'This does not exist'. See Moore (1936, 123).

11. Of course, Meinongians would claim that such an assertion would not be absurd. I argue against the Meinongian view in Chapter 4, Section 3.

12. For Russell, ordinary names are all used as short for definite descriptions (Russell 1912, 54). At one point (1918, 243), he suggests that 'Romulus did not exist' might mean, for instance, 'the person called "Romulus" did not exist'. Searle (1958, 171) endorsed a view on which a sentence of the form 'a did not exist' might mean something like 'The individual who has a sufficient number of the S_i did not exist', where the S_i are the properties commonly associated with the name a. (See also Plantinga 1974, 140.) On Donnellan's (1974) view, a negative existential 'a does not exist' might mean something like 'The individual to which the historical explanation of uses of a traces back does not exist'. (In fairness, Donnellan explicitly denies that he is providing an analysis of the meaning of sentences of the form 'a does not exist'; rather he says he is providing only the truth conditions for such sentences (p. 238).)

13. In particular, he suggests that 'some combination of the Searle- and Donnellan-like views' might be used to account for the meaning of serious uses of existentials containing names (1974, 146).

14. Though there is also the 'mixed view' mentioned in Chapter 2, on which individual constants are treated in both ways, some as names, some as descriptions.

15. It is similarly ironic that Strawson (1950) should have adopted Frege's theory of descriptions (without any mention of Frege) and then used it to argue that, contrary to Russell's theory, uses of sentences containing non-referring descriptions are neither true nor false (thus ignoring Russell's (1905) persuasive counterexamples). This is ironic since in treating descriptions this way, Strawson was in effect treating them as genuine terms ('logically proper names'), while in the same paper he vehemently denied (against Russell) that there are any such terms! [Frege's 1892a paper, 'On Sense and Reference', was first published in English translation in 1948 in *The Philosophical Review* 57 (May, 1948), 209–230.]

16. In stating a modal semantics of the standard 'possible world' variety, I do not wish to be taken to be committed to what might appear to be any of the radical metaphysical consequences that might intuitively seem to be implied. In particular, I do not wish to assume that the domain D can contain merely possible, nonexistent objects. I would prefer a view on which the domain elements, except for various concrete objects that exist in the actual world, are taken to be 'ersatz' possible objects such as pure sets. See, for instance, Menzel (1990).

17. A similar idea is applied in the modal semantics suggested by Christopher Menzel (1991, 361). My understanding of these matters has been helped in various ways by this useful and insightful paper.

18. In this paragraph, I leave out relativization to assignments f since I am only discussing *sentences*, which are true on an interpretation I at w if true on I on every assignment at w.

19. Both this example and its point are due to Richard Cartwright. (See his 1997, 76–80.) Cartwright also discusses the objection that the proposition C that Clinton is a politician would not exist in any world in which Clinton does not exist. Cartwright points out that this consideration, though correct, is not relevant to the question. As he says, we *have* Bill Clinton, and so we *have* the proposition C since they both *in fact* exist. And so we can intelligibly ask whether that proposition would be true or false with respect to a world in which neither Clinton nor it exists. In the case of C, the answer is that it would be *false* of such worlds. The literature on this topic is huge and still growing. But see especially Adams 1981, Plantinga 1983, Menzel 1991, and Hoffman 2003.

20. Here, $\varphi(a)$ is any formula containing a, and $\varphi(x/a)$ is the result of replacing a by x at one or more occurrences in $\varphi(a)$.

21. To evaluate (A) in the context of MNFL, we should of course assume that φ contains no individual constants.

22. (v1)–(v4) follow Lehmann's v_1-v_4 (Lehmann 2002, 227, 228, 234).

23. Note also that when $\forall x A$ and $\exists x A$ are closed formulae (sentences) that contain no individual constants and when the domain D of I is empty, then $\forall x A$ is trivially true under I (and any f), while $\exists x A$ is trivially false under I (and any f).

24. Many thanks to Dan Yeakel for bringing this fact to my attention.

25. Again, I don't wish to assume that D might contain merely possible nonexistent objects.

4 Some Alternatives to Using Neutral Free Logic

In this chapter, I will consider and criticize some alternatives to using neutral free logic. First, I will discuss the alternatives proposed by two prominent defenders of Direct Reference, David Braun and Nathan Salmon. Then I will consider two alternative types of quantification, Meinongian and substitutional, which some have suggested can avoid the existence assumptions of classical logic and so can provide cogent alternatives to free logic.

1. Braun's 'Gappy Propositions'

David Braun (1993) has suggested that sentences containing empty names express 'unfilled' or 'gappy' propositions that are always either true or false. The 'gap' occurs at the position in the propositional structure contributed by a sentence containing an empty name, a position that would normally be occupied by the name's referent. Braun claims that all atomic gappy propositions are false. If we treat 'exists' as a one-place predicate, then a sentence like 'Vulcan exists' will thus be false, and its negation ('Vulcan does not exist') will thus be true. Such a view of course commits Braun at most to *negative* free logic. The virtue of this view is that it allows existential sentences that contain empty names to be true or false, as they certainly seem to be, at least in some cases.

But despite having this virtue, Braun's view faces some serious difficulties. First, and perhaps most significant, is the fact that, given what propositions are supposed to be, there can be no propositions that are 'gappy'. For a proposition is a way that the world can be said to be. But when we use a sentence that contains an empty name that is used *as* a name, there is *no* way that the world is said to be by our use of that sentence. And so there is nothing about the way the world is that could make our sentence either true or false.

Even if we suppose that a sentence containing an empty name has some sort of semantic content, there is no good reason to think that this content would be something that is true or false. I would agree with Adams and Stecker (1994, 390) that the semantic content of an atomic sentence containing an empty name such as 'Vulcan is a planet' is precisely the content of the corresponding open sentence '*x* is a planet'. Since an empty name contributes no semantic value whatever to the content of the sentence containing it, the content of 'Vulcan is a planet' would seem to just be the content of the expression that results from *removing* the name 'Vulcan' from the sentence. Frege famously suggested that if we remove the name from such a sentence, the result is an 'unsaturated' predicate that 'contains an empty place', which in this case could be written ' ( ) is a planet'. (See Frege 1891, 31.) We could instead write this as an open sentence '(*x*) is a planet', with the free variable '*x*' marking the relevant gap. As is commonly held, I would say that such an open sentence has no truth value (except relative to an assignment of objects to the free variables).

A second difficulty with Braun's view is that he provides no good reason for his claim that gappy atomic propositions are false. Braun (1993, 463–464) proposes a truth condition for one-place atomic propositions from which it follows that

(1).   If P is a one-place atomic proposition whose subject position is unfilled, then P is not true.[1]

Braun goes on to suggest that such a gappy proposition would be false since not true. But in making the latter suggestion, Braun is choosing to ignore a *falsity* condition for atomic propositions that is exactly as plausible as (1). (1) is properly motivated since if we assert an unfilled one-place atomic proposition, then we fail to say anything that is *true* of any object. But by the same token, we also say nothing that is *false* of any object by asserting such a proposition. Thus the same reasoning behind Braun's (1) also justifies:

(2).   If P is a one-place atomic proposition whose subject position is unfilled, then P is not false.[2]

Of course, putting (1) and (2) together implies that *no* one-place atomic proposition ever has an unfilled subject position since if it did, that proposition would be neither true nor false and hence would not *be* a proposition. By merely assuming without argument that unfilled atomic propositions are false since not true, Braun has ignored one of the basic intuitions behind the no-proposition view, which I endorse. This is the intuition that an atomic sentence containing an empty name (used *as* a name) cannot be used to say anything false about anything and so is not false. By ignoring this intuition, Braun has left his view without any plausible motivation.[3]

Finally it should be emphasized that Braun's view cannot account for the fact, pointed out by Plantinga, that names can be used in positive and negative existentials to express substantive debates, disputes, discussions, and discoveries about existence. (See Chapter 3, Section 2.3.) This is a problem facing *any* view on which names can *never* be used as anything other than directly referring genuine terms. Braun's view, if correct, would explain how sentences containing empty names can be true or false. But his view does not solve Plantinga's problem.

Consider again the two classicists who disagree about Homer's existence. Classicist A asserts that Homer existed, classicist B asserts that Homer did not exist. Given that 'Homer' refers, then on Braun's view, A can only be pointlessly asserting a singular proposition that cannot be false (in the actual world), while B can only be absurdly asserting the denial of that singular proposition, a denial that cannot be true (in the actual world). Thus Braun's view has the false consequence that the use of *referring* names in positive and negative existentials is inevitably assertively pointless.

What happens when we assume that 'Homer' is empty? Then on Braun's view, A is asserting a *necessarily false* gappy proposition, while B is asserting the *necessarily true* denial of that gappy proposition. (See Braun 1993, 468, note 26.) Of course, neither A nor B has the slightest idea that they are respectively asserting and denying a gappy proposition that is necessarily false. So in this case, on Braun's view, A and B really *have no idea* whatever as to what their dispute is about, given that 'Homer' has no referent.

We have just found a second problem with the idea that the names used in substantive disputes about existence are being used as genuine terms. The first problem we saw in Chapter 3 is that when the names refer, the disputes turn out to be assertively pointless (as Plantinga pointed out). The new problem is that when the names fail to refer, either the participants have no idea what their dispute is about (on Braun's view) or their dispute is in fact about nothing (given that the relevant existentials fail to express propositions). In short, the problem is that if the names in the existence disputes are being used as genuine terms, then what such a dispute is literally *about* (if anything) will entirely depend on whether or not the relevant name refers. But whether or not the name refers is in effect precisely what the dispute is really supposed to settle! My idiom hypothesis, which I mentioned in Chapter 2 and which I will describe in detail in Chapter 5, provides a salutary solution to this problem. For if, as my hypothesis implies, the name *a* is being used as short for a description, then the proposition expressed by '*a* exists' can remain the stable subject of dispute, whether or not the name *a* refers. Note that when a substantive existence dispute is expressible by use of a proper name, then on my hypothesis, the major issue in dispute will be that of whether or not the property expressed by the name's reference-fixing description is uniquely satisfied. If the relevant property is uniquely satisfied, then the name, as it would *normally* be used *as a genuine term*, refers; otherwise the name as so used does not refer.

2. Maybe There *Are No* Empty Names: Salmon's View

I have been assuming all along, as Braun does, that there clearly are names, used as genuine terms, that have no semantic referents, are empty. Even so, it must be admitted that such uses of names are quite rare, relative to the vast majority of name uses that do have semantic referents. Most examples of empty names come from myth, legend, or fiction. A few other examples, like 'Vulcan', originate from disproven scientific hypotheses, or like 'Ossian', 'Bourbaki', and 'Piltdown Man', they originate from hoaxes.

But the class of empty names is even smaller than this initial survey suggests. Many authors, including Kripke (1973, 81), Plantinga (1974, 159), van Inwagen (1977, 301), and Currie (1990, 146–155), have pointed out that uses of names in fiction are only *pretend* uses rather than actual uses. When such pretend uses are not pretend uses of actual names (such as 'Napoleon' or 'London'), these pretend uses have no actual semantic referents. Moreover, it is wrong to classify such pretend uses as being uses of empty *names* since the expressions used are not actual names, but only pretend names, or *fictional* names. So such fictional names, not being actual names, are not examples of (actual) empty names either.

Kripke (1973) and van Inwagen (1977) independently suggested that literary critics and others engage in a secondary way of using pretend-names from fiction to talk about the *characters* that fictionally bear the names. Thus, *we* might truly say 'Sherlock Holmes is a fictional character'. Here, on the Kripke/van Inwagen view, we are using 'Sherlock Holmes' as the name of a certain character from fiction. In such a use, on this view, 'Sherlock Holmes' can be assumed to *directly refer* to the relevant character, which Kripke and van Inwagen take to be an abstract entity that is created in the writing of the fiction. So on this sort of view, neither the expressions used as pretend names in fiction nor the syntactically identical names secondarily used to talk about the characters of fiction can count as empty names: the former are not names, while the latter are not empty. Thus the entire class of 'names' both used in fiction and in talk about fiction fails to be a subset of the class of empty names!

My own view of the use of names taken from fiction has this same consequence. First, I agree that the expressions used as pretend names in fiction are not actual names and hence are not empty names. Second, while I will argue in Chapter 5 against the Kripke/van Inwagen view that the secondary uses of names from fiction refer directly to abstract characters, my own view of such uses has a similar consequence. I will argue that such secondary uses of fictional 'names' are short for Russellian definite descriptions. As such, the fictional 'names' are not really being used *as* names at all, and so they should not be classified as empty names.

For me, this consequence is especially important since it means that there can be no example of a sentence containing an empty name from *fiction* which yields an example of a non-bivalent sentence, that is, which provides any motivation for free logic.

Kripke (1973) suggested that names from myth are initially used (by believers in the myth) *as* names, though such names have no referents, and so the names as so used were empty. I agree with this view. But Kripke added that, in order to talk about the contents of myths, we have adopted a secondary way of using names from myth, on which the names are used to refer to abstract mythical entities. The latter names, as so used, are of course not empty. Again, as in the case of fiction, my view of such secondary uses is that in them, the 'names' used are short for descriptions, and so are not empty names.

Again, the class of empty names is considerably reduced: we are left with initially used empty names from myth and legend plus a few other cases like 'Vulcan' and 'Ossian'. Moreover, Nathan Salmon (1998) has proposed a view on which, contrary to Kripke's view (and mine), both initial uses of fictional names and initial uses of names in myth refer to abstract characters and mythical entities, respectively. Moreover, even in the case of 'Vulcan', Salmon maintains that in introducing this name as the name of a hypothetical planet whose orbit between the sun and Mercury explains disturbances in the orbit of Mercury, Le Verrier inadvertently both created a mythical planet and provided the name 'Vulcan' with an abstract mythical referent.

Salmon's view is very close to one on which there simply *are no* empty names. He seems to want to at least allow for the *possibility* of empty names since this seems to be the point of the example on which he (Salmon) stipulates that 'Nappy' is to refer to the new emperor of France, if there is one, and refers to nothing otherwise (1998, 305). Since it is wildly improbable that France has a new emperor, Salmon concludes that on his stipulation, 'Nappy' does not refer, and so is an example of an empty name. Apparently Salmon's reason for not saying that 'Nappy' refers to a mythical being in this case is that the one who stipulates this reference condition (Salmon himself) does not *believe* (in fact *disbelieves*) that the relevant reference condition is satisfied. Thus, the stipulator, unlike the case of 'Vulcan', has failed to create a mythical entity in making the stipulation.

But it is far from clear that one could rationally *introduce* a name (for use by speakers of the relevant language) without believing that the reference condition provided for the name is satisfied. Certainly Salmon instituted no *name practice* by his stipulation since neither he nor any other speaker would actually *use* 'Nappy' in a standard context while rationally *doubting* that 'Nappy' has a referent. This is simply due to the Direct Reference thesis, on which the sole function or purpose of using a name in a given sentence as a genuine term is to contribute the name's semantic referent to the proposition expressed by the sentence. Thus, no one who believed that the reference condition for a name is not satisfied and who therefore believed that the name has no referent would ever use that name *as* a name.

Since Salmon's stipulation fails to institute any name practice involving 'Nappy', no use of 'Nappy' would be subject to the reference condition provided by Salmon's stipulation. In short, Salmon's stipulation fails to have the result that 'Nappy' is semantically a name, and so he has failed to provide an example of an empty name.[4]

So it follows from Salmon's overall view that there neither are nor could be any empty names. He does not of course intend or endorse this consequence. His main goal seems to be that of turning aside one of the main objections to the DR-thesis, namely that many sentences containing empty names express truths. But in his zeal to overcome this objection, Salmon goes too far, and he ends up endorsing principles that prove too much. For me, the problem is that, if Salmon's view were correct, there would be no empty names, and so there would be no motivation for *any* form of free logic, including my neutral free logic.

But Salmon's view is not correct. The main culprit is Salmon's idea that sincere uses of names whose primary reference conditions are unsatisfied would end up referring to abstract mythical beings or objects. As far as I can tell, Salmon provides no evidence for this view. Moreover, the view is exceedingly implausible. Braun correctly points out that it is hard to see how Le Verrier's uses of 'Vulcan' could have ended up referring to the abstract mythical planet since the latter would satisfy virtually none of the characteristics that Le Verrier would have used to fix the reference of his uses of 'Vulcan' (2005, 614–615). The serious difficulty brought out by Braun's point is that Salmon in fact provides no account whatever as to how a name that fails to refer to any intended referent should miraculously end up referring to an abstract entity to which no user of the name ever intended to refer. I will return to this issue in Chapter 5. But it is perhaps more important to first emphasize that what Salmon claims to happen in the case of apparently empty names is just something that does not in fact happen.

Consider the ancient Greeks and their uses of names that were intended to refer to the various gods and creatures of their mythology. On Salmon's view, these name uses all failed to refer to any *actual* gods or creatures, but these uses *did* (somehow) succeed in referring to abstract *mythical* gods and creatures. Yet obviously the ancient Greek users of these names had no intentions or beliefs, indeed they did not have the slightest idea, that their uses of these names from their mythology referred to any abstract mythical entities; nor did they realize that the propositions they expressed and asserted by use of sentences containing these names were wildly false claims concerning abstract entities about which the name users had never intended to say anything at all. The very idea that the conventions which govern our uses of names could have such wildly counterintuitive consequences would seem to be a false empirical claim about language.[5]

What would the conventions that govern name use have to be on Salmon's view? Consider the case of 'Vulcan' again. In order for Salmon's view to work in this case, it seems that in introducing 'Vulcan', Le Verrier would have had to be subjecting himself (and others) to a reference rule like the following:

(V). For any utterance α of 'Vulcan' and any object x, (1) let α refer to x, if x is the planet whose orbit between Mercury and the sun explains discrepancies in the orbit of Mercury; but (2) if there is no such planet, let α refer to the mythical planet created by Le Verrier in his hypothesis that there actually is such a planet.

It is clear that Le Verrier subjected himself to no such rule as (V). First, it is highly unlikely that either Le Verrier or any other ordinary speaker would have endorsed (or even conceived of) the Kripke/Salmon ontology of abstract mythical entities.[6] Second, and more important, it obstructs communication and understanding for there to be reference rules that contain 'fallback' conditions like clause (2) of (V). For such conditions raise the possibility that when the primary condition such as (1) of (V) is not satisfied, speakers who are ignorant of this fact will end up referring to things (like mythical planets) that they never intended to refer to and would then end up saying things that they do not intend to say, are not aware that they are saying, and may not even understand.

Since reference rules like (V) undermine communication and understanding, it is highly unlikely that the semantic rules that govern name uses contain 'fallback' conditions as (V) does. A far more plausible hypothesis is that the relevant (reference-fixing) rules have the following form:

(N) For any utterance α of N and any object x, α is to refer to x if and only if x = the unique object that is F.[7]

Thus, in the cases of names from myth and legend, as well as in other cases like 'Vulcan', where the reference conditions for the names fail to be satisfied, the names, according to the relevant reference rules of the form (N), all fail to refer. So in the end, there is in fact a large class of empty names, including names from myth and legend as well as a few other cases, such as 'Vulcan', 'Ossian', 'Bourbaki', and 'Piltdown Man'.

3. Meinongian Quantification

In what I have said so far against classical first-order logic and in favor of neutral free logic, I have made the standard assumption that not only are the quantifiers of first-order logic objectual (as opposed to substitutional), but also that they range over domains that consist solely of *existing* objects. This assumption has been made by such classical logicians as Frege, Russell, Tarski, and Quine. It has also been made by all free logicians as well. Thus, $\forall x \exists y(x = y)$ is a theorem of both classical and free logics with identity, and it is interpreted to mean: *everything exists*. It is due to this interpretation of the quantifiers that it seems patently absurd to suppose that every sentence of the form $\exists x(x = a)$ is a logical truth since such sentences are understood to mean, in effect, *a exists*, and sentences such as 'Obama exists' and 'Pegasus exists' are obviously not logical truths. The desire to avoid this apparent consequence of classical logic is perhaps the primary motivation for free logic.

However, some have suggested that the (objectual) quantifiers of first-order logic need not be interpreted as ranging solely over existing objects. Richard Routley (1966) described various Meinongian systems on which the quantifiers are allowed to range over domains that may contain both existing and nonexistent (but possible) objects. Such interpretations can be provided that preserve the theorems of classical logic, but without the classic existence assumptions (p. 266). Routley uses 'π' as the universal quantifier, read 'for all' or 'for all possible'. Then making use of a predicate constant 'E' read 'exists', he defines additional quantifiers (p. 254) as follows:

$$(\Sigma x)A \quad \equiv_{Df} \sim (\pi) \sim A$$
$$(\exists x)A(x) \equiv_{Df} (\Sigma x)(A(x) \ \& \ E(x))$$
$$(\forall x)A(x) \equiv_{Df} \sim (\exists x) \sim A(x)$$

Here 'Σ' is read 'for some' or 'for at least one', while '$\exists$' is read 'there exists' (as usual), and '$\forall$' is read 'for all existing' (as usual). Routley's basic quantifiers 'π' and 'Σ' are existentially neutral and more general than '$\exists$' and '$\forall$' as usually understood since the latter are defined as restrictions of the former.

Routley's neutral interpretations of the quantifiers can be used to free classical logic of its existence assumptions while (syntactically) preserving its theorems. Thus all sentences of the form '$(\Sigma x)(x = a)$' can still be counted as logical truths. But this is no longer absurd since such a sentence is no longer understood to mean 'There exists an object identical with a' but rather to mean 'Some possible object is identical with a' or simply 'a is a possible object'.

Routley's idea, if it is acceptable, simply dispenses with the need for free logic since his version of classical first-order logic is itself free of existence assumptions. Moreover, the same idea, if acceptable, would solve the problem of reference failure since the Meinongian assumption is that there is no such thing: every meaningful singular term has a referent, either a possible object that exists or one that doesn't.

But in my view, Routley's Meinongian idea is not acceptable. This is a very large topic to which I cannot really do justice here, but I will try to explain some of the reasons why, like many other philosophers, I reject the suggestion that some objects that fail to exist in the actual world are nevertheless the actual referents of some of our singular terms, can have properties in the actual world, and can bear relations to actually existing things (like us).

My first reaction upon considering the proposal that domains of interpretation may contain both existing and non-existing (possible) objects is that I really don't understand the alleged distinction being made. Suppose we start with a set D whose members all exist. The Meinongian idea is that we can add nonexistent objects to D and thus obtain a *larger* set D^* that contains both existent and nonexistent objects. (That is, D^* is the union of D and some non-empty set N whose members are all nonexistent, so D is a proper subset of D^*.) But is this idea really comprehensible? What after all is the *result* of adding some nonexistent objects (Santa Claus, the golden mountain, Pegasus, etc.) to D? Isn't the result the same as that of adding *nothing* to D? That is, isn't a set N all of whose members are nonexistent simply the *empty* set, so that $D \cup N = D$? Routley (1966, 258) distinguishes between a domain that is *empty* (one that contains no *existing* objects) and a domain that is *null* (one that contains no objects that either exist or do not exist). But this is precisely the alleged distinction that seems to make no difference.

Of course this intuition of mine will neither persuade nor interest any Meinongians. They will, with some justice, say that I am begging the question or that I am merely exhibiting, as Meinong put it, 'the prejudice in favor of the actual' (Meinong 1904, 78). Still I think that the intuition is worth expressing, since it may well underlie much of the widespread antipathy towards the Meinongian idea.

Now I will try to give a (non-question begging) argument against the view that some of the objects to which we refer in language and thought are nonexistent. The conclusion of my argument will be that it is not possible in principle to provide any account of how nonexistent objects could be singled out, individuated, or specified in such a way that we can refer to these objects in language or thought. In the end, Meinongians just *assume* that such reference occurs, even though it really is impossible that it could occur since, I will argue, there are no stateable conditions under which reference to nonexistents (whether in language or thought) would be successful.[8]

Meinong believed that sentences of the following sort are necessarily true, whether or not they concern any existing object:

(3).   The golden mountain is both golden and a mountain.

Meinong and his followers all assume that every (closed) description of the form 'The φ' is a referring individual constant that either refers to an existing object that satisfies φ or, if no such object exists, refers to a nonexistent object. The alleged necessary truth of (3) illustrates Meinong's 'principle of independence', according to which an object's *Sosein* (its having the properties it in fact has) is independent of its *Sein* (its existence). (See Meinong 1904, 82.) But what properties does a nonexistent object like the golden mountain have? Meinong's answer is that nonexistent objects have precisely the properties that they are characterized as having! This is the famous *Characterization Principle* (CP), which Graham Priest has recently stated this way: 'Thus, if $A(x)$ is any property or conjunction of properties, we can characterize an object c_A, and be guaranteed that $A(c_A)$' (Priest 2005, 83).

Russell (1905, 45) famously objected to the CP by pointing out that it implies such contradictions as that the existent golden mountain both exists (by the CP) and does not exist (as a matter of fact). Priest raises both this objection plus a similar one that is more general and even more devastating: 'let A be any sentence one likes, and let B be $x = x \land A$. Apply the CP to B, and we get an object c_B such that $c_B = c_B \land A$, from which A follows' (Priest 2005, 83). Thus, the naïve version of the CP disastrously entails that every proposition is true, including contradictory propositions. Both Meinong himself and his more recent defenders [including Routley (1980, 496), Terence Parsons (1980, 23), and Dale Jacquette (1996, 81)] have attempted to avoid this type of objection by restricting the CP so that only specific types of 'nuclear' properties are allowed to characterize or determine objects. (Thus – hopefully – ruling out such properties as existence as well as being such that A.)[9]

Priest suggests that this as well as various other ways of restricting the CP are all unprincipled, *ad hoc*, and unmotivated. I agree. He instead proposes another sort of revision of the CP (2005, 83–85). On Priest's revision, any property or conjunction of properties $A(x)$ does determine a specific object c_A. But if $A(x)$ is an existence entailing property or conjunction of properties and c_A is nonexistent, then $A(c_A)$ will only be true in possible worlds in which c_A *exists* and will be *false* in the actual world. (Thus Priest's way of revising the CP requires denial of Meinong's 'principle of independence'.) On Priest's revision, the existent golden mountain is a perfectly fine object, but in the *actual* world, it neither exists, is golden, nor is a mountain (contrary to the naïve CP) since these are all existence-entailing properties that an object can have only in possible worlds in which it exists. On the other hand, on Priest's view, nonexistent objects like the golden mountain can and do have properties in the actual world, provided that the properties are not existence entailing. For instance, Priest holds (falsely, in my opinion) that the golden mountain has, in the actual world, such properties as that of *being thought of* by Meinong and of *being the referent of* 'the golden mountain' since these properties are (allegedly) not existence-entailing.

On Priest's view, the golden mountain is a possible object that, though it does not exist, *could* exist. Moreover, on that view, in every possible world in which the golden mountain exists, it is golden and a mountain (p. 84).

Now this latter doctrine may sound trivially true since it *sounds* like the doctrine that it is necessarily true (true in every possible world) that

(4). If the golden mountain exists, then the golden mountain is both golden and a mountain.

But note that, on the sense in which (4) is trivially true, the description 'the golden mountain' has narrow scope so (4) is not *about* any *particular* golden mountain. Rather (4) is necessarily true because in every possible world w, if there exists a unique golden mountain in w, then it is both golden and a mountain in w. But note that there is no limit to the number of possible distinct unique golden mountains that exist in various distinct possible worlds. The crucial question then is: *which* of all these nonexistent but possible golden mountains is the specific golden mountain that is (on Priest's view) supposed to be the referent of 'the golden mountain' in the *actual* world?

I think that no coherent answer can be given to this question. When Priest claims that in every world in which the golden mountain exists, it is both golden and a mountain, he does not mean that (3) is necessarily true in its trivial sense. Rather he means (using Routley's quantifiers):

(5). $(\Sigma x)(x =$ the golden mountain & $(\pi w)($if x exists in w, then x is a golden mountain in $w))$.

Now (5) is far from trivial. It says in effect that the golden mountain is *essentially* a golden mountain. This is an odd doctrine to say the least. A similar doctrine for the existing referents of descriptions is clearly false. Thus, the inventor of bifocals (Ben Franklin) is certainly *not* essentially an inventor of bifocals. But again, the most urgent question raised by a claim like (5) is, *Which* possible object is the referent in the actual world of 'the golden mountain' supposed to be?[10]

At various points, Priest seems to suggest a certain kind of answer to this question. He suggests that the referent of 'the golden mountain' might be, say, the unique possible golden mountain of which Meinong was thinking (in the actual world) when he thought of (or imagined) the golden mountain. Similarly, in the case of the fictional Sherlock Holmes, Priest suggests that the referent of the name 'Holmes' might be the possible object that was actually imagined or represented by Conan Doyle as being a detective who lived in Victorian London, in Baker St., etc. (Priest 2005, 141–143) In general, Priest suggests that the referent of a term that fails to refer to an existing object will be a possible (or in some cases an impossible) nonexistent object that a given person (perhaps the speaker who uses the term) directly has in mind in a given intentional act.

This idea is most explicitly suggested in the semantic theory that Priest provides for two types of terms that he calls 'indefinite descriptions' and 'definite descriptions'. As he explains: 'Indefinite descriptions are of the form "a(n)/one (particular) object, x, such that $A(x)$". I will write this as $\varepsilon x A(x)$' (2005, 91). Priest treats these terms as rigid designators whose referents are determined in part by speakers' intentions. 'Definite descriptions' are a specific sort of indefinite description whose matrix implies uniqueness. That is, Priest defines $\imath x A(x)$ as $\varepsilon x(A(x)\ \&\ {\sim}\Sigma y(A(y)\ \&\ y \neq x))$. These terms are also rigid, and their referents are also determined in part by speakers' intentions (p. 93).[11]

On Priest's semantics, a use of 'the golden mountain' used as what he calls a 'definite description' might refer to a certain nonexistent possible golden mountain to which the speaker in that use intends to refer (or which the speaker has in mind or mentally represents). But now it seems that there is no straightforward answer to my question, *Which* possible object is the referent of 'the golden mountain'? For apparently, the answer will have to depend on features of the specific *use* of the description: the referent might be the possible golden mountain that Meinong had in mind, or it might be any one of the various golden mountains that various speakers have in mind when they use this description. But then, as a consequence, there is no reason to think that in any of these uses, reference is ever made to the *same* nonexistent golden mountain as is made in any other use. And as a further consequence, Priest's view cannot explain how two speakers could ever use the same term in the same sentence to say the same thing about the same nonexistent object.

Suppose that in a philosophy class, intending to give an example of a true negative existential, I utter the true sentence

(6).   The golden mountain does not exist.

Now suppose that you utter the same sentence in your philosophy class for the same reason. Have we said the same thing? On Priest's view, by uttering (6) I've said, regarding the golden mountain *I* have in mind, that it does not exist, and you've said, regarding the golden mountain that *you* have in mind, that *it* does not exist. However, given the infinite number of possible nonexistent golden mountains, it would seem to be a miracle if you and I had managed to have *the same* possible golden mountain in mind, so that we succeeded in saying the same thing.[12]

But surely there should be no doubt that you and I can easily say the same thing by uttering (6). This means that there is a sense of (6) on which the description 'the golden mountain' is *not* being used as a kind of complex indexical whose referent is determined by context. Rather there must be a sense of (6) on which the relevant description's referent (if any) is determined independently of context.

Thus Priest's account of reference to nonexistents is radically *incomplete* since it cannot generally provide cogent answers to questions of the form 'Which possible nonexistent object is the referent of α ?', where α is a context-independent description or proper name, as opposed to an indexical description of the sort for which Priest provides a semantics.[13] Of course, as we mentioned earlier, Priest also suggests that we could pick out, say, the relevant possible golden mountain as 'the golden mountain that Meinong had in mind'. But this doesn't really help since again you and I can say the same thing using (6), even though neither of us knows of any particular person who has had thoughts about some particular possible golden mountain.

Not only does Priest provide answers for only a narrow range of cases as to how the possible but nonexistent referents of singular terms are determined, but the answers he does provide are, as Bob Hale has put it, 'mysterious and unsatisfactory' (Hale 2007, 107). Suppose that on a given occasion (perhaps as I now write), I vividly imagine a golden mountain with snowcaps and glaciers that looks quite similar to the Matterhorn; it appears golden and shiny from below the snowcaps down to the tree line, and it is composed of solid gold down to the foothills, etc. Priest claims that some specific nonexistent but possible golden mountain is part of the content of my act of imagination. But I claim that on the contrary, no such object is part of the relevant content. My reason is simple: It is that there is no feature of my act of imagination that could determine or make it true that, out of a no-doubt infinite number of distinct possible but nonexistent golden mountains, all of which have exactly the same features (in the worlds in which they exist) as my imaginary mountain, some specific one of these possible objects is *the one* that I am imagining. So in fact *no* such possible golden mountain is the one that I am imagining. Rather I am imagining *that there is* a golden mountain with such-and-such features. But *no* possible golden mountain is such that I am imagining *it* to have those features. Priest of course claims otherwise, but he gives no reason for this claim. Moreover, it does not seem possible to give such a reason. If my simple act of imagination actually somehow brought me into direct cognitive contact with some one, unique, possible golden mountain (out of the infinity of such objects), then that would be a miracle, a matter of sheer *magic*.

To Priest's credit, he alone among Meinongians has tried to provide an actual and intelligible theory of reference for at least *some* terms that allegedly refer to nonexistents. But on Priest's view, the types of conditions that an object must satisfy to be the nonexistent referent of one of the terms to which Priest's view applies, conditions such as 'the unique possible golden mountain imagined by Meinong', are conditions that in fact no object, possible or actual, ever satisfies. So such terms simply *do not refer*. Contrary to the Meinongian view then, reference failure is a real phenomenon.

The upshot is that a revision of classical first-order logic using Routley's neutral quantifiers will not work. For to work, Routley's classical interpretations must provide a referent from the relevant domain of possible objects for every individual constant, whether or not the constant refers to an existing member of the domain. But this requires that on some interpretations, some individual constants must refer to possible but nonexistent objects, and as we've just seen, reference to such objects is not possible. So to avoid the existence assumptions of classical logic, it surely seems that a free logic that allows for non-referring terms is required after all.

4. Substitutional Quantification

It has been suggested by some that the mistaken existence assumptions of classical logic can be avoided by use of substitutional quantification and that this tactic is preferable to the strategy of free logic, on all forms of which the quantifiers are interpreted objectually and as ranging over domains of existing objects. [See, for instance, Alex Orenstein (1978, Chapter 3, and 1990). A similar suggestion seems to be made in a recent series of papers by Thomas Hofweber (2000, 2005, 2009).] In classical logic, the truth of quantified formulae, under any interpretation I and assignment a, is determined as follows (where $a(d/x)$ is the assignment exactly like a, except that it assigns object d to x):

(O)   a. $\exists x A$ is true under I and a if there is at least one object $d \in D$ such that A is true under I and $a(d/x)$; otherwise $\exists x A$ is false under I and a.

   b. $\forall x A$ is true under I and a if, for every object $d \in D$, A is true under I and $a(d/x)$; otherwise $\forall x A$ is false under I and a.

By contrast, if we use 'Σ' and 'Π' for the substitutional particular and universal quantifiers respectively, the truth under I of quantified sentences is determined as follows [where $A(c/x)$ is the result of substituting c for x in A]:

(S)   a. $\Sigma x A$ is true under I if there is an individual constant c such that $A(c/x)$ is true under I; otherwise $\Sigma x A$ is false under I.

   b. $\Pi x A$ is true under I if, for every individual constant c, $A(c/x)$ is true under I; otherwise $\Pi x A$ is false under I.[14]

On the objectual conditions (O), the truth value of a quantified sentence or formula such as $\exists x A$ is always determined by the truth value, on an assignment to the free variables, of the relevant embedded open formula $A(x)$. By contrast, on the substitutional conditions (S), the truth value of a quantified sentence $\Sigma x A$ is not determined by any semantic features of the embedded open formula $A(x)$, and so assignments to the free variables are not necessary; rather it is the truth value of one or more *instances* $A(c/x)$ of $\Sigma x A$ that determines the truth value of $\Sigma x A$. [Note that the righthand sides of the conditions (S) involve metalinguistic but *objectual* quantification.]

I want to argue that substitutional interpretations of the particular and universal quantifiers cannot provide any acceptable alternative to objectually quantified free logic as a means of avoiding the unacceptable existence assumptions of classical logic. But I should stress that there are no serious *formal* problems with substitutional quantification. Kripke (1976) shows (among other things) that any language L_o without substitutional quantifiers can be extended to a language L that contains substitutional quantifiers, where the set of truths of L is determined by and coincides with the set of truths in L_o. (Kripke 1976, 328–332) Kripke also shows that the set of valid sentences of the pure predicate calculus with the quantifiers interpreted objectually can be the same as the set of valid sentences with the quantifiers interpreted substitutionally. As Kripke puts it:

> The important fact is this: *one and the same formal system* can be used to prove all the valid formulae of both the pure referential and the pure substitutional predicate calculi.
>
> (Kripke 1976, 336; Kripke's emphasis)

But while substitutional quantification is formally unproblematic, it cannot possibly be used to avoid the problems for classical logic raised by the free logicians. This is simply because these problems are not formal. Rather the problems arise when we attempt to *apply* the classical notion of a model or interpretation to the first-order fragment of a natural language like English. Again the crucial cases are existence sentences such as

(7). There exists an object that is identical with Obama.
(8). There exists an object that is identical with Pegasus.

Since these sentences are translations of sentences of first-order logic of the form $\exists x(x = a)$ and since sentences of this form are true on every classical interpretation, application of classical logic to English has the absurd consequence that (7) and (8) are both logical truths. The fact that the quantifiers of pure first-order classical logic can be given an adequate substitutional interpretation (as Kripke showed) is simply irrelevant to the problem raised by sentences of English like (7) and (8). Since the English quantifier 'there exists' in (7) and (8) is objectual, application of classical logic to these sentences requires use of the objectual interpretation of the quantifier '∃', and we straightforwardly obtain the absurd result that (7) and (8) are logical truths, whether English also contains substitutional quantifiers or not.

As Kripke has emphasized, there can't really be any serious question as to whether natural languages like English contain objectual quantifiers, use of which carries ontological commitment, uses such as 'there are men', 'there exist men', 'there are rabbits', and so on. (Kripke 1976, 379). So to apply first-order logic to the fragment of English that contains such objectual quantifiers, we have to use a first-order logic with objectually interpreted rather than substitutional quantifiers. Thus an applicable form of first-order logic that avoids the absurd consequences of classical logic must be a free logic that uses objectual quantifiers which range over domains of existing objects.

Are there quantifiers in English and other natural languages that have substitutional interpretations? Before closing this chapter, I want to argue that such quantifiers do not exist. This is strictly a side issue at this point since the simple defense of free logic that I've just given is perfectly consistent with the existence of both objectual and substitutional quantifiers in English. But it will be useful to discuss this issue now since it is relevant to my defense in Chapter 5 of the Direct Reference thesis against such alleged counterexamples as sentences (1)–(5) mentioned in Chapter 2.

4.1 Substitutionalism

The primary alleged advantage of the hypothesis that the quantifiers of natural languages like English have substitutional interpretations is that so interpreted, the quantifiers would be *ontologically neutral*. Thus such sentences as

(9). Something is a flying horse; and
(10). There is an object that does not exist.

can innocently follow (without ontological commitment) from such (allegedly) obvious truths of common sense as:

(11). Pegasus is a flying horse; and
(12). Pegasus does not exist,

respectively. [Again, see Orenstein (1978 and 1990) and Hofweber (2000, 2005, and 2009).] The idea is that quantified sentences like (9) and (10) are ontologically innocent because they follow (by substitutional particular generalization) from true sentences like (11) and (12) that contain non-referring names. I will call this idea, which requires there to be substitutional interpretations of the English particular and universal quantifiers, 'substitutionalism'.

First, it is important to emphasize that given Direct Reference and given that the substitution class for the substitutional quantifiers is restricted to individual constants, that is, proper names when used as names, substitutionally quantified sentences are precisely as ontologically committal as their objectual counterparts. Consider, for instance, a substitutional reading of 'There is an object that is identical with *a*' together with any of its instances:

(13) a. $\Sigma x (x = a)$
     b. $t = a$,

where *t* is any individual constant, perhaps *a* itself. Given the DR-thesis, no case of (13b) is true unless *t* and *a* refer to the same existing member of the relevant domain. Since (13a) is true only if an instance of the form (13b) is true and since any such instance logically implies $\exists x (x = a)$, (13a) also implies $\exists x (x = a)$, and so (13a) is ontologically committed to the existence of an object identical with *a*.[15] The same sort of ontological commitment holds for all sentences of the form $\Sigma x \varphi$, where φ is atomic, and on my preferred version of neutral free logic, it holds for *any* φ, atomic or not.

Following Michael Hand (2007, 654), call the semantics for the atomic sentences of a language the language's *base* semantics, and call that base semantics *referential* when it requires that an atomic sentence be true only if the individual constants in the sentence all refer to existing objects in the relevant domain.[16] On the DR-thesis, the base semantics of natural languages are all referential, so any substitutionally quantified sentence of the form $\Sigma x \varphi$, where φ is atomic, logically implies $\exists x \varphi$, and so is ontologically committal. To avoid existential commitment of this sort, a language's base semantics must be *non*-referential and must allow some atomic sentences to be true even when they contain non-referring constants. The semantics of positive free logic is an example of this since it allows such sentences as 'Pegasus is a flying horse' and 'Pegasus = Pegasus' to be true, so that their substitutional generalizations '$\Sigma x (x$ is a flying horse)' and '$\Sigma x (x = \text{Pegasus})$' would both be true and would not logically imply either '$\exists x (x$ is a flying horse)' or '$\exists x (x = \text{Pegasus})$'. Of course, as I argued in Chapter 2, this sort of base semantics is simply false since it is inconsistent with the DR-thesis. I will return to this issue in a few paragraphs and again at length in Chapter 5.

The previous consideration undermines the basic motivation for substitutionalism since the DR-thesis implies that sentences containing non-referring names such as (11) and (12) are not true and so cannot be used to justify the idea that there are ontologically neutral (substitutional) quantifiers. But in addition, we can argue *independently* of the DR-thesis that there are in fact no substitutional quantifiers in English. Next, I will give several arguments against various forms of substitutionalism. These different forms vary according to which types of singular terms are allowed to be in the 'substitution class', that is, are allowed to occur in the relevant substitution instances of quantified sentences. The arguments I give will differ, depending on whether the form of substitutionalism allows only *proper names* in the substitution class or whether it also allows *demonstrative pronouns* or *definite descriptions* in the substitution class. My arguments will all have the same general form. In each case, I will show that the relevant form of substitutionalism implies that certain quantified sentences of English are false or that they are true, but in each case, it will be completely obvious that the relevant quantified sentences *have no senses* in English on which they have the relevant truth values. Thus, I will conclude there are *no* (first-order) substitutional quantifiers in English.

4.2 When the Substitution Class Contains Only Proper Names

There is already available a well-known, frequently mentioned, and apparently conclusive argument against substitutionalism, given that the substitution class is restricted to *proper names*. The argument is similar to the one that Kripke suggested (1976, 380), and it raises what Michael Hand has called *the problem of too few names* (Hand 2007, 650; Baldwin 1979, 174). Suppose I say to my wife (as I have in fact said on a number of occasions):

(14). There is a skunk in our backyard.

With its quantifier interpreted objectually, (5) means

(15). $\exists x(x$ is a skunk $\&$ x is in our backyard),

and so understood, suppose (14) is true even though the skunk in question has no name. (We can also assume that only one skunk is involved in this episode.) But if (14) is given a substitutional interpretation, so that it means

(16). $\Sigma x(x$ is a skunk $\&$ x is in our backyard),

then (14) would be *false* since there is no true instance of my use of (14) that has the form 'n is a skunk $\&$ n is in our backyard', where n is a name. Yet it seems abundantly clear that my use of (14) *has no reading in English* on which it would be false (in the circumstances). But then, since my use of (14) *would* have such a reading if the quantifier 'there is' had a substitutional interpretation in English, it follows that 'there is' is not a substitutional quantifier in English, at least not when the substitution class is restricted to *proper names*.

Now consider the substitutional universal quantifier, again restricting the substitution class to proper names. It is highly unlikely that any physical object that weighs one microgram or less has a name. In this case, there would be a sense in which it is *true* that

(17). $\Pi x($if x is a physical object, then x weighs more than one microgram), since every instance of (17) containing a name of an object in place of variable x would be true. Hence, given that the quantifier 'all' has a substitutional meaning in English, there would be a sense in English in which it would be *true* that

(18). All physical objects weigh more than one microgram.

There would then also be senses in which it is true that there are no neutrinos, electrons, molecules, or atoms since these things all weigh one microgram or less. But clearly there are *no* senses in which *any* of these things are true in English. Hence 'all' and 'no' also do not have substitutional interpretations in English. And clearly, similar arguments can be given for all other English counterparts of the first-order quantifiers, including 'some', 'at least one', 'something', 'every', and 'everything'. Thus, there are no first-order substitutional quantifiers in English, given that the substitution class is restricted to proper names.

4.3 Has the 'Too Few Names' Problem Already Been Solved?

In my opinion, the problem of too few names obviously refutes the version of substitutionalism on which the substitution class is restricted to proper names. But I have heard it suggested that the problem can be easily avoided by adopting either of two ways of revising the standard Tarskian treatment of the quantifiers, one proposed by Benson Mates (1972, 60–63) and the other proposed by Martin Davies (1981, 114–123). Since this suggestion may be responsible for the persistence of sympathy for substitutionalism in the literature, I should briefly discuss it.

Mates's elegant model theory for the first-order quantifiers is based on the notion of an interpretation I being a *β-variant* of an interpretation I', where I is a β-variant of I' if and only if I and I' are either the same or differ at most in what they assign to the individual constant β. Then a sentence of the form $\forall x A$ is true under I if and only if $A(\beta/x)$ is true under every β-variant of I and $\exists x A$ is true under I if and only if $A(\beta/x)$ is true under some β-variant of I (where β is the first individual constant not occurring in A; see Mates 1972, 60).

Mates's motivation for proposing this alternative to the standard Tarskian model theory for the quantifiers is that he wants (1) to ensure that (closed) *sentences* rather than open formulae are the primary bearers of truth value so that (2) it is also ensured that the truth functional connectives, while they are used as operators on open formulae in the scope of quantifiers, nevertheless have their fundamental senses as operators on the bearers of truth value, that is, as operators on sentences. (See Mates 1972, vi.)

As far as I can tell, the motivation that Davies has for his proposal is exactly the same as Mates's, but Davies provides another way of achieving the same goals. To provide truth conditions for the quantified sentences of a given language L which does not contain a name for every object in the domain D of its intended interpretation I, Davies proposes that we introduce an extended language L^+ that contains a name for every member of D and which contains the same predicates, names, and connectives with the same meanings as under I. Call the closely related interpretation I^+. Then a sentence $\forall xA$ is true under I if and only if, for every name c of L^+, $A(c/x)$ is true under I^+, and $\exists xA$ is true under I if and only if, for some name c of L^+, $A(c/x)$ is true under I^+. (See Davies 1981, 114–118.)[17]

Now do the truth conditions provided for the quantifiers by either Mates or Davies imply that the quantifiers are *substitutional*? It is true that on both proposals, the truth conditions for quantified sentences are given *via* substitution instances with names replacing the relevant free variables. But on Mates's proposal, the substitution instances' semantic features are provided by a perhaps infinite number of β-variant interpretations which are all distinct from the interpretation I relative to which the interpretation is being given. By contrast, on substitutional interpretations of the quantifiers, the truth conditions of quantified sentences under a given interpretation I are provided by the truth or falsity of substitution instances under *that very* interpretation I. [See the condition (S).] And on Davies's proposal, most of the relevant substitution instances will be sentences of L^+ rather than the language L for which truth conditions are being given, while on substitutional interpretations, the substitution instances will be from the very language for which truth conditions are being given. [Again, see (S).]

So it is far from clear that either of the proposals by Mates and Davies imply that the quantifiers are substitutional. Neither Mates nor Davies ever say or suggest that they are proposing forms of substitutional quantification, even though both discuss substitutional quantification at other points in the works cited. (See Mates 1972, 62–63 and Davies 1981, 142–148.) Moreover, their motivations for their proposals really have nothing to do with substitutional quantification. Rather their goal, as Davies nicely puts it (1981, 117–118) is to provide an account of an open formula's being *true of* an object in terms of *truth*, period. By contrast, the Tarskian method can define 'truth of' at best in terms of truth relative to an assignment. But all three ways of defining 'truth of' yield the same *objectual* way of understanding the quantifiers, namely that a sentence $\forall xA$ is true under I if and only if A is true of every object in the domain D of I, while a sentence $\exists xA$ is true under I if and only if A is true of some object in the domain D of I.

Ernest LePore and Kirk Ludwig (2007, 64–75) discuss and make use of both Mates's and Davies's proposals, but they also never suggest that the proposals are committed to some form of substitutional quantification. Rather at one point they correctly suggest that at least Mates's proposal and Tarskian semantics 'do the same work' (2007, 71). It has been frequently pointed out that in Tarskian semantics, free variables are treated as 'temporary names'. [See, for instance, Neil Tennant (1978, 25–26).] Similarly, LePore and Ludwig suggest here that the assignment functions that provide referents for the free variables on Tarskian semantics in effect turn the variables into (temporary) names and thus turn open sentences into (temporary) substitution instances (relative to an assignment *a*) of the relevant quantified sentence.

Those who take the proposals of Mates and Davies to provide versions of substitutional quantification that avoid the 'too few names' problem seem to be assuming that *any* semantics on which the truth values of quantified sentences are determined by the truth values of name-containing substitution instances of those sentences (no matter what the relation of those instances to the language in question or to the interpretations being characterized) is *thereby* a semantics on which the quantifiers are substitutional. But this assumption is false since if it were true, it follows (absurdly) that even on a *Tarskian* semantics, the quantifiers are substitutional, since as we've seen, a Tarskian semantics also relies on the truth values of name-containing substitution instances (relative to a given assignment) to provide the truth conditions of quantified sentences. So again, the assumption is false: on Tarskian semantics, as on the proposals of Mates and Davies, the quantifiers are objectual, not substitutional.[18]

4.4 *When Demonstratives Are Allowed in the Substitution Class*

So I take it that the problem of too few names flatly refutes the version of substitutionalism on which the substitution class contains only proper names. Thomas Baldwin (1979, 174–175) agrees with this, but he goes on to suggest that the problem of too few names can be overcome if we allow demonstrative pronouns (such as 'he', 'she', 'it', 'this', 'that', and 'that man') to also be members of the substitution class. Baldwin would then say, regarding my case of the backyard skunk, that the substitutionally quantified sentence (19):

(19). $\Sigma x(x$ is a skunk & x is in our backyard)

would be true after all, since a substitution instance of (19), namely

(20). *That* is a skunk and *that* is in our backyard,

would be true in the context.

But note that no one utters or *uses* the instance (20) in my example. In my view of demonstratives, this implies that the demonstrative 'that' has no semantic referent in the context, contrary to Baldwin's view, and thus the instance (20) would not be true in the context. This in turn is due to the fact that in my view, the semantic referent of 'that' in a context must be the object to which the *speaker* refers with a use of 'that' in the context. (See McKinsey 1983, 8 and 1984, 494.)[19] Given that no speaker in the context (including me) refers to any object with 'that', it follows that 'that' has no semantic referent in the context, and so again, (20) would not be true in the context.

David Kaplan's view of demonstratives has the same consequence regarding (20). In his 'Demonstratives' (1977, 489–491), Kaplan held that an object cannot be the semantic referent of 'that' in a context unless the speaker *demonstrates* the object in the context, where a demonstration might be an act of physical pointing. Later Kaplan changed his view, so that a demonstration is taken to be a 'directing intention' of the speaker (1989, 582–584). Since in my view a speaker refers to an object with a demonstrative term only if the speaker *intends* to refer to that object with the term, Kaplan's later view and my view are very similar.[20] Details aside, it seems completely clear that, contrary to Baldwin's view, the mental states and acts of the speaker in using a demonstrative play a crucial role in determining the demonstrative's semantic referent in a context.

In the case of substitutional universal generalizations like (17), addition of demonstratives to the substitution class certainly provides *more* instances than can be provided by names alone. For instance, various particular fundamental particles are sometimes detected by physicists in a laboratory setting and so can be referred to by use of a demonstrative such as 'that neutrino'. In this case, there could be false instances of the form 'if t is a physical object, then t weighs more than 1 microgram' where t is a demonstrative, so (17) would also be false. But even if we agree that there actually are such instances that are false (in various contexts), this fact doesn't really help. For it will still be true that

(21). Πx(if x is a physical object, then either x weighs more than one microgram or x has been detected by someone),

since every instance of 'if t is a physical object, then either t weighs more than one microgram or t has been detected by someone' will be true, whether t is a name or a demonstrative. But again, as in the case of (17), there is *no* sense in English on which it is true that all physical objects either weigh more than one microgram or have been detected by someone.

We may conclude that there are no first-order substitutional quantifiers in English, at least not when the substitution class is restricted to proper names and demonstrative pronouns.

4.5 Adding Definite Descriptions to the Substitution Class

Some have suggested that the substitution class for the English substitutional quantifier should also include *definite descriptions*, both those that refer and those that do not.[21] If so, then this would considerably mitigate the problem of too few names. However, there are grave problems with allowing the relevant substitution class to contain definite descriptions. First, I maintain, the correct view of definite descriptions is that of generalized quantifier theory, on which definite descriptions are themselves (objectual) *quantifiers* and are not singular terms.[22] So on this well-established view (inspired in part by Russell's theory), it certainly seems that sentences containing descriptions could not thereby be first-order *instances* of other quantified sentences in any intelligible sense.[23] For I take it that the substitution class for any first-order quantifier would, by definition, have to be restricted to *singular terms*. But in any case, even with definite descriptions allowed in the substitution class, we will once again obtain interpretations of many English sentences that simply do not exist.

For instance, James Tomberlin (1990, 575–576) pointed out that if both referring and non-referring descriptions are allowed in the substitution class, then no substitutional interpretation of *any* universal generalization of any open atomic formula would ever be true. Where '*Fx*' is any open atomic formula, '$\prod x Fx$' will always be false since it will always have a false instance of the form

(22). The unique object that is not *F* is *F*.

$$[F(\imath x)(\sim Fx)]$$

One especially damaging such false instance that I'd suggest would be:

(23). The unique object that is not self-identical is self-identical.

$$[\imath x(x \neq x) = \imath x(x \neq x)]$$

On Russell's theory of descriptions (and on negative free description theory),[24] (23) is false, a fact that (on substitutionalism) implies the falsehood of

(24). $\prod x(x = x)$.

Tomberlin never tells us exactly what problem for this version of substitutionalism is raised by the fact that such generalizations as (24) would be false on this version. But the problem is pretty obvious: if, for example, (24) is false, then according to substitutionalism, it follows that *there is a sense* of the English sentence 'Everything is self-identical' on which this sentence is false. But of course it is quite obvious that there is *no* such sense. So even with descriptions allowed in the substitution class, universal quantifiers such as 'everything' are still not first-order substitutional quantifiers in English.

Other types of cases, not considered by Tomberlin, raise similar problems for the substitutional particular quantifier 'Σx'. Consider the following three cases:

(25). It is not the case that the present king of France = the present king of France.
(26). Ralph believes that the oldest spy is a spy.
(27). The number of planets = 8, but it is possible that the number of planets < 8.

On the assumption that the English quantifier 'there is' is a substitutional quantifier on one of its meanings and allowing descriptions in the substitution class, it follows that each of (25q)–(27q) would have a sense in which it is logically implied by (25)–(27), respectively:

(25q).   There is someone who is not self-identical.

$$\left[\Sigma x \sim (x = x) \right]$$

(26q).   There is someone such that Ralph believes that he/she is a spy.

$$\left[\Sigma x (\text{Ralph believes that } x \text{ is a spy}) \right]$$

(27q).   There is something such that it = 8, but it is possible that it < 8.

$$\left[\Sigma x \left(x = 8 \,\&\, \Diamond (x < 8) \right) \right]$$

However, it is quite clear that there are *no* senses of (25q)–(27q) on which they follow from (25)–(27).[25] Hence, even with definite descriptions allowed in the substitution class, 'there is' is not a first-order substitutional quantifier in English.

First, with 'it is not the case' given largest scope, I take it that (25) is true in English. For since the description 'the present king of France' has no existing referent, (25) is true on both negative free logic and on Russell's theory of descriptions. But there is clearly no sense in English on which (25q) is true. So there is no sense of (25q) on which it follows from (25). Second, there is no sense of (26q) in English on which it follows from (26). As Robert Sleigh (1967, 28) first pointed out, it simply does not follow from (26) that Ralph believes someone in particular to be a spy. But I can see no *other* sense (in English) on which (26q) could be true. Finally, (27) is true in English.[26] Yet there is clearly *no* sense on which it is true that something is both identical with 8 and yet possibly less than 8. So there is no sense of (27q) on which it follows from (27).

Thus, even when definite descriptions are allowed in the substitution class, there are still plenty of cases to show that English contains no first-order substitutional quantifiers.

4.6 Meinongian Generalizations

Finally, it is worth noting that the same considerations which show that (25)–(27) fail to validly imply (25q)–(27q) also show the invalidity of the arguments often used by both Meinongians and substitutionalists to defend the claim that it's simply obvious and trivial that

(28). There are things that [or: *Some things*] do not exist.

Note that the inferences from (25)–(27) to (25q)–(27q), respectively, are really just simple *scope fallacies*. The senses of (25)–(27) on which they would be true all demand that some of the descriptions in the sentences occur in the scope of negation [in (25)] or in the scope of an intensional operator [in (26) and (27)]. Existential generalization on these small-scope occurrences of descriptions is simply invalid, as we showed previously. The (false) suggestion that there are first-order substitutional quantifiers in natural languages like English has had the unfortunate effect of giving the impression (to some philosophers) that what is in fact a type of obviously specious scope fallacy can really be understood as an innocent form of obviously valid quantificational inference!

The following kind of argument is an especially important and often-used example of this odd phenomenon:

(29). a. The round square does not exist.
   Hence,
   b. There is something that does not exist.

(See, for instance, Orenstein 1990, 252 and Hofweber 2000, 252.) Russell, in 'On Denoting' (1905), showed in effect that this inference commits a scope fallacy. On the sense in which (29a) is true, the description 'the round square' has small scope relative to 'not'. In this sense, (29a) expresses the same proposition as

(29a$_S$). ~(There exists a unique round square).

But obviously, nothing of the form (29b) follows from (29a$_S$). For as Russell pointed out, on the sense in which it is true, (29a) is simply a true *negation* of a false sentence ('the round square exists'). Thus the inference from (29a) to (29b) is fallacious for the same reason that, as we saw previously, the inference from (25) to (25q) is fallacious. Of course the inference (29) may *appear* valid since it may *appear* that the description 'the round square' has large scope in (29a). But as Russell pointed out, 'the round square' does *not* have large scope in (19a), at least not in the only sense in which (29a) is true. If (29a) is read with the description given large scope, then it is read as ascribing non-existence to the round square. But if read in this (Meinongian) way, then for (29a) to be true, the description 'the round square' must *refer* to the (nonexistent) round square, and of course it doesn't.

Oddly enough, the substitutionalist agrees with the Meinongian that (29) is a valid inference, but for a quite different reason. The substitutionalist can agree with Russell that (29a) is true only when the non-referring description 'the round square' has smallest scope in (29a), so it means

(30). ~(The round square exists).

But even so, the substitutionalist claims, (30) validly implies the conclusion (29b), provided that (29b) is read as

(31). $\Sigma x \sim (x \text{ exists})$

(where we can read 'exists' as a one-place atomic predicate). But again, there simply is *no* sense of (29b) in English in which it could be read this way. For if there were such a sense, then there would for instance also be a sense in which (25q) is true in English, that is, a sense in which it is true that someone (namely the present king of France) is not self-identical.

I suspect that there will be many who are not convinced by my argument, who will continue to insist that it is just *obvious* that in some sense it must be true that

(32). There are (many) things that do not exist,

given the truth of (29a) and many other similar examples such as Santa Claus, Pegasus, the golden mountain, the Fountain of Youth, and so on, none of which exist. But I have given strong evidence that there is no literal sense of (32) on which it is true. For I have shown that the first-order English quantifier 'there is' has no substitutional meaning in English (where the substitution class consists of singular terms). Hence, the plural quantifier 'there are' also has no substitutional meaning in English. I agree that there are many *examples* of true *denials* of existence like (29a), (29a$_s$), and (30). Such examples no doubt lead speakers of English to say things like 'There are lots of examples of *things* that don't exist'. But I take such sayings as sloppy speech that, while based on there being true denials of existence, is not itself literally true.

5. Conclusion

In this chapter, I have discussed and given reason to reject four views that provide alternatives to the use of neutral free logic as ways of dealing with the phenomenon of reference failure. First, I argued against Braun's view that atomic sentences containing empty names express false gappy propositions. I contended that, by definition, no propositions are gappy and (following Adams and Stecker) also contended that the semantic contents of atomic sentences containing empty names are merely the semantic contents of open sentences that are neither true nor false. I also argued that Braun provides no reason for his claim that atomic gappy propositions are false, and I pointed out that Braun's view cannot solve Plantinga's problem as to how positive and negative existentials containing names can be used to express substantive disputes, discussions, and discoveries about existence.

Second, I considered Salmon's view which, I contended, entails that there are no empty names. I then suggested that the aspect of Salmon's view which entails this unhappy result is a false assumption to the effect that sincere uses of names whose primary reference conditions are not satisfied would end up referring to abstract mythical beings or objects. I argued against this assumption on the grounds that it has the absurd consequence that believers in myths who use names from the myths would succeed in referring to, and would end up saying wildly false things about, abstract mythical entities that they had no conception of and to which they had never intended to refer.

Third, I considered Routley's Meinongian semantics for classical logic, on which the quantifiers range over domains that may contain both existing and non-existing objects. This semantics, if acceptable, dispenses with the need for free logic since it can retain all the theorems of classical logic while being free of existence assumptions. However, this semantics requires that some individual constants can refer (in the actual world) to nonexistent objects, and I argued that such reference is unintelligible: it is not possible to provide any stateable conditions under which reference to nonexistents (in either language or in thought) would be successful. In particular, I considered Graham Priest's recent account of reference to nonexistents and argued that he fails to provide any explanation of how a term with no existing referent could nevertheless refer to a specific one of the infinite number of possible objects that satisfy (in some possible worlds) the characteristics in the term's descriptive content.

Finally I considered use of substitutional quantification as a possible way of providing an alternative to free logic. I first pointed out that since natural languages like English obviously contain objectual quantifiers that range over domains of existing objects, only a free first-order logic that uses similar objectual quantifiers can both be applied to natural languages while at the same time also avoiding the existence assumptions of classical logic. The possibility that such natural languages might *also* contain substitutional quantifiers is simply irrelevant to the problems with classical logic that free logic is designed to avoid. I went on to give arguments that natural languages like English do not in fact contain substitutional quantifiers, whether the substitution class is restricted to proper names or whether it also contains demonstratives and definite descriptions. I also used some of the latter arguments to show in addition that, contrary to common opinion, true negative existentials such as 'the round square does not exist' cannot validly be used to support any (innocent appearing) claim to the effect that there are things that do not exist.

Notes

1. The full statement of truth conditions that Braun provides is:

> If P is a proposition having a single subject position and a one-place property position, then P is true iff the subject position is filled by one, and only one, object and it exemplifies the property filling the property position. If P is not true, then P is false.
>
> (1993, 463)

2. Here is the full falsity condition:

> If P is a one-place atomic proposition, then P is false iff the subject position in P is filled by just one object, and that object does not exemplify the property filling the property position.

3. Adams and Stecker (1994, 397) also point out that this aspect of Braun's view is, as they put it, 'undermotivated'.
4. In McKinsey (2010, 348–349), I provide an analysis of what it means to use an expression as a proper name, an analysis from which it follows that one cannot use an expression as a name without both believing that the use has a referent and without the use being an instance of a proper name practice.
5. Salmon may have been anticipating this sort of objection when he pointed out that the ancients may have intended 'Hesperus' to refer to a *star* and nevertheless the name ended up referring to a *planet* (1998, 305). But as Braun has pointed out, there are serious relevant disanalogies between this sort of case and the case of 'Vulcan' (2005, 618–619). I would add that the same disanalogies hold between the 'Hesperus' case and the ancient Greeks' uses of names from their mythology. The most important disanalogy is that, as Braun points out, Le Verrier clearly had *no* intention whatever that 'Vulcan' refer to a mythical planet, under any circumstances. The same point holds for the ancient Greeks' uses of names from their mythology. But the ancients who introduced 'Hesperus' had various intentions to the effect that the name refer to a certain object, where that object in fact turned out to be a planet and not a star. (Thus they also intended that 'Hesperus' refer to the brightest *heavenly body* on the evening horizon and that it refer to *that* heavenly body *over there*.)
6. Kripke (1973, 151, note 13) makes a similar point.
7. I have proposed in several places that the reference rules for names have this form. See, for instance, McKinsey 1984, 507 and 2010, 343. Note that Salmon's stipulation regarding 'Nappy' has precisely the form (N).
8. This sort of objection is briefly suggested by Bob Hale (2007, 107) in his review of Priest (2005).
9. For a nice survey of the various strategies for revising the CP, see Maria Reicher (2012, 20–25).
10. Glüer-Pagin and Pagin (2014) suggest a view on which 'the golden mountain' refers to the possible unique golden mountain that exists in the possible world that is closest to the actual world among those worlds where a unique golden mountain exists. But why should we assume that there is a *closest*

such world? Surely there could be a many-membered proper subset S of the set P of possible worlds in which there is a unique golden mountain and where each member of S is such that no member of P is closer to the actual world than it. (Perhaps the golden mountain in each member of S is qualitatively identical with, but numerically distinct from, all the other golden mountains in each member of S.)

11. Priest's view that indefinite descriptions are rigid singular terms (on at least one of their meanings) is quite controversial. (See, for instance, Ludlow and Neale 2006, 307–310.) I myself prefer a Russellian view on which 'a φ is ψ' is a quantified sentence of the form [an x:φx]ψx, which expresses the same proposition as $\exists$x(φx & ψx). However, I'll waive this objection since in my view, there are rigid demonstrative descriptions of the form 'that φ' whose semantics is almost exactly the same as that of Priest's indefinite descriptions. In my view, a use of 'that φ' rigidly refers to an object x if x is a φ to which the speaker intends to refer with that use; Priest's 'definite descriptions' would correspond to my demonstrative descriptions of the form 'that unique φ'. See McKinsey (1979).

12. Of course, you and I could say the same thing, if I said, 'The golden mountain that I have in mind does not exist' and you said, 'The golden mountain that McKinsey has in mind does not exist'. But what I am claiming is that you and I could say the same thing by each of us uttering (6) *alone*.

13. Priest suggests that the name of a nonexistent fictional object such as Sherlock Holmes can be introduced by a description that refers to the object. However, in his view, the description in question must apparently always involve mention of a particular person that has had the object in mind, such as 'the object represented by Doyle as living in Baker St., etc., etc.' (Priest 2005, 141). But again, you and I can both say the same thing using sentences containing the name 'Sherlock Holmes', such as 'Sherlock Holmes does not exist'. Yet to say this, neither of us needs to know the name of the author of the Holmes stories. Nor does the referent of 'Sherlock Holmes' as I use it have to be determined by which object I have in mind, as opposed to the object that you have in mind. For if it were so determined, then again, it would be wildly unlikely that you and I would be saying the same thing by use of the sentence 'Sherlock Holmes does not exist'.

14. In stating these conditions, I am restricting the substitution class of expressions of a language that provide the relevant instances of substitutionally quantified sentences to the class of individual constants of the language. But in fact there need be no restrictions at all on the syntactical items that can belong to such a substitution class. (See Kripke 1976, 329.) My restriction here to individual constants is both standard and convenient since the resulting interpretation, in Quine's words, 'comes closest to objectual quantification' (1969, 107).

15. Here I'm assuming an extension of a first-order formal language that contains both substitutional and objectual quantifiers.

16. Hand (2007) provides a very clear and useful account and critical discussion of all the various forms of and motivations for substitutional quantification.

17. Davies is really only interested in providing truth conditions for languages, the meanings of whose vocabulary are already given, so he does not need to define the general notion of *true under I*. But my generalization of his proposal is in the spirit of that proposal, and it allows for comparison with Mates's proposal and with (O) and (S) in this chapter.

18. I should note that there can be languages and interpretations on which the quantifiers would be *both* objectual *and* substitutional. For instance, the quantifiers of a first-order language L would be both objectual and

substitutional on an interpretation I, given that each object in the domain D of I is the referent on I of a name in L, every name of L has a referent in D, and where the truth conditions under I of the quantified sentences of L are provided by substitution instances containing names, in the manner of principle (S). Of course, no actual natural language would be both objectual and substitutional in this sense, due to the problem of too few names.

19. On the distinction between speaker's reference and semantic reference, see Kripke (1977).

20. But the two views are apparently not the same. In Kaplan's view, a demonstrative's linguistic meaning is not sufficient to determine its referent in every context – an associated demonstration is also needed (1989, 490). But in my view, it is precisely a demonstrative's linguistic meaning that *requires* the term's referent to be demonstrated (referred to) by the speaker.

21. Hofweber (2000) seems to be suggesting this, though he does not do so explicitly. See, for instance, his sentence (37), (2000, 266) and his remark about "true instances of the quantifiers . . . with names or *terms* that do not stand for anything that exists" (2000, 269; my emphasis). See also Orenstein 1990, 252.

22. For explanation and defense of this view, as well as a nice introduction to generalized quantifier theory, see Neale 1990, Chapter 2.

23. I was thus surprised to find that Hofweber (2005, 187) explicitly endorses generalized quantifier theory and its view of descriptions as quantifiers. I do not see how he can consistently also endorse the view that descriptions are singular terms in the substitution class of the first-order substitutional quantifiers (as he seems to do in Hofweber 2000).

24. For a statement and defense of negative free description theory, see Burge 1974. There Burge provides a persuasive argument (independent of Russell's theory) that sentences of the form $t = t$ are false when t is a non-referring description (1974, 320–323).

25. Here, I'm assuming that the descriptions in (25) and (26) have smallest scope and that the second occurrence of 'the number of planets' in (27) also has smallest scope. The lines in brackets in each of (25q)–(27q) represent the logical forms of the (alleged) substitutional generalizations of (25)–(27).

26. Assuming of course that Pluto is not a planet. If it is, change the example to one that is about the number 9.

5 Truths Containing Empty Names

In this chapter, I will try to make good on the promissory note that I offered at the beginning of this monograph, a note to the effect that I would later explain how various sentences that contain empty names can express true or false propositions, sentences such as

(1). Santa Claus exists.
(2). Santa Claus does not exist.
(3). Sylvia believes that Santa Claus will bring her a doll for Christmas.
(4). Zeus is the most powerful of the Greek gods.
(5). Sherlock Holmes is a brilliant detective.

Again my view is that in such cases, the empty names are not being *used* *as* genuine terms, not being used as names. Rather the names are being used as short for Russellian definite descriptions, which are quantifiers, as I argued in Chapter 2.

To explain how such uses are possible, I will motivate and develop the idea that such uses are *idiomatic*, being based on two different conventional idioms that arise from two different ways in which names are used in natural language. One of these idioms involves the use of names from fiction to provide a way to talk about fiction, as in example (5). A second more general and important idiom derives from the typical and fundamental use of names as genuine terms, but where the names are of a special sort which, following the terminology of Gareth Evans (1979), I call 'descriptive names'. It is this second idiom that applies to cases like (1)–(4). I will discuss this second idiom first. After I've explained and defended my overall view, I will go on to explain and argue for my view of the ways we use names from myth and fiction, and I will argue against the commonly held view that in such uses, we use these names as genuine terms to refer to abstract mythical beings and abstract fictional characters. Finally I will explain how my idiom hypothesis can be used to provide a partial solution to another classic problem for DR, namely the apparent failure of substitution of co-referring names in cognitive contexts to preserve truth.

1. Descriptive Names

We saw earlier in Chapter 3 (Section 2.3) that while proper names can be meaningfully used as directly referring genuine terms in both positive and negative existentials, uses of this sort that are *assertive* are pointless: positive such uses cannot be false, while negative such uses cannot be true. (See also Section 1 of Chapter 4.) But then, as Plantinga (1974) pointed out, it follows that when names are used in serious discussions or disputes about existence, the names are *not* being used as genuine terms, as names. How then *are* the names being used? As Plantinga also suggested, it seems that in such cases, the names are being used as short for definite descriptions since there in fact seems to be no reasonable alternative. (See Chapter 4, Section 1 and Section 3 for justification of this.) It is clear that when a given name *a* is being used in a serious discussion or dispute about existence, the speakers are not presupposing the existence of the name's referent, as they would be if the name were being used as a genuine term. In my view, the best hypothesis is that the name *a* is being used as short for a description understood according to Russell's theory of descriptions. Understood this way, positive and negative existentials such as 'Homer existed' and 'Homer did not exist' express propositions that are either true or false, whether or not the name 'Homer' refers.

Of course, if Plantinga is right, as I think he is, then the very difficult question arises as to how directly referring names like 'Homer' should come to be meaningfully used as short for specific descriptions. What features of natural language could possibly account for its happening that a given proper name of a sort that is typically used as a genuine term that has no descriptive content should nevertheless come to be useable in certain contexts (such as positive or negative existentials) as synonymous with some specific definite description?

The difficulty of this question is considerably ameliorated if we note at the outset that the vast majority of proper names that speakers commonly use as names simply cannot be reasonable candidates for acquiring the additional meaning of a specific definite description. If a single description commonly associated with a name by speakers of a given language did in fact determine or fix the semantic reference of that name, then of course that description would be a semantically salient feature of the name. But Kripke (1972a) provided strong evidence that the reference of most names is not determined or fixed by any commonly associated descriptions. As we saw in Chapter 1, he did this with his famous Gödel-Schmidt case and other cases like it. Practically the only thing that most speakers know about Gödel is that he discovered the incompleteness of arithmetic. But as Kripke points out, speakers' uses of 'Gödel' would still refer to Gödel even if not Gödel but an unknown high school teacher named 'Schmidt' had discovered that arithmetic is incomplete. Since the same point can be made regarding all the accomplishments for which

Gödel is famous, it is clear that the semantic referent of 'Gödel' is not determined by any description like 'the discoverer of incompleteness' that might be commonly associated with the name. So it surely seems that the referents of most proper names are not determined by any commonly associated descriptions. Thus, in the case of most names, there will simply be no semantically salient description that would allow us to interpret positive or negative existentials containing the name as expressing anything other than an assertively pointless proposition.

Nevertheless, as I have argued elsewhere (McKinsey 1999) and as Kripke himself pointed out (1972a, 301), there do exist names of natural language which are both used as genuine terms and whose referents are determined or fixed by commonly associated definite descriptions. Again, following Evans's (1979) terminology, I call such names 'descriptive names'. Names like this are in fact exceedingly rare, though in the examples of philosophers, they are not rare but frequent. For as we shall see, it is precisely the members of this relatively small class of names which provide most of the examples of names like 'Homer' that can be used in positive and negative existentials that are substantive rather than pointless and which, when they lack referents, can provide examples of truths and falsehoods that contain empty names, such as (1), (2), (3), and (4).

The crucial common feature of descriptive names is that their referents (if any) are *epistemically remote* from all speakers in the same way, so the users of such a name have to base their referring use of the name on the same small set of properties or descriptions. A good example of this, suggested by Kripke (1972a, 291) is the name 'Jack the Ripper', used to refer to whoever committed the grisly murders of a specific group of prostitutes in Victorian era London, but about whom nothing else is known. The two names of the planet Venus, 'Hesperus' and 'Phosphorus', are also good examples, especially as they were used by the ancient Greeks, since cognitive access to Venus was then based solely on sightings of the planet in different locations of the sky and at different times of day. Other good candidates for being descriptive names would include: 'Vulcan' (used as the name of an alleged planet between Mercury and the Sun); names of deities such as 'Zeus' and 'God'; names of mythical persons and creatures such as 'Faffner' and 'Pegasus'; names of historically remote figures about whom little is known, like 'Homer', 'King Arthur', and 'Robin Hood'; and pen names such as 'Mark Twain' and 'George Sand', at least before their referents' identities become publicly known.

Note that my examples of descriptive names do not include any names from *fiction*, such as 'Sherlock Holmes'. Our use of such names to talk about fiction, as we shall see in Section 8, is not at all based on any actual speakers' referential uses of the names *as* names that happen to be descriptive in the sense I just explained.

Whether or not a name is descriptive is of course always an empirical question. But we can sometimes provide good evidence to settle the question by using a strategy derived from Kripke's Gödel-Schmidt case. (Again, see McKinsey 1999, 536–538.) In that case, we ask whether or not it is consistent with the way we actually use the name 'Gödel' to suppose that it is not Gödel who uniquely satisfies a given description 'The F', but rather it is someone else, Schmidt say, who uniquely satisfies 'The F'. If the answer is 'Yes', then the description 'The F' is irrelevant to determining the reference of 'Gödel'. But if the correct answer is 'No', then the name is descriptive.

Consider, for instance, whether the following expresses a live semantic possibility:

(6).   It wasn't Jack the Ripper who murdered all those prostitutes in Victorian era London; rather those murders were all committed by some *other* man named 'Schmidt'.

Such a pronouncement strikes me as absurdly false, but not because it expresses an impossible proposition. It is absurd simply because if Schmidt had committed the relevant murders, then he would just *be* Jack the Ripper, the very one to whom we had been referring all along with that name. Thus even though there are possible worlds in which Jack did not do the heinous deeds, the actual semantics of the name 'Jack the Ripper' guarantees that (6) is false. Thus, 'Jack the Ripper' is a descriptive name.[1]

It is worth noting that descriptive names can either refer or fail to refer, depending on whether the description that determines or fixes the referent of the name is or is not uniquely satisfied. In either case, if the name is descriptive, it will pass the Gödel-Schmidt test. For example, it surely seems that the name 'God' passes the test since it would, I think, be absurd to say:

(7).   It isn't God who is the purely spiritual, omniscient, omnipotent, maximally benevolent creator of the universe by intelligent design; rather it is some *other* being (named 'Schmidt'?) who has these characteristics.

Whether or not one believes that God exists, one can see the semantic absurdity of (7), and hence one can see that the name 'God' is descriptive, whether it refers or not.

2. The Idiomatic Use of Descriptive Names

I should emphasize that on the view I have been outlining and motivating, descriptive names like 'Homer' and 'Jack the Ripper' are in the first place used as genuine terms and, as such, function only to introduce referents into the propositions expressed by sentences containing the descriptive names. The descriptions that are commonly associated with descriptive names serve only to *fix the reference* of the relevant names, for each individual user of the name. There is *no* sense in which the description that fixes the reference of a given descriptive name provides the *meaning* of that name, as it is used as a genuine term. That a given name is descriptive is thus, I take it, solely a matter of *fact* and *not* a matter of meaning. The fact that matters, as I mentioned earlier, is the epistemic remoteness of the name's putative referent. It may be that there is little or even no good evidence for the putative referent's existence, as in the case of names of historically remote persons and the beings of religion and myth. Here, names' referents (if any) must be fixed either by the scant historical evidence or by the narrow confines of myth or religious doctrine. On the other hand, there may be very good, even conclusive, evidence for the referent's existence, as in cases like 'Jack the Ripper' and 'Hesperus'; but here, the *body* of good evidence is itself very small, so all users of the name must base their reference with the name on a narrow class of descriptions or properties.

Given the existence of a class of descriptive names, each of which has its semantic referent determined by a commonly associated description, each such description will become a semantically salient feature of the relevant name, for the speakers of a given language. My hypothesis is that in such conditions, it is natural for a general *idiomatic* convention to arise on which each descriptive name is allowed, in certain types of sentential contexts, to be used as short for the description that normally fixes the name's reference. I will call this 'the idiom hypothesis'. As far as I can tell, there are just three types of context in which a descriptive name is allowed to be used as short for the relevant description: (i) existential contexts, where as we've seen, use of a descriptive name as short for the relevant description allows speakers to use a positive or negative existential containing the name to express or assert interesting discoveries or subjects of significant debate regarding existence, as opposed to expressing assertively pointless propositions; (ii) cognitive contexts, such as sentence (3), in which a small-scope descriptive name's use as short for a description can be used to express an agent's way of thinking about a (putative) object without committing the speaker to such an object's existence; and (iii) contexts involving the use of names from myth to talk about what is true (or false) in a given myth. (Note again that the idiom just described does not apply to uses of names from *fiction*. Such uses, as I mentioned earlier, are instances of a distinct idiom, which I will describe in Section 5.)

One of the most important consequences of my idiom hypothesis is that when we ask, say, whether Homer existed or not, we are in effect also asking whether the reference condition for the descriptive genuine term 'Homer' is uniquely satisfied or not. Suppose the reference condition for this type of use of 'Homer' is that 'Homer' is to refer to a given object x if and only if x = the poet of ancient Greece named 'Homer' who composed the *Iliad* and the *Odyssey*. Abbreviate this description as 'the F'. Then we have the consequence that 'Homer' refers if and only if the F exists. In everyday parlance, this equivalence would be expressed as: 'Homer' refers if and only if Homer exists. It is commonly assumed that in such locutions, the name *referred to* is semantically the same as the name that is *used* in the relevant existential. This is a serious error. For in these locutions, the name 'Homer' referred to is a directly referring genuine term, while the 'name' used in the relevant existential is not used as a name at all since it abbreviates 'the F'.

3. An Alternative Pragmatic Explanation

A few defenders of the DR-thesis have suggested that, while some sentences containing empty names may appear to be true (or false), such sentences never literally express true or false propositions. Fred Adams and Robert Stecker (1994) suggest that a sentence like

(8).   Vulcan does not exist,

may appear to express a true proposition, but this is only because use of the sentence will 'pragmatically impart' such information as that there is no planet between Mercury and the sun (p. 313). They allege that this sort of pragmatic fact explains why people (like me) have the mistaken intuition that (8) is true (p. 394).

Of course in my view, Adams and Stecker are wrong. 'Vulcan' is a descriptive name in its use derived from the astronomer Le Verrier since in this use, the semantic reference of 'Vulcan' is fixed for most speakers by the description 'the planet whose orbit between Mercury and the sun explains discrepancies in the orbit of Mercury'. Given the idiom hypothesis, 'Vulcan' is used as short for this description in (8), so that on one of its meanings, this sentence in fact expresses the true proposition that

(9).   The planet whose orbit between Mercury and the sun explains discrepancies in the orbit of Mercury does not exist.

But why prefer my idiom hypothesis to a view like that of Adams and Stecker? I think the main reason is that, as Adams and Stecker agree, it is *extremely* counterintuitive to claim that no negative existential that like (8) contains an empty name is ever true. (See also Adams and Dietrich 2004, 126.) Attempts to explain away the intuition that many negative existentials such as (8) are true are, in my opinion, unpersuasive, given the robustness, persistence, and pervasiveness of this sort of intuition. My view has the distinct advantage of explaining how such intuitions can be correct, while requiring only minimal revision of the DR-thesis. [See principles (DR) and (NP) in Chapter 2.]

Adams and Stecker seem to be worried that if they accepted the idea that a negative existential like (8) expressed a descriptive proposition like (9), then they would be committed to a short for descriptions theory of names, which (like me) they correctly think is false (1994, 394). But this worry is misplaced. Again, my view is that names are typically and fundamentally used as genuine terms, and in such uses they are of course never short for descriptions. But this allows for a statistically rare class of exceptions, where in a *few* types of context (existentials, cognitive ascriptions, and talk about myth), a *small class* of descriptive names are idiomatically allowed by the conventions of natural language to be used as short for descriptions.

A second reason why I prefer the idiom hypothesis is that I have yet to see a plausible pragmatic explanation of why we persistently have the firm intuition that sentences like (8) are true. Adams *et al.* merely rely on the fact that various descriptions are often *associated* with empty names. But as Mitchell Green (2007, 432–433) has pointed out, it is difficult to see how mere association of 'Vulcan' with a given description could cause one to think that 'Vulcan does not exist' is true, given that one did not think this in the first place. Adams and Dietrich (2004, 145, note 7) suggest that their associated-descriptions explanation is somehow Gricean in nature, but in fact Adams *et al.* never explicitly make any use of Grice's ideas.

Still it is useful to consider how the intuition that 'Vulcan does not exist' is true might be given a Gricean explanation. If, like Adams and Stecker, we assume that the only literal meaning that a negative existential like (8) could have is a meaning on which the relevant name is being used as a genuine term, then when we hear someone assertively utter (8), we will take the speaker to be absurdly attempting to predicate non-existence of the referent of 'Vulcan'. Since such a sentence is at best false (when 'Vulcan' has a referent) and at worst without truth value (if 'Vulcan' is empty), the speaker is violating Grice's maxim of Quality ('speak truly'), and thus the speaker seems to be conversationally uncooperative in Grice's sense. But if the speaker otherwise seems to be cooperating, the hearer will infer that the speaker is trying to communicate something other than what (8) literally expresses. (See Grice 1989, 26–27.) Since the referent of 'Vulcan' is fixed by the description in (9), the hearer will naturally infer that by uttering (8), the speaker means the true proposition expressed by (9).

This is the best Gricean explanation of the intuition that (8) is true that I can think of. Yet the explanation is seriously defective. It assumes that one who hears a speaker assertively utter (8) will only hear the utterance either as an absurd attempt to assert a blatantly false singular proposition or as being neither true nor false. But on the contrary, I seriously doubt that anyone would *ever* (even tacitly) hear an assertive utterance of (8) this way. Thus my Gricean explanation simply cannot get off the ground. The speaker will not be heard as literally saying something that must be false or truth-valueless and so will not seem to be uncooperative. So the hearer will not be driven to figure out what else the speaker might mean. In my view, an assertive utterance of (8) – where 'Vulcan' is understood as in its uses derived from Le Verrier – is always heard in just *one* of its *two* literal meanings, namely the descriptive meaning on which (8) means (9). The other literal meaning of (8) will simply not be heard since being assertively pointless, it is just not ever salient in an assertive context.

Another serious difficulty with attempting to use Gricean mechanisms to explain how uses of negative existentials like (8) could 'pragmatically impart' descriptive information like (9) is that on Grice's view, conversational implicatures are always *cancelable* in the following sense:

(C). If a person *x* uses a sentence S to say or assert that p, where S literally expresses p, then *x*'s use of S conversationally implies that q only if q is *cancelable*, that is, only if there are contexts in which someone may say or assert that p while consistently adding *but not q* or *I don't mean to imply that q*. (Grice 1989, 44–46)[2]

The problem is that a speaker *x* who both assertively utters (8) ('Vulcan does not exist') and who, like the rest of us, would be following Le Verrier's usage of 'Vulcan' could not rationally cancel the implicature of (9), saying *but I do not mean to imply that the planet whose orbit between the sun and Mercury explains discrepancies in the orbit of Mercury does not exist*. To say this would be irrational on Le Verrier's usage of 'Vulcan' since in this usage, 'Vulcan' is a descriptive name whose reference is fixed by the description 'The planet whose orbit between the sun and Mercury explains discrepancies in the orbit of Mercury'. Thus, any speaker *x* who failed to accept (9) would accept that the name 'Vulcan' does have a referent, and so *x* would not assertively utter (8). Thus the implication of (9) by one who assertively utters (8) is no mere pragmatic implicature since the implication is not rationally cancelable.

We may conclude that, contrary to the view of Adams and Stecker, it is highly probable that the very strong intuition that there are true negative existentials such as (8) is not merely a mistaken intuition that can be explained away by use of pragmatic Gricean methods.[3]

4. Names From Mythology

Our uses of names from mythology and fiction are derived from uses of the same expressions in mythology and fiction. As we shall see, these two origins of our uses of such names are significantly different from each other, and moreover, our ways of using these two classes of names both differ significantly from our use of other empty descriptive names.

Originally, names from myth were used to express stories that were told as fact and widely believed to be fact. The names used to express such stories, and parts of such stories, were thus originally used *as* names, as genuine terms. These names, in my view, were all what I call descriptive names, whose referents were fixed by descriptions gleaned from the myths. Thus the names from Greek mythology could well have been used by the ancient Greeks to express substantive disputes as to whether, say, Zeus existed or did not exist. If so, the ancient Greek language would have contained an idiomatic convention of the kind that, in my view, exists in contemporary natural languages like English, a convention that allows descriptive names to be used in certain types of context as short for the descriptions that fix their reference. As I suggested earlier, empty names from myth can be used by contemporary speakers in three different ways. First, there are 'metamythic' uses in which the names are used to make true (or false) statements about what is true in a given myth,[4] such as

(10). In Greek mythology, Zeus is both immortal and extremely powerful.

Second, empty names from myth can be used in cognitive contexts to make true (or false) statements such as

(11). The ancient Greeks believed that Zeus is both immortal and extremely powerful.

And finally, empty names from myth can be used to make (false) positive existential statements and (true) negative existential statements, such as 'Zeus existed' and 'Zeus did not exist'.

My view is of course that in all of these three types of use, the relevant name is being used not as a name, but as short for a description. But it is a far from trivial matter to determine which description a contemporary use of a name from myth would be short for. For instance, ancient Greek users of a name like 'Zeus' would no doubt have had a far more detailed and extensive conception of the putative referent of this name than do modern users. So it seems unlikely that we use the name as short for the same, perhaps complex, description that commonly fixed the reference of the ancients' uses of 'Zeus'. Contemporary uses of such names from Greek mythology are probably based upon whatever cursory knowledge that modern speakers might have of the most important and distinctive characteristics that were alleged in the myths to be possessed by the various gods. For instance, in the myths, Zeus was considered the most powerful of the gods, a 'sky god' who controlled the occurrence of rain, thunder, and lightning.[5] So one good candidate for the description that our uses of 'Zeus' might be short for would be 'the most powerful of the gods, who is named "Zeus"'. The chief criterion that any such candidate description must satisfy is that it yields truths upon substitution for 'Zeus' in true statements about the relevant myth and about the myth's believers' cognitive states. Substitution of the description 'the most powerful of the gods, who is named "Zeus"' for 'Zeus' in (10) and (11) results in true (if somewhat redundant) statements.

Earlier, in Chapter 3, Section 2.3, in Chapter 4, Section 1, and in this chapter, Section 3, I provided good evidence that when descriptive names occur in substantive existentials, they are being used as short for descriptions. Once this is accepted, we then have additional evidence that empty mythical names are also used as short for descriptions in metamythic and cognitive contexts like (10) and (11). Consider sentences involving pronominal anaphora such as:

(12). Zeus does not exist, but in Greek mythology, *he* is both immortal and extremely powerful.
(13). Zeus does not exist, but the ancient Greeks believed that *he* is both immortal and extremely powerful.

Since the anaphoric pronoun 'he' has the name 'Zeus' as antecedent in both (12) and (13), it surely seems that these occurrences would just be going proxy for 'Zeus' as it is meant in the left conjuncts of (12) and (13). Thus in both cases, 'he' would be short for the same description as 'Zeus' is short for. But then, the right-hand conjuncts of (12) and (13) as so understood would express the same truths as (10) and (11). So in both metamythic and cognitive contexts, names from myth can be used as short for descriptions.

Kripke (1973) has persuasively argued for the view that contemporary users of names from both myth and fiction often use such names as *genuine terms* that refer directly to abstract mythical or fictional beings or objects.[6] I will discuss Kripke's contention further in Section 6. But it is already apparent that in both metamythic and cognitive contexts, names from myth are *not* used as names of abstract objects. For instance, (10), which I take to be true, would be false if the occurrence of 'Zeus' in (10) referred to an abstract mythical being. For it is clearly *not* true in Greek mythology that any abstract mythical being is both immortal and extremely powerful. Nor is it true that the ancient Greeks (absurdly) believed of some abstract mythical being that it is both immortal and extremely powerful. Thus (11) would also be false, if in (11) 'Zeus' referred to an abstract mythical being. I take it that these arguments can be generalized in an obvious way to show that in no metamythic or cognitive contexts containing names from myth are the names used to refer to abstract objects. It remains to be seen whether there are any *other* types of contexts in which names from myth are used as names of abstract entities. Kripke clearly thinks that there are such contexts, but I disagree. I will discuss this issue at length in Section 9.

5. Names From Fiction

The origin of our uses of names from fiction is quite different from the origins of our uses of descriptive names, including names from myth, as short for descriptions in special contexts. These latter uses derive from real uses of the descriptive names *as* names, as genuine terms. But as many authors have pointed out, fictional names are never actually used *as* names in fiction.[7] Rather, in fiction it is merely *pretended* that given expressions are used as names of various characters in the fictions. But since these are only pretend uses, they are not actual uses, and so they have no actual semantic properties: such uses have no referents, and sentences in fiction containing them express no propositions.[8]

Thus my idiom hypothesis cannot be applied to explain how we use 'names' from fiction since these fictional names are not really used as names at all, let alone as descriptive names. The idiom that provides meanings for our uses of (syntactic) names to make true or false statements *about* fiction must be an idiom that is specific to talk about fiction. My hypothesis will again be that the relevant terms that we borrow from fiction to talk about fiction are used as short for descriptions. We can again justify this hypothesis for what Currie (1990, 158) calls 'metafictive' uses of names by using constructions involving anaphoric back-reference to negative existentials, such as

(14). Sherlock Holmes does not exist, but in the Holmes-stories, *he* is a brilliant detective.

Again, assuming that in the left conjunct of (14) 'Sherlock Holmes' is used as short for a definite description, then the anaphoric pronoun 'he' in the right conjunct must be short for the same description. But this right conjunct would clearly have the same meaning as

(15). In the Holmes-stories, Sherlock Holmes is a brilliant detective.

Thus, as in the metamythic cases, the 'names' used in metafictive contexts can be used as short for definite descriptions.[9]

And again, as in the metamythic cases, we can show that no 'name' used in a metafictive context is ever used as a genuine term that refers to an abstract fictional character.[10] Consider, for instance

(16). Holmes is an abstract fictional character, and in the Holmes-stories, Watson believes that Holmes plays the violin.

On the assumption that in (16) 'Holmes' is used as the name of an abstract entity, it would follow from (16) by existential generalization that

(17). $\exists x(x$ is an abstract fictional character, and in the Holmes-stories, Watson believes that x plays the violin).

But surely, contrary to (17), it is simply *not true* in the Holmes-stories that Watson has a (wildly false) belief about an abstract entity to the effect that it plays the violin.

My view of how names work in metafictive contexts is largely derived from Gregory Currie's thorough, clear, and persuasively argued theory of fiction in his book *The Nature of Fiction* (1990). Currie also endorses the view that in metafictive contexts, where we use 'names' derived from a given fiction to make claims about what is true in that fiction, the names are being used as short for a certain sort of definite description. As we shall see, my view of what these descriptions are differs significantly from Currie's view. But even so, my view is inspired by Currie's compelling theory of truth in fiction. I will write this theory as follows:

> (TF) In fiction S, it is true that p if and only if it is reasonable (to degree r) for the informed reader of S to infer that the fictional author of S believes that p. (Currie 1990, 92)

Currie's concept here of the fictional author of a fiction is especially important for my purposes. Currie points out that when we read a given story, we make believe that we are being told the story by a reliable teller who has complete and knowledgeable access to all the facts of the story being told. As Currie puts it:

> The fictional author (as I shall call him) is that fictional character constructed within our make-believe whom we take to be telling us the story as known fact. Our reading is thus an explanation of the fictional author's belief structure.
>
> (Currie 1990, 76)

Since the actual author of a story will not in fact believe most of the propositions that make up the story, the actual author should not be confused with the fictional author. Moreover, while some fictions have characters who narrate the fiction, as Watson narrates the Holmes-stories, Currie argues that we also should not confuse the fictional author with the fictional narrator (if any): he points out (p. 124) that fictional narrators like Watson often have beliefs that are simply not true in the fiction.

Currie (1990, 149–150) proposes that the total content of a given fiction is the Ramsey sentence obtained by replacing each name t_i in the fiction $F(t_1 \ldots t_n)$ by a distinct variable and then writing the existential closure of the result, as follows:[11]

(18) $\exists x_1 \ldots \exists x_n \left[F(x_1 \ldots x_n) \right]$.

Then (certain niceties aside), Currie uses a procedure invented by David Lewis (1970) to form the definite descriptions for which each metafictive use of a name from fiction is an abbreviation. Supposing for instance that 'x_1' is the variable that replaces 'Holmes' in the original regimentation of the fiction $F(t_1 \ldots t_n)$, we can then define the name 'Holmes' thus:

(19)   Holmes $=_{df} \iota x_1 \exists x_2 \ldots \exists x_n [F(x_1 \ldots x_n)]$.[12]

On this idea, every fictional name in a metafictive statement about a fiction S is short for a definite description that expresses the *entire content* of S. This has the implausible consequence that even the best-informed reader would have at best only a partial and schematic grasp of the hugely complex propositions expressed by use of even quite simple metafictive sentences such as

(20). In the fiction H, Holmes is a pipe smoker,

(where 'H' refers to the fiction composed of all the Holmes-stories). But surely a correct semantic account of the use of names in talk about fiction should *not* imply that, in the case of fairly long fictions, no speaker of the relevant language could possibly understand, let alone know the truth of, even the simplest metafictive sentences such as (20).

My alternative suggestion is that when a fictional name N from a given fiction S is used in a given metafictive sentence about S, N is short for a metalinguistic description of the form 'the person [or object] to whom [or which] the fictional author of S refers with N'. I will abbreviate this form as 'the referent$_{FAS}$ of N'. So, for instance, (20) would then mean

(20a). In the fiction H, the referent$_{FAH}$ of 'Holmes' is a pipe smoker.

Similarly, the negative existential 'Holmes does not exist' would mean

(21). The referent$_{FAH}$ of 'Holmes' does not exist.

(21) is true on my proposal simply because the fictional author of H, being fictional, does not exist. Hence the person to whom the fictional author of H refers with 'Holmes' also does not exist. Note that it turns out on my proposal not only that 'Holmes does not exist' is true, but also that it is *necessarily* true. Since at no possible world will there exist a *fictional* author of anything, the description 'the person to whom the fictional author of H refers with "Holmes"' will fail to refer at every possible world. Thus my proposal is both consistent with and explains Kripke's important insight that not only does Sherlock Holmes not exist, but it is not even *possible* that he exists. (See Kripke 1972b, 764 and 2013, 40–42.)

One minor problem for my proposal is raised by the fact that there can be fictions in which two or more persons have the same name. Thus in

The Adventure of the Greek Interpreter, Holmes's brother Mycroft Holmes appears. In such a case, the description for which the relevant name is short might have to be minimally revised so as to achieve unique reference in the fiction. In the Holmes stories, we can achieve this by slightly revising the relevant description to 'the person named "Sherlock" to whom the fictional author of H refers with "Holmes"'. (Occurrences of 'Holmes' in which Mycroft is the pretended referent can then be replaced by another suitably revised description.)

A more serious problem arises when we try to further analyze a proposal like (20a) in terms of Currie's analysis (TF) of truth in fiction. The result is

(20b). It is reasonable (to degree r) for the informed reader of H to infer that the fictional author of H believes that the referent$_{\text{FAH}}$ of 'Holmes' is a pipe smoker.

The problem here is that if we read the metalinguistic description 'the referent$_{\text{FAH}}$ of "Holmes"' as having small scope relative to 'believes that', then we get a false result. For (20b) would then imply the falsehood that the fictional author believes that his story H has a fictional author! To avoid this problem, we need to add a clause to (TF) stipulating that, for any fictional name N that occurs in the relevant instance of 'p' in the *definiens* of (TF), N must have large scope relative to the operator 'the fictional author of S believes that' and small scope relative to 'infers that'. The resulting revision of (20b) is then unproblematic:

(20c). It is reasonable (to degree r) for the informed reader of H to infer that the referent$_{\text{FAH}}$ of 'Holmes' is such that the fictional author of H believes that *he* is a pipe smoker.

This revised proposal has the nice effect that metafictive uses of fictional names really only ascribe *de re* beliefs about various characters in the fiction to the fictional author, so the *truths* of fiction expressed by our metafictive uses of names are all pretended to be *singular* propositions, even though in our uses, the names are short for descriptions.[13]

6. Abstract Mythical Beings and Fictional Characters

Kripke (1973) provides a plethora of useful and persuasive examples in his attempt to show that we often use names from myth and fiction as genuine terms to refer to abstract mythical beings and fictional characters.[14] Van Inwagen (1977) and Currie (1990) also provide useful examples to the same end in the case of names from fiction. I am not convinced by these examples, most of which I take to be disguised metamythic or metafictive uses of names, in which, as I argued previously, the names are used as short for descriptions. For instance, Kripke (1973) gives the following examples:

(22). Hamlet is a fictional character. (61)
(23). There is such a fictional character as Hamlet. (72)

I take it that a 'fictional character' is by definition a character in fiction that does not actually exist, as opposed to being an existing object such as Napoleon who is also a character in various fictions. Thus I also take it that (22) is logically equivalent to

(22a).   There is a fiction F such that Hamlet is a character in F, but Hamlet does not actually exist.

I would also suggest that to be a character in a fiction is to be a subject of predication in that fiction, so (22) and (22a) are both equivalent to

(22b).   There is a fiction F such that Hamlet is a subject of predication in F, but Hamlet does not actually exist.

As I argued previously, any name in a (partly metafictive) context like this is being used as short for a description, and so is not being used as a name of an abstract entity.

   While (22) is true on my analysis, Kripke's example (23) is false. (23) certainly *seems* to be true since it appears to be logically equivalent to (22), which is true. But (22) and (23) are equivalent only if the context 'is a fictional character' is extensional. But in my analysis of (22), this context is not extensional, and so (22) does not imply (23). In fact, given the analysis (22a), (22) implies that (23) is false.

   Another class of cases which Kripke (1973) discusses at length are cases where it appears that a person is said (truly) to bear a two-place relation to a mythical being or fictional character, cases such as

(24). The ancient Greeks worshipped Zeus.
(25). Jones [a literary critic] admires Desdemona.

One oddity of Kripke's appeal to such cases is that, rather than supporting his view, these cases actually seem to *refute* that view. For while (24) is true and (25) could be true, they would both be false if in them the names 'Zeus' and 'Desdemona' referred to abstract entities. For surely, the Greeks did *not* worship any abstract entity when they worshipped Zeus; nor would any literary critic be admiring an abstract entity when admiring Desdemona or be pitying an abstract entity when pitying Anna Karenina.

   It remains to explain how sentences like (24) and (25) could be true. I will have to skip discussion of cases like (25) since their explication would require a full theory of emotion in fiction.[15] I will concentrate instead on Kripke's discussion of (24). Kripke argues that the verb 'worship' expresses a two-place relation. I agree that on *one* of its meanings, 'worship' expresses the mental two-place relation that a person x bears to an entity y just in case x 'reveres, adores, or venerates' y as a deity. (See Webster's *New World Dictionary*, 1982 edition.) But in this meaning, (24) will just be either false or without truth value since 'Zeus' will either be an empty name or description or perhaps will be a name that refers to an abstract object (which no one has ever worshipped).

However, 'worship' has a second meaning in which it is an *intransitive* verb meaning to *engage* in worship, that is, to perform various ritualistic activities such as prayer, sacrifice, etc. (Again, see Webster's *New World Dictionary*.) In this sense, 'worship' resembles the intensional verbs 'seek', 'look for', 'search for', and 'want', as they were discussed by Alonzo Church (1956), 8, note 20) and W. V. O. Quine (1960, 155–156). Church gave the example

(26). Schliemann sought the site of Troy.

Church pointed out that there is a sense in which (26) would be true, even had the site of Troy never existed. So he suggests that 'sought', rather than expressing a two-place relation, is an operator that forms intensional contexts. Kripke (1973, 68–69) discusses Church's suggestion at length, arguing that the suggestion will not work for 'worship' on the grounds that 'worship' expresses only a two-place extensional relation. But again, Kripke is wrong about this.

Church's example (26) can usefully be understood as

(26a).   Schliemann sought with the intention (purpose, goal) of finding the site of Troy.

Similarly, the oft-mentioned example 'Ponce de Leon searched for the fountain of youth' becomes

(27). Ponce de Leon searched with the intention (purpose, goal) of finding the fountain of youth.

The verbs 'seek' and 'search for' form intensional contexts because they express types of action that are necessarily *goal directed*. The intransitive sense of 'worship' also expresses a type of necessarily goal-directed activity. Thus Kripke's sentence (24) ('The ancient Greeks worshipped Zeus') has a reading similar to (26a) and (27):

(24a).   The ancient Greeks engaged in various ritualistic activities with the intention (purpose, goal) of expressing their devotion to, reverence for, or adoration of Zeus.

Here, the fact that 'Zeus' is an empty term does not affect the truth of (24a) since 'Zeus', which I take to be short for a description like 'the most powerful of the gods, whose name is "Zeus"', occurs in the scope of a cognitive operator.

Before closing, I should discuss cases of the sort that Currie (1990, 171) calls *transfictive*. Here are three transfictive cases:

(28). Holmes's methods are quite different from those of Poirot. (Currie 1990, 171)

(29). There are characters in some nineteenth-century novels who are presented with a greater wealth of detail than any character in any eighteenth-century novel. (van Inwagen 1977, 302)

(30). Falstaff and Iago are two of the most charming characters in literature. (Kripke 1973, 62)

Kripke, van Inwagen, and Currie are all convinced that in cases like (28) and (30), the names must be taken to refer directly to abstract characters. My own view is that such cases are all metafictive. When the relevant fiction operators are missing, I hold that they are implicit, which frequently happens, as in sentences about fiction like 'Holmes is a pipe smoker'.

First, consider Currie's example (28). Currie holds that here, the names 'Holmes' and 'Poirot' refer to abstract entities that he calls *roles*. According to Currie, (28) says that the methods of detection that partly define the Holmes role are quite different from the methods of detection that partly define the Poirot role (1990, 174). I agree that (28) does say something much like this, but we don't need to suppose that 'Holmes' and 'Poirot' *refer* to the relevant roles in (28). Rather we can simply say

(28a). In the fiction H, Holmes uses a set of methods M, while in the fiction P, Poirot uses a set of methods M*, and the methods in M are quite different from the methods in M*.

Here, we may assume that the names 'Holmes' and 'Poirot' are short for the relevant descriptions as before.

Both van Inwagen and Currie claim that van Inwagen's example (29) involves quantification over fictional characters. But this claim becomes doubtful when we give the phrase 'in some nineteenth-century novels' largest scope in (29). If we simplify somewhat by replacing the plural quantifiers in (29) with singular ones, (29) can be plausibly understood to mean

(29a). There is at least one nineteenth-century novel F such that in F, d_1 is the degree of detail provided by the properties ascribed to a given character, and for every eighteenth-century novel G and any set of properties S, if in G, S is ascribed to some character, then the degree d_2 of detail provided by S is less than d_1.

My overall suggestion is that comparisons of characters across fictions amount to comparisons of aspects of the *sets of properties* ascribed to characters in the relevant fictions.

In (29a), I used a suggestion by Edward Zalta that comparisons of fictional characters can often be analyzed in terms of the *degrees* to which the characters have given properties. (See Zalta (2000), 130–134.) The same device also provides an adequate analysis of Kripke's challenging case (30). Let 'H' name the combination of the two *Henry IV* plays in which Falstaff appears, and let 'O' abbreviate *Othello*. Then we can analyze (30) as

(30a).   In H, Falstaff has charm to degree d_1, and in O, Iago has charm to degree d_2, and d_1 and d_2 are among the highest degrees of charm in the set D, where a degree d is a member of D if and only if in some fiction F, some character has charm to degree d.

As in (28a), the names in (30a) occur in metafictive contexts, and so are short for the relevant descriptions as before.

My metafictive analyses of examples (28), (29) and (30) provide good *prima facie* evidence that the names in such cases do not refer directly to abstract characters. So given our previous discussion of other examples in Sections 4, 5, and 6, the best general hypothesis would seem to be that in our talk about both myth and fiction, names from myth and fiction are used as abbreviated definite descriptions.

7. The Use of Names in Cognitive Contexts

I have now completed my overall explanation of how certain forms of sentence that contain empty names can express true or false propositions. This explanation, I think, provides a plausible solution to one of the major classical problems facing the Direct Reference thesis, as it applies to proper names. As a defender of DR, my strategy has been to (a) simply accept that sentences like (1)–(5) are counterexamples to an over-general way of stating DR, (b) restrict the scope of DR to the typical and most fundamental uses of names, and then (c) explain how certain narrow classes of names (descriptive names and 'names' used to talk about fiction) are idiomatically allowed to be used as abbreviated definite descriptions in just four types of sentential contexts.

Before concluding, it is of some importance to see the extent to which my idiom hypothesis based on descriptive names provides a solution to a second classical problem that faces DR, namely the apparent fact that substitution of co-referring proper names in cognitive contexts can fail to preserve truth value. This is 'the substitution problem'.

In the discussion to follow, keep in mind that in my idiom hypothesis, descriptive names that are ordinarily used as genuine terms can be used as short for the descriptions that fix their reference, but *only* in existential, cognitive, and metamythic contexts. In all other sentential contexts, descriptive names *must* be used as names and not as short for descriptions. Moreover, *all* names may be used as directly referring genuine terms in both existential and cognitive contexts. This implies that both existential and cognitive contexts that contain descriptive names are invariably ambiguous and so will have different meanings depending on whether the relevant descriptive name is or is not being used as short for a definite description.

Now consider the following classic example of an argument in which substitution of one co-referring name for another in a cognitive context can apparently lead from true premises to a false conclusion:

(HP) (1) The ancients believed that Hesperus appears in the evening.
  (2) Hesperus = Phosphorus.
  ∴ (3) The ancients believed that Phosphorus appears in the evening.

Given that both 'Hesperus' and 'Phosphorus' are used as directly referring genuine terms throughout the argument (HP), then (HP) is valid. For if the second premise 'Hesperus = Phosphorus' is true, then the first premise and the conclusion must express precisely the same singular proposition about the planet Venus, to which both 'Hesperus' and 'Phosphorus' refer. There are various ways of explaining what this singular proposition is. My preferred explanation is that, since by assumption 'Hesperus' refers directly to Venus in premise (1), (1) ascribes to Venus the property that an object x has if and only if the ancients believed that x appears in the evening. Thus, even though (1) and (3) are both *structurally de dicto*, with both 'Hesperus' and 'Phosphorus' having small scope within 'believes that', these sentences are in fact *semantically de re*, when the names in them are used as genuine terms. Understood this way, premise (1) expresses the *de re* proposition that

(1*). Hesperus is such that the ancients believed that it appears in the evening,

while the conclusion (3) expresses the same *de re* proposition, with 'Phosphorus' replacing 'Hesperus'. (For fuller discussion, see McKinsey 1994, 317–318 and McKinsey 1999, 521–522.) With premise (1) and conclusion (3) understood this way, (HP) is plainly valid.

On the other hand, my idiom hypothesis implies that since 'Hesperus' and 'Phosphorus' are both descriptive names occurring in cognitive contexts in premise (1) and conclusion (3) of (HP), each name can be used in (1) and (3) as short for the description that normally fixes its reference.

There are then three possibilities: (i) *both* 'Hesperus' and 'Phosphorus' abbreviate descriptions in (1) and (3); (ii) 'Hesperus' does abbreviate a description in (1), but 'Phosphorus' does *not* abbreviate a description in (3); and (iii) 'Hesperus' does *not* abbreviate a description in (1), but 'Phosphorus' does abbreviate a description in (3). In all three of these cases, (HP) is invalid for quite obvious reasons.

In case (i), substitution of 'Phosphorus' for 'Hesperus' in premise (1) to yield conclusion (3) is clearly invalid, assuming that 'Hesperus' and 'Phosphorus' have distinct descriptive meanings in premise (1) and conclusion (3). For even though 'Hesperus' and 'Phosphorus' have the same referent, it is still possible for the ancients to have the descriptive belief ascribed by premise (1) without having the descriptive belief ascribed by the conclusion (3). In case (ii), it's possible for the ancients to have the descriptive belief ascribed by (1) without having the *de re* belief that would be ascribed by the conclusion (3). And finally, in case (iii), where 'Hesperus' is used as a genuine term in premise (1) and 'Phosphorus' abbreviates a description in conclusion (3), the substitution of 'Phosphorus' for 'Hesperus' yields a (semantically) *de dicto* descriptive belief ascription that does not follow by substitution from the (semantically) *de re* premise (1).

In general, where α and β are proper names, Φ is a sentence containing either α or β in the scope of a cognitive operator, and at least one of α and β is a descriptive name, then arguments of the forms

$$(C) \qquad \frac{\Phi}{\alpha = \beta} \qquad \frac{\Phi}{\alpha = \beta}$$
$$\therefore \Phi(\beta//\alpha) \quad \therefore \Phi(\beta//\alpha)$$

will both have at least one (actual) interpretation on which they are valid and at least one (actual) interpretation on which they are invalid. (Here, $\Phi(\beta//\alpha)$ is the result of replacing at least one (but not necessarily every) occurrence of α in Φ by β.)

I had earlier proposed in McKinsey (1999) a (partial) solution to the substitution problem that is also based on appeal to descriptive names. On that solution, I maintained that descriptive names contribute their descriptive linguistic meanings to determine the cognitive properties that are ascribed by cognitive predicates of the form 'Cs that p'. On this idea, the premise (1) and conclusion (3) of an argument like (HP) will express different propositions, even though the descriptive names 'Hesperus' and 'Phosphorus' are taken to be unambiguous directly referring genuine terms. There are two reasons why I now prefer my idiom hypothesis to this earlier idea. First, and most important, my idiom hypothesis is more general in its application: it not only provides a (partial) solution to the substitution problem as did my earlier idea, but it *also* explains how both existential and metamythic contexts that contain empty names can be true (or false). Second, since I gave my earlier proposal, I have found new persuasive arguments for the conclusion that proper names (when used as names) have no lexical meanings in natural language (McKinsey 2010). This conclusion of course is inconsistent with my earlier (1999) hypothesis that descriptive names have descriptive linguistic meanings in natural language.[16]

I said previously that the solution to the substitution problem that is provided by my idiom hypothesis is partial. That is because there are arguments in which substitution of one co-referring name for another in a cognitive context appears to lead from truth to falsehood, even though the names *are not descriptive*. Suppose, for instance, that Sally has heard of Cary Grant and knows that he was a famous movie star, but she does not have the slightest idea that his original name was 'Archibald Leach'. Then it may appear that the following argument has true premises but a false conclusion:

(CA) (1) Sally believes that Cary Grant was a famous movie star.
    (2) Cary Grant = Archibald Leach.
    ∴ (3) Sally believes that Archibald Leach was a famous movie star.

Here, the intuition that (3) is false would seem to be based on the assumption that Sally is unaware that Cary Grant was named 'Archibald Leach'. This in turn suggests that the relevant intuition is based on the assumption that the conclusion (3) says something false about the name 'Archibald Leach'. But how could this be?

Steven Rieber (1997) has suggested that substitution of co-referring names can lead from truth to falsehood, when one or both of the names occurs in the context of implicit 'complex quotation', in which the relevant name is both used and mentioned. On this idea, the conclusion (3) of (CA) could be understood to mean:

(3a). Sally believes that 'Archibald Leach' was a famous movie star,

which Rieber (p. 224) suggests would in turn mean:

(3b). Sally believes that 'Archibald Leach' refers to someone who was a famous movie star,

which of course is assumed to be false in the example.

Since (3b) can be false when the premises (1) and (2) of (CA) are both true, the argument (CA) has an actual interpretation on which it is invalid. The invalidity is explained by the fact that the conclusion (3a) does not result from proper substitution of 'Archibald Leach' for 'Cary Grant' in premise (1). This in turn is due to the fact that in the identity premise (2), the name 'Archibald Leach' refers to Cary Grant, whereas in (3a) the quotation name " 'Archibald Leach' " refers to the name 'Archibald Leach'.

When we combine my idiom hypothesis with Rieber's use of implicit complex quotation, we obtain the means of explaining the apparent invalidity of a vast number of arguments in which the apparent substitution of co-referring names is in fact invalid, where these explanations are all perfectly consistent with the principle of direct reference DR. Since I have found no case of apparent substitution failure of co-referring names in cognitive contexts that is not susceptible to one of these two kinds of explanation, I think it is highly probable that the conjunction of these two types of explanation provides a complete solution to this classic problem for DR.

8. Conclusion

The Direct Reference thesis is often assumed to imply that names are *never* used as abbreviated definite descriptions. But this assumption results in an unfortunately narrow and inaccurate account of the way names work in natural language. What is true is that the fundamental, dominant way in which names are used is their use as directly referring genuine terms and not as short for descriptions. But this allows for the possibility that natural languages contain *idioms* in which in a few types of contexts, names *can* be used as short for descriptions. Here, I've proposed a way in which such an idiom might be based on the semantic properties of one relatively rare class of names, the descriptive names. The great advantage of this hypothesis is that it provides a general account of most of the examples of sentences containing empty names that are nevertheless regarded as obviously true by most speakers. In particular, I contended that the idiom hypothesis provides the only plausible account of the way names are used in substantive (as opposed to pointless) positive and negative existentials, and I argued against an alternative pragmatic explanation proposed by Adams and Stecker.

Extending the idiom hypothesis to uses of names from myth, I argued that such names are short for descriptions in both metamythic and cognitive contexts as well as in positive and negative existentials. I gave similar arguments for similar consequences regarding names from fiction as used in both metafictive contexts and in existentials. With the help of Currie's theory of truth in fiction, I proposed an idiom in which, in our talk about fiction, we use names from fiction as abbreviations of a certain form of definite description. Finally I surveyed some of the main types of example that have been used to support the view that the names from myth and fiction in these examples must be used as directly referring genuine terms whose referents are abstract objects. I proposed analyses of these cases in which the names are not used to refer to abstract entities but are rather used as short for descriptions. One advantage of my view is that it provides a unified account of the semantics of names, as we use them to talk about myth and fiction.

Finally I explained how my idiom hypothesis can also be used to provide a partial solution to the other classic problem facing Direct Reference, namely the apparent failure of substitution of co-referring names in cognitive contexts to preserve truth. I suggested that when this partial solution is combined with Rieber's use of complex quotation, we obtain a complete solution to the classic problem of substitution.

Notes

1. A referee raised an interesting problem for the test I propose for determining whether or not a given proper name is a descriptive name. The referee correctly points out that 'Laotze existed' and 'Laotze didn't exist' both express perfectly good (though incompatible) propositions. I would say that both of these sentences express descriptive propositions since here the syntactic name is short for a definite description. But the referee claims that 'Laotze' does not pass my test for when a name is descriptive, pointing out that the sentence 'It wasn't Laotze who was the author of the *Daodeging* but a committee' makes perfect sense. I agree that the sentence makes perfect sense. But this fact doesn't show that 'Laotze' is not a descriptive name. Rather it just shows that the referee has chosen the wrong description for the test. If we choose instead the description 'the original and major contributor of philosophical doctrines to the *Daodeging*', then the name 'Laotze' passes my test.

2. A minor difficulty with the application of (C) to the present issues is that on the Adams/Stecker view, sentences like (8) containing empty names can literally express no propositions. But note that use of a sentence like S that contains an empty name does not prevent that use from having cancelable implicatures. Consider, for instance, 'Santa gave me some of my presents; in fact I believe he gave me all of them'. In this case, 'I believe he gave me all of them' cancels the implicature of the first sentence that the speaker believes that Santa did not give her all of her presents. It is a simple matter to slightly revise Grice's (C) so that it can deal with such cases.

3. Another approach that is pragmatic but non-Gricean proposes that, given the satisfaction of certain contextual conditions, sentences can be used to *assert* propositions other than, and in addition to, the propositions that the sentences semantically express, given their literal meanings. For example, Soames (2002, 2004) suggests that sentences containing directly referring names can be used to assert propositions that specify the names' referents *descriptively*, even though these descriptive propositions are not semantically expressed by the sentences used. I argued against this proposal at some length in McKinsey (2005).

4. My coinage of 'metamythic' is derived from Currie's (1990) useful term 'metafictive' to describe statements about what is true in a given fiction. In general, metamythic and metafictive contexts are always either prefixed by explicit myth or fiction operators such as 'in myth M' or 'in fiction F' or such an operator is implicit.

5. See Hamilton (1953, 27).

6. For an extremely thorough defense of this view, see Amie Thomasson (1999).

7. See, for instance, Plantinga (1974, 159), Kripke (1973, 81), van Inwagen (1977, 301), and Currie (1990, 146–155).

8. Here I am ignoring the names that are used in fiction as names of actual objects, such as 'Napoleon' and 'London'. These names are of course names used *in* fiction, but they are not *fictional* names.

9. Cases like (14) and (15) also provide counterexamples to Predelli's (2017, 143) recent 'paratactic' analysis of talk about fiction since the sentences embedded in such metafictive contexts as (14) and (15) are clearly being *used*, not mentioned.

10. Contrary to the views of Salmon (1998, 302–303) and Zalta (2000, 128–129).

11. As Currie notes (p. 146), this idea was first suggested by Plantinga (1974, 159–163.)

12. See Currie's definition (8) (Currie 1990, 160).

13. This *de re* effect also allows my view to avoid various nice problems regarding *modal* truths in fiction that were brought home to me by Ben Caplan (in correspondence). One such problem goes like this. It certainly should be true that

    (i).   In the fiction H, it is possible that both Holmes exists and 'Holmes' has no referent.

    But if in (i), as I propose, 'Holmes' is short for 'the referent$_{FAH}$ of "Holmes"', then (i) would be false, if 'Holmes' has small scope relative to 'it is possible that'. But on the revised analysis of (i) that I just proposed, the problem disappears, for we just get the truth:

    (ii). It is reasonable (to degree r) for the informed reader of H to infer that the referent$_{FAH}$ of 'Holmes' is such that the fictional author of H believes it is possible both that *he* exists and that 'Holmes' has no referent.

14. Anthony Everett calls this view regarding names from fiction 'fictional realism', and in his 2005a, he raises some serious problems for the view. Schnieder and von Solodkoff (2009) propose objections to Everett's arguments, and Caplan and Muller (2014) defend Everett's arguments against these objections. My objections to the Kripke/van Inwagen view are distinct from Everett's objections, and my view of the semantics of fictional names is distinct from Everett's view.

15. See, for instance, the theory of emotion in fiction proposed by Currie in Chapter 5 of his (1990). Given this theory, it is not difficult to construct a plausible explication of sentences like (25) in which the relevant names from fiction do not refer to abstract characters.

16. However, I still endorse the other major features of my earlier (1999) view of the meaning and logical form of cognitive ascriptions: (1) the linguistic meaning of, and not merely the proposition expressed by, a sentence p in the scope of a cognitive operator 'C's that' will determine the cognitive property expressed by the predicate 'C's that p'; (2) the cognitive verbs, in their fundamental senses, do not express relations between persons and propositions; and (3) cognitive states and acts are in general not individuated by their propositional contents, when these contents are wide, singular propositions. (See McKinsey 1986, 1994, and 1999.)

Bibliography

Abbott, B. (2002). "Definites and Proper Names: Some Bad News for the Description Theory". *Journal of Semantics* 19: 203–207.

Abbott, B. (2004). "Proper Names and Language". In *Reference and Quantification: The Partee Effect*, edited by G.N. Carlson and F.J. Pelletier, 63–82. Stanford: CSLI Publications.

Adams, F. and Dietrich, L. (2004). "What's in a(n Empty) Name". *Pacific Philosophical Quarterly* 85: 125–148.

Adams, F. and Stecker, R. (1994). "Vacuous Singular Terms". *Mind and Language* 9: 387–401.

Adams, R. (1981). "Actualism and Thisness". *Synthese* 49: 3–41.

Bach, K. (1987). *Thought and Reference*. Oxford: Oxford University Press.

Bach, K. (2002). "Giorgione Was So-called Because of His Name". *Philosophical Perspectives: Language and Mind* 16: 73–103.

Baldwin, T. (1979). "Interpretations of Quantifiers". In *Philosophy of Logic*, edited by D. Jacquette, 169–182. Oxford: Blackwell's, 2002.

Barwise, J. and Cooper, R. (1981). "Generalized Quantifiers and Natural Language". *Linguistics and Philosophy* 4: 159–219.

Bencivenga, E. (1986). "Free Logics". In *Handbook of Philosophical Logic*, Vol. III, edited by D. Gabbay and F. Guenthner, 373–426. Dordrecht: Reidel.

Bencivenga, E., Lambert, K., and van Fraassen, B. (1991). *Logic, Bivalence and Denotation*. Atascadero: Ridgeview.

Braun, D. (1993). "Empty Names". *Noûs* 27: 449–469.

Braun, D. (2005). "Empty Names, Fictional Names, Mythical Names". *Noûs* 39: 596–631.

Burge, T. (1974). "Truth and Singular Terms". *Noûs* 8: 309–325.

Caplan, B. (2005). "Against Widescopism". *Philosophical Studies* 125: 167–190.

Caplan, B. and Muller, C. (2014). "Against a Defense of Fictional Realism". *Philosophical Quarterly* 64: 211–224.

Cartwright, R. (1962). "Propositions". In *Analytic Philosophy* First Series, edited by R.J. Butler, 81–103. Oxford: Basil Blackwell.

Cartwright, R. (1997). "On Singular Propositions". In *Meaning and Reference*, edited by A.A. Kazmi, 67–83. Calgary: University of Calgary Press.

Church, A. (1956). *Introduction to Mathematical Logic*. Princeton: Princeton University Press.

Crossley, J. and Humberstone, I. (1977). "The Logic of 'Actually'". *Reports on Mathematical Logic* 8: 11–29.

Currie, G. (1990). *The Nature of Fiction*. Cambridge: Cambridge University Press.

Davidson, D. (1964). "Theories of Meaning and Learnable Languages". *Logic, Methodology, Philosophy of Science*, edited by Y. Bar-Hillel. Amsterdam: North-Holland.

Davies, M. (1981). *Meaning, Quantification, Necessity*. London: Routledge & Kegan Paul.

Donnellan, K. (1970). "Proper Names and Identifying Descriptions". *Synthese* 21: 335–358.

Donnellan, K. (1974). "Speaking of Nothing". *The Philosophical Review* 83: 3–32.

Dummett, M. (1973). *Frege: Philosophy of Language*. New York: Harper and Row.

Elbourne, P. (2005). *Situations and Individuals*. Cambridge, MA: MIT Press.

Evans, G. (1977a). "Pronouns, Quantifiers, and Relative Clauses (I)". *Canadian Journal of Philosophy* 7: 467–536.

Evans, G. (1977b). "Pronouns, Quantifiers, and Relative Clauses (II)". *Canadian Journal of Philosophy* 7: 777–797.

Evans, G. (1979). "Reference and Contingency". *The Monist* 62: 161–189.

Evans, G. (1982). *Varieties of Reference*. Oxford: Clarendon Press.

Everett, A. (2005a). "Against Fictional Realism". *Journal of Philosophy* 102: 624–649.

Everett, A. (2005b). "Recent Defenses of Descriptivism". *Mind and Language* 20: 103–139.

Fitch, G. (1981). "Names and the De Re—De Dicto Distinction". *Philosophical Studies* 39: 25–34.

Frege, G. (1891). "Function and Concept". In *Translations from the Philosophical Writings of Gottlob Frege*, edited by P. Geach and M. Black, 21–41. Oxford: Basil Blackwell, 1966.

Frege, G. (1892a). "On Sense and Reference". In *Translations from the Philosophical Writings of Gottlob Frege*, edited by P. Geach and M. Black, 56–78. Oxford: Basil Blackwell, 1966.

Frege, G. (1892b). "On Concept and Object". In *Translations from the Philosophical Writings of Gottlob Frege*, edited by P. Geach and M. Black, 42–55. Oxford: Basil Blackwell, 1966.

Frege, G. (1904). "Selection from the Frege-Russell Correspondence". In *Propositions and Attitudes*, edited by N. Salmon and S. Soames, 56–57. Oxford: Oxford University Press, 1988.

Gabbay, D. (1976). *Investigations in Modal and Tense Logic with Applications to Problems in Philosophy and Linguistics*. Dordrecht: D. Reidel.

Garson, J. (1984). "Quantification in Modal Logic". In *Handbook of Philosophical Logic, Volume II: Extensions of Classical Logic*, edited by D. Gabbay and F. Guenthner, 249–307. Dordrecht: D. Reidel.

Garson, J. (1991). "Applications of Free Logic to Quantified Intensional Logic". In *Philosophical Applications of Free Logic*, edited by K. Lambert, 110–142. Oxford: Oxford University Press.

Garson, J. (2006). *Modal Logic for Philosophers*. Cambridge: Cambridge University Press.

Geach, P. (1967). "Intentional Identity". *Journal of Philosophy* 64: 627–632.

Geurts, B. (1997). "Good News About the Description Theory of Names". *Journal of Semantics* 14: 319–348.

Glanzberg, M. (2006). "Quantifiers". In *The Oxford Handbook of Philosophy of Language*, edited by E. LePore and B. Smith, 794–821. Oxford: Clarendon Press.

Glüer-Pagin, K. and Pagin, P. (2014). "Vulcan Might Have Existed and Neptune Not: On the Semantics of Empty Names". In *Empty Representations: Reference and Non-Existence*, edited by M. Garcia-Carpintero and G. Marti, 117–141. Oxford: Oxford University Press.

Green, M. (2007). "Direct Reference, Empty Names, and Implicature". *Canadian Journal of Philosophy* 37: 419–448.

Grice, H.P. (1969). "Vacuous Names". In *Words and Objections*, edited by D. Davidson and J. Hintikka, 118–145. Dordrecht: Reidel.

Grice, H.P. (1989). *Studies in the Way of Words*. Cambridge, MA: Harvard University Press.

Hale, B. (2007). "Into the Abyss". *Philosophia Mathematica (III)* 15: 94–110.

Hamilton, E. (1953). *Mythology*. New York: The New American Library.

Hand, M. (2007). "Objectual and Substitutional Interpretations of the Quantifiers". In *Handbook of the Philosophy of Science, Philosophy of Logic*, edited by D. Jacquette, 650–674. Oxford: Elsevier B.V.

Higgenbotham, J. and May, R. (1981). "Questions, Quantifiers and Crossing". *Linguistics Review* 1: 41–79.

Hintikka, J. (1959). "Existential Presuppositions and Existential Commitments". *Journal of Philosophy* 56: 125–137.

Hoffmann, A. (2003). "A Puzzle About Truth and Singular Propositions". *Mind* 112: 635–651.

Hofweber, T. (2000). "Quantification and Non-Existent Objects". In *Empty Names, Fiction, and the Puzzles of Non-Existence*, edited by A. Everett and T. Hofweber, 249–273. Stanford: CSLI Publications.

Hofweber, T. (2005). "A Puzzle About Ontology". *Noûs* 39: 256–283.

Hofweber, T. (2009). "Ambitious, Yet Modest, Metaphysics". In *Metametaphysics*, edited by D. Chalmers, D. Manley, and R. Wasserman, 260–289. Oxford: Clarendon Press.

Hudson, J. and Tye, M. (1980). "Proper Names and Definite Descriptions with Widest Possible Scope". *Analysis* 40: 63–64.

Hughes, G. and Cresswell, H. (1968). *An Introduction to Modal Logic*. London: Methuen.

Jacquette, D. (1996). *Meinongian Logic. The Semantics of Existence and Non-existence. Perspectives in Analytical Philosophy*, Vol. 11. Berlin-New York: de Gruyter.

Justice, J. (2001). "On Sense and Reflexivity". *Journal of Philosophy* 98: 355–364.

Kaplan, D. (1970). "What Is Russell's Theory of Descriptions?" In *Physics, Logic, and History*, edited by W. Yourgrau, 277–288. New York: Plenum.

Kaplan, D. (1973). "Bob and Carol and Ted and Alice". In *Approaches to Natural Language*, edited by J. Hintikka, J.M. Moravcsik, and P. Suppes, 490–518. Dordrecht: D. Reidel.

Kaplan, D. (1977). "Demonstratives". In *Themes from Kaplan*, edited by J. Almog, J. Perry, and H. Wettstein, 481–563. Oxford: Oxford University Press, 1989.

Kaplan, D. (1989). "Afterthoughts". In *Themes from Kaplan*, edited by J. Almog, J. Perry, and H. Wettstein, 565–614. Oxford: Oxford University Press.

Katz, J.J. (1994). "Names Without Bearers". *Philosophical Review* 103: 1–39.

Katz, J.J. (2001). "The End of Millianism". *Journal of Philosophy* 98: 137–166.

Kleene, S.C. (1950). *Introduction to Metamathematics*. Princeton: D. van Nostrand.

Kripke, S. (1963). "Semantical Considerations on Modal Logic". *Acta Philosophica Fennica* 16: 83–94.

Kripke, S. (1972a). "Naming and Necessity". In *Semantics of Natural Language*, edited by D. Davidson and G. Harman, 253–355. Dordrecht: Reidel.

Kripke, S. (1972b). "Addenda". In *Semantics of Natural Language*, edited by D. Davidson and H. Harman, 763–769. Dordrecht: D. Reidel.

Kripke, S. (1973). *Reference and Existence: The John Locke Lectures*. Oxford: Oxford University Press, 2013.

Kripke, S. (1976). "Is There a Problem About Substitutional Quantification?" In *Truth and Meaning*, edited by G. Evans and J. McDowell, 325–419. Oxford: Clarendon Press.

Kripke, S. (1977). "Speaker's Reference and Semantic Reference". In *Midwest Studies in Philosophy* 2, edited by P. French, T. Uehling, and H. Wettstein, 255–276. Minneapolis: University of Minnesota Press.

Lambert, K. (1963a). "Existential Import Revisited". *Notre Dame Journal of Formal Logic* 4: 288–292.

Lambert, K. (1963b). "Notes on E!III: A Theory of Descriptions". *Philosophical Studies* 13: 51–59.

Lambert, K. (1964). "Notes on E!IV: A Reduction in Free Quantification Theory with Identity and Definite Descriptions". *Philosophical Studies* 15: 85–88.

Lambert, K. (2001). "Free Logics". In *The Blackwell Guide to Philosophical Logic*, edited by L. Gobel, 258–279. Oxford: Blackwell Publishing.

Larson, R. and Segal, G. (1995). *Knowledge of Meaning*. Cambridge, MA: The MIT Press.

Lasonen-Aarnio, M. (2008). "Why the Externalist Is Better Off Without Free Logic: A Reply to McKinsey". *Dialectica* 62: 535–540.

Lehmann, S. (1994). "Strict Fregean Free Logic". *Journal of Philosophical Logic* 23: 307–336.

Lehmann, S. (2001). "No Input, No Output Logic". In *New Essays in Free Logic*, edited by E. Morscher and A. Hieke, 147–155. Dordrecht: Kluwer Academic Publishers.

Lehmann, S. (2002). "More Free Logic". In *Handbook of Philosophical Logic*, 2nd Edition, Vol. 5, edited by D. Gabbay and F. Guenthner, 197–259. Kluwer Academic Publishers.

LePore, E. and Ludwig, K. 2007. *Donald Davidson's Truth-theoretic Semantics*. Oxford: Clarendon Press.

Lewis, D. (1970). "How to Define Theoretical Terms". *Journal of Philosophy* 67: 427–446.

Linsky, L. (1977). *Names and Descriptions*. Chicago: University of Chicago Press.

Ludlow, P. and Neale, S. (2006). "Descriptions". In *The Blackwell Guide to the Philosophy of Language*, edited by M. Devitt and R. Hanley, 288–313. Oxford: Blackwell.

Maier, E. (2009). "Proper Names and Indexicals Trigger Rigid Presuppositions". *Journal of Semantics* 26: 253–315.

Mates, B. (1972). *Elementary Logic*, 2nd Edition. New York: Oxford University Press.

Mates, B. (1973). "Descriptions and Reference". *Foundations of Language* 10: 409–418.

Matushansky, O. (2008). "On the Linguistic Complexity of Proper Names". *Linguistics and Philosophy* 21: 573–627.

McKinsey, M. (1978a). "Names and Intentionality". *The Philosophical Review* 87: 171–200.

McKinsey, M. (1978b). "Kripke's Objections to Description Theories of Names". *Canadian Journal of Philosophy* 8: 485–497.

McKinsey, M. (1979). "The Ambiguity of Definite Descriptions". *Theoria* 45: 78–89.

McKinsey, M. (1983). "Psychologism in Semantics". *Canadian Journal of Philosophy* 13: 1–25.

McKinsey, M. (1984). "Causality and the Paradox of Names". *Midwest Studies in Philosophy* 9: 491–515.

McKinsey, M. (1986). "Mental Anaphora". *Synthese* 66: 159–175.

McKinsey, M. (1987). "Apriorism in the Philosophy of Language". *Philosophical Studies* 52: 1–32.

McKinsey, M. (1991). "The Internal Basis of Meaning". *Pacific Philosophical Quarterly* 72: 143–169.

McKinsey, M. (1994). "Individuating Beliefs". *Philosophical Perspectives, Philosophy of Logic and Language* 8: 303–330.

McKinsey, M. (1999). "The Semantics of Belief Ascriptions". *Nous* 33: 519–557.

McKinsey, M. (2002). "Forms of Externalism and Privileged Access". *Philosophical Perspectives* 16, Language and Mind: 199–224.

McKinsey, M. (2005). "Critical Notice of Scott Soames, *Beyond Rigidity*". *Canadian Journal of Philosophy* 35: 149–168.

McKinsey, M. (2006). "Direct Reference and Logical Truth: A Reply to Lasonen-Aarnio". *Dialectica* 60: 447–451.

McKinsey, M. (2010). "Understanding Proper Names". *Linguistics and Philosophy* 33: 325–354.

McKinsey, M. (2016). "Truths Containing Empty Names". In *Philosophical Approaches to Proper Names*, edited by P. Stalmaszczyk and L. Fernández-Moreno, 175–202. Bern: Peter Lang GmbH.

Meinong, A. (1904). "The Theory of Objects". In *Realism and the Background of Phenomenology*, edited by R. Chisholm, 76–117. Atascadero: Ridgeview, 1960.

Menzel, C. (1990). "Actualism, Ontological Commitment, and Possible World Semantics". *Synthese* 85: 355–389.

Menzel, C. (1991). "The True Modal Logic". *Journal of Philosophical Logic* 20: 331–374.

Meyer, R. and Lambert, K. (1968). "Universally Free Logic and Standard Quantification Theory". *Journal of Symbolic Logic* 33: 8–26.

Mill, J.S. (1843). "Of Names". In Book I, Chapter II, *A System of Logic*, 29–44. New York: Harper and Brothers, 1893.

Montague, R. (1970). "English as a Formal Language". In *Formal Philosophy: Selected Papers of Richard Montague*, edited by R. Thomason, 188–221. New Haven: Yale University Press, 1974.

Moore, G.E. (1936). "Is Existence a Predicate?" In *Philosophical Papers*, 112–125. New York: Collier Books, 1959.

Neale, S. (1990). *Descriptions*. Cambridge, MA: The MIT Press.

Nelson, M. (2002). "Descriptionism Defended". *Nous* 36: 408–436.

Nelson, M. and Zalta, E. (2012). "A Defense of Contingent Logical Truths". *Philosophical Studies* 157: 153–162.

Orenstein, A. (1978). *Existence and the Particular Quantifier*. Philadelphia: Temple University Press.

Orenstein, A. (1990). "Is Existence What Existential Quantification Expresses?" In *Perspectives on Quine*, edited by R.B. Barrett and R.F. Gibson, 245–270. Oxford: Basil Blackwell.

Parsons, T. (1980). *Nonexistent Objects*. New Haven: Yale University Press.

Perry, J. (1977). "Frege on Demonstratives". *The Philosophical Review* 86: 474–497.

Perry, J. (1979). "The Problem of the Essential Indexical". *Noûs* 13: 3–21.

Perry, J. (1997). "Indexicals and Demonstratives". In *A Companion to Philosophy of Language*, edited by B. Hale and C. Wright, 586–612. Oxford: Blackwell Publishing.

Plantinga, A. (1974). *The Nature of Necessity*. Oxford: Clarendon Press.

Plantinga, A. (1978). "The Boethian Compromise". *American Philosophical Quarterly* 15: 129–138.

Plantinga, A. (1983). "On Existentialism". *Philosophical Studies* 44: 1–20.

Predelli, S. (2017). *Proper Names: A Millian Account*. Oxford: Oxford University Press.

Priest, G. (2005). *Towards Non-Being*. Oxford: Clarendon Press.

Prior, A.N. (1963). "Is the Concept of Referential Opacity Really Necessary?" *Acta Philosophica Fennica* 16: 189–198.

Pryor, J. (2006). "Hyper-Reliability and Apriority". *Proceedings of the Aristotelian Society* 106: 327–344.

Putnam, H. (1970). "Is Semantics Possible?" Reprinted in *Naming, Necessity, and Natural Kinds*, edited by S. Schwartz, 102–118. Ithaca: Cornell University Press, 1977.

Quine, W. (1960). *Word and Object*. Cambridge, MA: MIT Press.

Quine, W.V.O. (1969). "Existence and Quantification". In *His Ontological Relativity and Other Essays*, 91–113. New York: Columbia University Press.

Recanati, F. (1993). *Direct Reference*. Oxford: Blackwell.

Reicher, M. (2012). "Nonexistent Objects". In *The Stanford Encyclopedia of Philosophy*, Fall Edition, edited by E.N. Zalta. Forthcoming URL = <http://plato.stanford.edu/archives/fall2012/entries/nonexistent-objects/>

Reichenbach, H. (1947). *Elements of Symbolic Logic*. New York: The Macmillan Company.

Rieber, S. (1997). "A Semiquotational Solution to Substitution Problems". *Philosophical Studies* 86: 267–301.

Routley, R. (1966). "Some Things Do Not Exist". *Notre Dame Journal of Formal Logic* 7: 251–276.

Routley, R. (1980). *Exploring Meinong's Jungle and Beyond*. Canberra: RSSS, Australian National University.

Russell, B. (1903). *Principles of Mathematics*. Oxford: Routledge.

Russell, B. (1905). "On Denoting". Reprinted in *Logic and Knowledge: Essays 1901–1950*, edited by R.C. Marsh, 39–56. New York: The Macmillan Company, 1956.

Russell, B. (1910–11). "Knowledge by Acquaintance and Knowledge by Description". *Proceedings of the Aristotelian Society* 11: 108–128.

Russell, B. (1912). *The Problems of Philosophy*. Oxford: Oxford University Press, 1959.

Russell, B. (1918). "The Philosophy of Logical Atomism". Reprinted in *Logic and Knowledge: Essays 1901–1950*, edited by R.C. Marsh, 177–281. New York: The Macmillan Company, 1956.

Russell, B. and Whitehead, A.N. (1910). *Principia Mathematica to *56*. London: Cambridge University Press, 1962.

Sainsbury, R.M. (2005). *Reference Without Referents*. Oxford: The Clarendon Press.

Salmon, N. (1981). *Reference and Essence*. Princeton: Princeton University Press.

Salmon, N. (1986). *Frege's Puzzle*. Cambridge, MA: The MIT Press.

Salmon, N. (1998). "Nonexistence". *Noûs* 32: 277–319.

Scales, R.D. (1969). *Attribution and Existence*. Ann Arbor: University Microfilms International.

Schnieder, B. and von Solodkoff, T. (2009). "In Defense of Fictional Realism". *Philosophical Quarterly* 59: 138–149.

Schock, R. (1968). *Logics Without Existence Assumptions*. Stockholm: Almquist and Wiksell.

Scott, D. (1967). "Existence and Description in Formal Logic". In *Bertrand Russell: Philosopher of the Century*, edited by R. Schoenman, 181–200. Boston: Little, Brown & Co.

Searle, J. (1958). "Proper Names". *Mind* 47: 166–173.

Sharvy, R. (1969). "Things". *The Monist* 53: 488–504.

Sleigh, R.C. (1967). "On Quantifying into Epistemic Contexts". *Noûs* 1: 23–31.

Smiley, T. (1960). "Sense Without Denotation". *Analysis* 20: 125–135.

Soames, S. (1987). "Direct Reference, Propositional Attitudes, and Semantic Content". *Philosophical Topics* 15: 47–87.

Soames, S. (1998). "The Modal Argument: Wide Scope and Rigidified Descriptions". *Nous* 32: 1–22.

Soames, S. (2002). *Beyond Rigidity: The Unfinished Semantic Agenda of Naming and Necessity*. New York: Oxford University Press.

Soames, S. (2004). "Naming and Asserting". In *Semantics vs. Pragmatics*, edited by Z.G. Szabo, 357–382. Oxford: Oxford University Press.

Soames, S. (2010). *Philosophy of Language*. Princeton and Oxford: Princeton University Press.

Soames, S. (2014). *The Analytic Tradition in Philosophy, Volume 1, The Founding Giants*. Princeton and Oxford: Princeton University Press.

Sosa, D. (2001). "Rigidity in the Scope of Russell's Theory". *Nous* 35: 1–38.

Stalnaker, R. (1994). "The Interaction of Modality with Quantification and Identity". In *Modality, Morality, and Belief*, edited by W. Sinnott-Armstrong, D. Raffman, and N. Asher, 12–28. Cambridge: Cambridge University Press.

Strawson, P.F. (1950). "On Referring". *Mind* 59: 320–344.

Strawson, P.F. (1963). *Individuals*. Garden City, NY: Anchor Books.

Tennant, N. (1978). *Natural Logic*. Edinburgh: University of Edinburgh Press.

Thomasson, A. (1999). *Fiction and Metaphysics*. Cambridge: Cambridge University Press.

Tomberlin, J. (1990). "Belief, Nominalism, and Quantification". *Philosophical Perspectives* 4: 573–579.

van Fraassen, B. (1966). "Singular Terms, Truth-Value Gaps, and Free Logic". *Journal of Philosophy* 43: 481–495.

van Fraassen, B. and Lambert, K. (1967). "On Free Description Theory". *Zeitschrift für Mathematische Logik und Grundlagen der Mathematik* 13: 225–240.

van Inwagen, P. (1977). "Creatures of Fiction". *American Philosophical Quarterly* 14: 299–308.

Westerståhl, D. (2001). "Quantifiers". In *The Blackwell Guide to Philosophical Logic*, edited by L. Gobel, 437–460. Oxford: Blackwell Publishing.

Wiggins, D. (1980). "'Most' and 'All': Some Comments on a Familiar Programme, and on the Logical Form of Quantified Sentences". In *Reference, Truth, and Reality*, edited by M. Platts, 318–346. London: Routledge & Kegan Paul.

Woodruff, P.W. (1970). "Logic and Truth-Value Gaps". In *Philosophical Problems in Logic*, edited by K. Lambert, 121–142. Dordrecht: D. Reidel.

Zalta, E. (1988). "Logical and Analytic Truths That Are Not Necessary". *Journal of Philosophy* 85: 57–74.

Zalta, E. (2000). "The Road Between Pretense Theory and Abstract Object Theory". In *Empty Names, Fiction, and the Puzzles of Non-Existence*, edited by A. Everett and T. Hofweber, 117–147. Stanford: CSLI Press.

Index

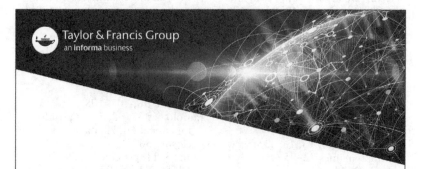

Taylor & Francis Group
an **informa** business

Taylor & Francis eBooks

www.taylorfrancis.com

A single destination for eBooks from Taylor & Francis
with increased functionality and an improved user
experience to meet the needs of our customers.

90,000+ eBooks of award-winning academic content in
Humanities, Social Science, Science, Technology, Engineering,
and Medical written by a global network of editors and authors.

TAYLOR & FRANCIS EBOOKS OFFERS:

A streamlined
experience for
our library
customers

A single point
of discovery
for all of our
eBook content

Improved
search and
discovery of
content at both
book and
chapter level

REQUEST A FREE TRIAL
support@taylorfrancis.com

 Routledge
Taylor & Francis Group

 CRC Press
Taylor & Francis Group

9781032337760